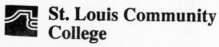

St. Louis Community College

Forest Park
Florissant Valley
Meramec

Instructional Resources
St. Louis, Missouri

GAYLORD

FORM AND REASON

Essays in Metaphysics

EDWARD HALPER

STATE UNIVERSITY OF NEW YORK PRESS

Published by
State University of New York Press, Albany

For information, address State University of New York
Press, State University Plaza, Albany, N.Y., 12246

Production by E. Moore
Marketing by Theresa A. Swierzowski

Library of Congress Cataloging-in-Publication Data

Halper, Edward C., 1951-
    Form and reason : essays in metaphysics / Edward Halper.
        p.   cm.
    Includes bibliographical references and index.
    ISBN 0-7914-1581-3 (acid-free). — ISBN 0-7914-1582-1 (pbk. : acid-free)
    1. Metaphysics.   I. Title.
BD111.B17   1993
110—dc20   92-29106
                                                                        CIP

10 9 8 7 6 5 4 3 2 1

To my children:
Yehuda, Daniel, and Aaron

CONTENTS

ACKNOWLEDGMENTS

A briefer version of "The 'Socrates' of Plato's Early Dialogues" was presented at the Second International Conference on Greek Philosophy: The Philosophy of Socrates, held in August 1990, in Samos, Greece, in honor of Gregory Vlastos, and appears in the conference proceedings, *The Philosophy of Socrates: Elenchus, Ethics, and Truth* edited by K. J. Boudouris, vol. 2 (Athens: International Center for Greek Philosophy and Culture, 1992), pp. 81–87. Permission of the Editor and the International Association for Greek Philosophy to reprint portions of the original article is gratefully acknowledged.

"Plato and Aristotle on Friendship" was presented at the Ninth Joint Conference of the Society for the Study of Islamic Philosophy and Science and the Society for Ancient Greek Philosophy, at an Emory University Philosophy Department Colloquium, and at an American Philosophical Association, Pacific Division meeting. Discussions on all three occasions were lively, and Tom Tuozzo delivered a very helpful set of comments on the last occasion. Paul Sunstein, Ronna Burger, and Vicky Davion kindly commented on an earlier version.

Versions of "The Rational Basis of Aristotle's Virtue" were delivered at an annual meeting of the Southern Society for Philosophy and Psychology and at the Eighteenth World Congress of Philosophy in Brighton. I am also grateful for comments from David McNaughton and Paul Sunstein on later versions.

"Two Problems in Aristotelian Ethics" was inspired by a conference at the University of Dayton on Aristotle's Metaphysics and Ethics (November 1987). The papers of Julia Annas and Stephen A.

White were particularly helpful; a conversation with Jerome Schiller helped me formulate my ideas. I am grateful to the conference organizers, Ray Herbenick and Jane Zembaty. Versions of the chapter were presented at conferences of the American Philosophical Association (Central Division) and the Canadian Philosophical Association. I would like to thank my commentators on these occasions, Christine Korsgaard and John Baker, and the audiences (especially Roger Shiner and Janet Sisson) for lively discussions.

A portion of "Aristotle on Knowledge of Nature" was presented at a meeting of the American Philosophical Association, Pacific Division and commented upon by Al Spangler. It later appeared in the *Review of Metaphysics* 37 (1984): 811–35. Permission of the editor to reprint it here is gratefully acknowledged.

"Ackrill, Aristotle, and Analytic Philosophy" was originally published in *Ancient Philosophy* 2 (1982): 142–51. I gratefully acknowledge permission of the editor and Mathesis Publications to reprint it here.

A version of "Some Problems in Aristotle's Mathematical Ontology" was presented before the Boston Area Colloquium in Ancient Philosophy. The present version benefited from discussions with students and faculty at Boston College, from the comments of John Cleary, my commentator on that occasion, as well as from comments by Ian Mueller and Henry Mendell. It was published in the colloquium's proceedings, vol. 5 (1989): 247–75.

"Is Creativity Good?" appeared in the *British Journal of Aesthetics* 28 (1989): 47–56. I gratefully acknowledge permission of Oxford University Press to reprint it here.

"Hegel and the Problem of the Differentia" was presented at the tenth biennial meeting of the Hegel Society of America, where it was commented upon by Martin Donougho. It appears in the conference's proceedings, *Essays in Hegel's Logic*, edited by George di Giovanni, pp. 191–202 (Albany: State University of New York Press, 1989).

Work on this manuscript was supported, in part, by a Senior Faculty Research Grant from the University of Georgia Research Foundation.

INTRODUCTION

Only lately laid to rest as an unfortunate mistake in the history of philosophy, metaphysics has once again been resurrected. It appears in various guises on the current scene: as a realism/nominalism debate, as disputes about ontological commitment, as a resurgent pragmatism, and as hermeneutics. These recent approaches to metaphysics distinguish themselves from the older, seventeenth-century style of metaphysics that sought, as Richard Rorty put it, to mirror nature with mental representations. Recent metaphysics takes its start not from nature but from language: the issue is not how to capture the world in ourselves, but whether or how our usage of natural and artificial signs could extend beyond ourselves to the world. And what is problematic here is that all attempts to specify something beyond language must themselves use language and so, it would seem, fail to extend beyond language. We must see the world with linguistic glasses, as it were. Unable to speak objectively of the world, current metaphysicians fall back on a merely "internal realism" or on comparing stories we tell about the world.

The conclusion that metaphysics must take some such form is at odds with the reasoning upon which it rests. For in order to agree that the world is beyond our reach we must know what it is that we mean by "world"—but this is just what the argument claims we cannot know. In other words, even to formulate the problem requires a grasp of the world that we are not supposed to be able to have. The utter simplicity of this criticism renders it no less devastating.

Some will object to this criticism by asking what we could mean by "world" other than the object that we *do* refer to with language. I

1

do not need to answer this question because my point is not that we can make sense of such an object but that proponents of contemporary metaphysics unwittingly assume this object. It will be further objected to my criticism: the philosophical community is able to engage in metaphysics without any reference to this object. So far as I can see, an appeal to the practices of the philosophical community will not solve this problem: there may be some or, even, many philosophers who are able to engage in philosophical discourse without stumbling on this problem, but that could only solve the problem if the community provided the standard, and the notion that the community does provide the standard is just based upon our supposed inability to get beyond language. The philosophical community may well agree that metaphysics does not depend upon speaking about an object that cannot be spoken of, but the reason to accept the authority of the community is just the supposition that the world, as it truly is, cannot be grasped. So, in this case, appeals to the community beg the question.

Appeals to the standards and practices of a community have mired current metaphysics in relativism. Because it is rarely—if ever—possible to achieve the agreement of the entire community of philosophers, it has come to be assumed that doing philosophy consists in the philosopher's defending her unjustifiable commitments against the attacks of others who hold different convictions. In this clash of beliefs there can be no true victors because there is no objective basis for adjudicating competing claims.

This philosophical impasse has made studies in the history of philosophy more attractive. Besides the goal of deflating claims to objectivity and proof, contemporary scholars have sought from historical figures insights that they could bring to bear on contemporary problems. Thus the literature abounds with studies on Aristotle's philosophy of language, his examinations of the usage of terms, and his method of common opinion. The contemporary scene, with its emphasis on the linguistic perspective, so colors accounts of classical texts that we read them as if they, too, treated contemporary problems.

The essays collected in this volume concern texts of classical metaphysicians. However, rather than bringing contemporary concerns to these texts, I have sought to examine them in their own terms. What strikes me as particularly interesting is just their difference from contemporary perspectives. In particular, the philosophers examined here are all realists of some sort. They think that it is possible to peer behind our human perspective to see the world as it really is. What I am concerned with here is how they managed to justify this notion and just what they found. How can we cast aside our linguistic glasses, common opinions, and community's practices?

What I want to show is why certain thinkers have thought they could get a handle on the way some types of things are, and how they went about it. What this requires is to link somehow our experience with something beyond it that makes it possible. In other words, the issue is, just what must the world be like in order that we have the sort of experiences and perceptions that we do? Since action, choice, and value are parts of our experience, it is part of this same question to ask, what must the world be like in order that we have ethical experiences? How—to mention a few of the topics to be considered— could there be right action, regular change, and distinctions?

The link between experience and the world is indicated by the title, form and reason. The key feature that characterizes our experience is the capacity to exercise reason, and what makes this possible is the existence of forms. It is just to the extent that form exists in the world that the world is intelligible; and, conversely, experience itself comes to have the character of form when rational reflection is realized. But this link breaks down in certain respects because world and experience are neither fully formal nor fully rational. At issue here is just the extent to which the world is intelligible.

This is not to say that readers will find here a thorough treatment or compelling arguments for realism. These essays are more preliminary. Indeed, a casual reader could miss this issue; for the essays presented here focus explicitly on individual scholarly topics and could be so read. But these scholarly topics are manifestations of deeper philosophical difficulties. It is in order to focus attention on these deeper problems at issue in the essays that I have collected them together here: one way to see the forest is to look at a lot of different trees. The textual details that could obscure the philosophical points will, I hope, serve here rather as a sphere in which to make them manifest. For the most part I do not argue for a position here. Instead, I try to elucidate arguments of classic texts so as to show what about the world and reason is at issue.

All the essays here concern reason and form, and I take them to be the key concepts for Plato and Aristotle. Recent scholars have not often placed these two at center stage, and I will appear to them to be reverting to traditional interpretations. But the real traditionalists will probably derive little comfort from these essays because I have actually strayed from the tradition and because, despite my amassing the textual details to support my case, my real concern is not to demonstrate my interpretation but to come to grips with philosophical problems and their solutions.

At first consideration, it may seem that "reason" refers to language or thought and "form" to a character in the world; for a central Greek term for reason, *logos*, could also be rendered as language or speech, and form is what makes things be. But the classical terms are broader; for it is equally appropriate to say that form makes us what we are, that our use of language and thought is in accordance with or, even, is our form, and that thought and language grasp and express forms. Likewise, reason is in us, but it is also appropriate to say that reason is present in the orderly process of nature. So the classical terms, reason and form, could *each* include both language and world. The latter contemporary terms lack this flexibility. There are well-known arguments advanced by Quine and others that the proper logical unit is not the proposition but the sentence on the ground that sentences are public and that what can be expressed by propositions can be equally well expressed by sentences. Clearly, though, it could make sense, provided other conditions were met, to say that laws of nature exist in nature as propositions: thought could govern nature— leaving aside whether or not this is true. But it is hard to imagine how to give any sense to a claim that a sentence expressing the law could be in or govern nature. So the terms do make a difference.

The first group of essays address topics in Greek ethics. It is appropriate to include them here in a group of essays on metaphysics because the Greeks think that being good consists of acquiring a form. Thus, ethics depends upon the existence of certain metaphysical entities, forms. To show that our ethical activity presupposes the existence of forms is a way of grasping a reality beyond human experience or, at any rate, beyond the experience of most of us. The essays contained in this section work together to refine the notions of form advanced by Plato and Aristotle.

In "The 'Socrates' of Plato's Early Dialogues" I challenge the widely held view that Plato's early dialogues represent an historical Socrates who does not posit transcendent forms. Rather than consider the presuppositions implicit in "what is X?" questions—a path that has proven inconclusive—I consider (1) the parallel structures of several early dialogues and (2) a group of arguments that I take to be "unity of virtue" arguments, the most famous of which appear in the *Protagoras*. First, I argue here that the author has structured many early dialogues so as to indicate a particular conclusion. Second, I show that Socrates argues that—contrary to all experience—virtue must be one in order to show that form can only exist beyond sensible experience. Though the dialogues are Platonic, they remain faithful to the historical Socrates insofar as the character Socrates never states the conclusion implicit in the dialogue.

Plato's early account of friendship in the *Lysis* conforms to this pattern. By setting this dialogue against Aristotle's account of friendship in the *Nicomachean Ethics*, "Plato and Aristotle on Friendship" aims to show the key position of knowledge in those accounts and to challenge some current interpretations of both philosophers. First, I argue that the *Lysis* expounds two apparently contradictory requirements for friendship: reciprocity and utility. Through much of the dialogue, Plato shows the difficulty of meeting both criteria, but his implicit aim is to show they can be met if the good is transcendent. Second, the essay explains how Aristotle thinks he can meet Plato's requirements for friendship without positing a transcendent good. Despite this difference, Aristotle, too, advances a triadic account of friendship that contrasts sharply with current notions.

Aristotle's own description of the virtues in the *Nicomachean Ethics* is usually supposed to be based on the moral practices and the common opinions of his contemporaries. "The Rational Basis of Aristotle's Virtue" argues that, contrary to the usual view, Aristotle thought these virtues are rationally justifiable and that he attempted to offer such a justification in his account. What is crucial here is to explain how the moral virtues can have a rational basis when (1) reason cannot by itself determine the action that is virtuous and (2) the moral virtues are not merely means to intellectual virtue but ends in their own right. In showing what sort of rational basis the moral virtues have, the essay also shows how to resolve the problem of Aristotle's intellectualism, his final endorsement of the theoretical life as the best life.

"Two Problems in Aristotelian Ethics" aims to examine and clarify the account of form that emerges from the preceding chapter by addressing two problems that have been raised about Aristotelian ethics: (1) how can some lives be happier than others if, as Aristotle says, a happy life lacks nothing? and (2) are external goods intrinsically or instrumentally valuable? I argue that these problems arise from trying to understand Aristotle's response to, respectively, a utilitarian and a Kantian. Both problems can be resolved by recognizing the character of happiness as an actuality. First, happiness should not be understood quantitatively. Second, acts in accordance with moral virtue are not acts that are distinct from such ordinary acts as eating, caring for children, and being with friends; they are ways of performing these ordinary acts and, for that reason, intrinsically connected with the so-called external goods.

What emerges from the essays on ethics is the notion of a peculiar entity, an actuality. The essays collected under the heading "metaphysics" try to come to grips with this entity. Since, though, there are actualities of various types, it is necessary to consider different types of entities. These essays explore questions of the ontological status of different entities: what kinds of things are numbers? how do causes exist? what sort of an entity is language? what must things be like if they are to be the object of knowledge? So far as I can see, Aristotle does not answer these questions by analyzing language; indeed, that would beg the question just because the status of language, the things it describes, and its relation to these things are all in question. Instead, he addresses ontological problems and advances doctrines that will resolve them. It is a token of our current notions of metaphysics that these ontological problems are often overlooked and that Aristotelian problems are thought to turn on reconciling various commitments, such as commitments to empiricism and to the existence of metaphysics.

Once again, the first essay in the group shows why examining human faculties leads us to posit the existence of entities beyond ourselves. "Aristotle on Knowledge of Nature" examines Aristotle's response to Plato's arguments against the possibility of knowing what moves. Whereas Plato thinks that knowledge claims could be falsified unless the objects of knowledge are eternal, Aristotle maintains that the objects of knowledge need only be complete and unchanging, characters he ascribes to forms or actualities. By identifying some of what would ordinarily be called motions as actualities, he produces an account of sensibles that escapes Plato's objections to knowledge.

"Ackrill, Aristotle, and Analytic Philosophy" is a brief examination and critique of J. L. Ackrill's linguistic interpretation of Aristotle. In support of the linguistic interpretation are Aristotle's inquiries into the many ways that a word is said and his examinations of what other thinkers have said about an issue. However, Aristotle differs from ordinary language philosophers in at least three respects. First, he is not concerned with language in order to clarify our concepts but to get a handle on the way things are. Second, he does not, as Ackrill supposes, criticize philosophical opponents by pointing to their misunderstandlng of linguistic usage. Considering the arguments from *Physics* I that Ackrill discusses, I show that they turn, instead, on ontological considerations. Third, Aristotle pays attention to language because he thinks that we all share a human capacity to grasp forms or essences and this grasp of reality is manifested in language. The mistake of the linguistic interpretation is to emphasize language without the forms upon which it depends.

It is not easy to see how all things could be forms; mathematical entities pose a special difficulty. "Some Problems in Aristotle's Mathematical Ontology" begins by developing two ontological problems that concern Aristotle's numbers and arise from his metaphysical positions: (1) it seems that each attribute is an attribute of some individual substance, numbers are attributes, but numbers do not belong to individuals; and (2) Aristotle denies that attributes can have attributes, numbers are attributes, but arithmetic investigates the attributes of numbers. The essay uses these problems as touchstones to evaluate several prominent accounts of Aristotelian mathematics, accounts according to which: (1) mathematicals are abstracted from sensible substances (G. Martin), (2) mathematicals are defined by counting or by the sortal concepts through which we count (J. Klein), and (3) mathematicals are characterized by Aristotle in both ways (J. Annas). None of these accounts is able to resolve the problems. Drawing upon Aristotle's account of the infinite in *Physics* III, I develop an interpretation of Aristotelian arithmetic that does resolve them. By examining possible objections, I round out the account and bring it to bear on several other problems in Aristotle's mathematical ontology. My account combines realist and constructivist elements, and it suggests a way that Aristotle might have responded to some of Frege's criticisms.

One of the most troubling problems of Aristotelian metaphysics is how there could be an "accidental cause." The phrase indicates more than an partially specified cause; it suggests that even if all causal factors are present, an event may or may not occur. The issue in "Aristotle's Accidental Causes" is what nature must be like if there are to be accidents. After showing that the pertinent texts provide no definitive solution and arguing against the view that reigns in the literature, that Aristotle's accidents are uncaused, I reconstruct what I take to be Aristotle's account. I argue that accidents occur because of the character of Aristotelian metaphysics. Because he accounts for events by treating them as attributes of individual substances, any interaction between two substances is understood as two events, each of which has two causes. Because each of these events depends upon some substance other than the one in which it inheres, it cannot inhere in a substance solely in virtue of the substance. To inhere in a substance in virtue of the substance is to belong to it per se, and what does not so belong is accidental. Hence, any event that depends on the interaction of two substances must be accidental. In other words, accidents exist because substances are the pertinent principles of explanation and no one of them can fully account for its interactions with others. Though this is a failing, the attempts of modern philosophers to solve the problem of interaction generate the problem of free will. I show here why Aristotelian ethics is not subject to this latter problem.

What emerges from the essays of the "metaphysics" section is both the power and the limitations of the notion of actuality. On one hand, Aristotle can treat virtually any entity as an actuality, a self-subsistent entity. On the other hand, just because he thinks in terms of self-subsistent entities, there are inherent problems in accounting for interactions among them. An actuality is an intelligible entity. Hence, insofar as the world consists of actualities, it is intelligible. Thus, Aristotle and other Greek thinkers regard rationality as a feature of objects in the world. The final group of essays explores two different approaches to reason. Nietzsche virtually eliminates it; Hegel makes it all important.

In "Is Creativity Good?" I criticize Nietzsche's *Thus Spoke Zarathustra* by examining the consequences it would have. Nietzsche is interpreted to advance the twofold thesis that whatever is new is valuable for its own sake and that rationality is an obstacle to creativity that must be overcome. Such a position is implicit in much artistic experimentalism of this century and, especially, in works that aim to depict the primitive and nonrational. This essay argues that because these experimental works must rely on some conceptual scheme, their denial of the importance of reason is self-contradictory. It concludes that Nietzsche's mistake is to separate reason from creativity.

The problem of the differentia ("Hegel and the Problem of the Differentia") is whether or not the differentia belongs to the genus it differentiates. There are plausible arguments for both including it in and excluding it from the genus. This essay shows how the problem arises for Aristotle, and it argues that it is part of a more general problem inherent in drawing philosophical distinctions. The chief contention of this essay is that Hegel solves this problem by using a category to differentiate itself. The process of self-differentiation transforms a category into a new, richer category and, thus, drives the dynamic development of Hegel's categories.

Taken together, the essays in this book show how reason can be more than a process of human thought and how form can be more than a fixture of the world. To think of the world as some nonlinguistic item involves us immediately in the contradiction of describing something that does not admit of description. If instead we consider our actions and our knowledge and ask, what must things be like if we are to be what we are, we are led to posit a very different world— a world whose forms manifest rationality. Reason is not simply a set of human mental processes; as order, organization, and regular processes, reason is a constituent of nature. Again, if we pose the puzzle as how to express in language something that can only be nonlinguistic, we will be stymied. If, though, we can see the issue as how to grasp the world by means of reason, then solution is possible if the world is rational. Language and the world, as typically conceived, belong to distinct categories; reason and the world do not.

PART I

ETHICS

It might seem surprising to begin a collection of essays on Metaphysics with studies of topics in ethics. However, the ontological status of what we term "values" is indeed a topic for metaphysics. Historically, it was the beginning point for Socrates, for it was he who first sought definitions of virtues—at least if Aristotle's account is to be believed (*Metaphysics* XIII.4.1078b17–19). In seeking these definitions, Socrates must have supposed—as he often asks his interlocutors to do—that the virtues are something, and this amounts to ascribing ontological status to them. Aristotle's account continues: Socrates did not separate the forms; others—presumably Plato and the Academy—separated them from sensible things (1078b30–32). Aristotle himself rejected this separation. This well-known scheme is often repeated. However, taking it as a kind of thumbnail sketch of ancient *metaphysics*, we forget that the controversy it describes really concerns the good and the virtues—that is, that the controversy belongs to ethics. The result is that the sketch becomes a wooden statement of doctrinal differences. To understand the historical development and, more importantly, to understand the philosophical point at issue, we need to move the controversy back to the problem of virtue. The four papers in this section aim to come to grips with the arguments for forms, for their separation, and against their separation that stem from concerns about the nature of virtue and the good. For the most part, they are not deductive but are what I call "heuristic" arguments. They seek to find the nature of virtue or the good by finding its characteristics, and then they look for entities that possess the requisite characteristics. Their aim is not to deduce the nature of form but to show that nothing in our experience could do the job or, contrariwise, that there is indeed something that could have the requisite characteristics.

"The 'Socrates' of Plato's Early Dialogues" presents arguments for transcendent forms—not the standard Academic arguments, but the arguments that emerge from the inquiries into the virtues presented in Plato's early dialogues. "Plato and Aristotle on Friendship" shows why the consideration of friendship also leads Plato to posit the existence of a transcendent good. This chapter then argues that it is possible to satisfy Plato's criteria for friendship without positing such an entity. Aristotle meets these criteria by treating friendship as a joint activity, a type of actuality. The last two chapters in this group try to come to grips with actuality by examining problems in Aristotelian ethics. In "The Rational Basis of Aristotle's Virtue" I show how to construe acts of moral virtues as acts that are in accordance with reason. If this is right, then acts of moral virtue are not only actualities but derivable from our nature. The two problems that I consider in the last essay of this section both arise from failing to grasp what it means for human happiness to be an actuality. One of them stems from taking happiness quantitatively, as utilitarians do, the other from taking happiness qualitatively, in the way that Kant did. We can skirt both problems by understanding that insofar as happiness is an actuality it is a self-subsistent entity. In short, by treating particular problems in ancient ethics, the first four essays show us what it means to be an actuality and why it is necessary that there be actualities.

Chapter 1

The "Socrates" of Plato's Early Dialogues

In the *Phaedo*, Plato has Socrates make the following remarks:

> So long as we keep to the body and our soul is contaminated with this imperfection, there is no chance of our ever attaining satisfactorily to our object, which we assert to be truth. . . . If no true knowledge is possible in the company of the body, then either it is totally impossible to acquire knowledge or it is possible only after death. . . . It seems that so long as we are alive, we shall continue closest to knowledge if we avoid as much as we can all association with the body. . . . In fact the philosopher's occupation consists precisely in the freeing and separation of soul from body. (66b–67d, Tredenick trans.)

Socrates goes on to speak of his favorable prospects for gaining knowledge of courage and moderation after death (68c–e).

This text, often taken as a paradigm of Platonism, casts an extremely interesting light on the earlier dialogues: The failure of

Socrates and his interlocutors to arrive at adequate definitions of courage, moderation, piety, and so forth was, it would now seem, inevitable. Tied to his body and, thus, to sensible experience, Socrates was no more able than his interlocutors to attain knowledge of objects that are intrinsically nonsensible, objects that transcend sensible experience. It is precisely their transcendence, their separate existence, that renders forms indefinable *to us*. Plato's early dialogues were, it would now seem, inconclusive for a good reason.[1]

Conversely, the inconclusive character of the early dialogues supports the *Phaedo*'s claim that forms are separate. To put this point ironically, the very failures of the early dialogues to define the virtues amount to partial successes, for our apparent inability to define courage, moderation, and so forth, marks out their essential feature, their transcendence. So understood, the early dialogues not only provide support for the separation of forms that Plato asserts in the *Phaedo*: they argue, albeit inconclusively, for it.

This, I submit, is Plato's view of the early dialogues. The question that I want to pursue here is whether it is to be found in the early dialogues. Is it the perspective he held when he wrote those dialogues or is it the view of the mature Plato anxious to assimilate the work of his youth and the teachings of his master to a new scheme?

I

Before tackling this question, we need to raise another: what counts as evidence for ascribing any doctrine to the author of the early dialogues? The currently prevailing answer is that either the doctrine must be explicitly asserted in a text or some explicit argument must presuppose it as an implicit premise. Testimony from reliable contemporaries counts also, but it is thought less important than textual evidence. I shall call this view "evidentiary literalism."

Applying this standard to the question of "an early theory of forms," scholars acknowledge that no text in the dialogues usually dated early (on stylistic grounds) explicitly asserts the existence of separate forms. Consequently, the debate about an early theory of forms has centered on whether forms are assumed somewhere. Some have claimed that they are presupposed by "what is X?" questions or by the arguments answering them.[2] Others, however, have argued that these discussions can be given a good sense without supposing an early theory and that such an interpretation is preferable because interlocutors in the dialogues would hardly agree to claims that assumed a theory of forms.[3] This latter is today the most widely held view. We have it from Aristotle that, unlike others (Plato and the Academy, presumably), the historical Socrates never separated the forms (Met. XIII.4.1078b30–31). Since the early dialogues do not explicitly refer to separate forms and need not, it has seemed, presuppose their existence, most scholars have come to regard these dialogues as representations of the historical Socrates.[4]

Though it is my aim here to challenge this widely held view, I want to acknowledge that it is a formidable interpretation. Much of the credit for it belongs to Gregory Vlastos. His careful attention to detail and dogged insistence on finding what is really in the text have produced a clear, sane, and highly plausible interpretation.[5] A token of its cogency is that to challenge it I need to introduce new standards of evidence.

To motivate this change let us suppose for the moment that Aristotle is right when he says that Socrates never separated the forms. Writing shortly after the death of Socrates, Plato might well have wished to retain the style and substance of Socrates' views, especially when part of his audience would have been familiar with the original. Nevertheless, he could have decided that these views support an inference that Socrates himself never drew, that the forms must be separate, and he could, accordingly, have written the dialogues so that readers would draw this conclusion even though it is never stated in the dialogues. Though I think this scenario is accurate, my point now is not its accuracy, but that if we insist that only what is said or assumed counts as evidence, we cannot even consider it seriously. Evidentiary literalism rules this hypothesis and others like it out of court without a hearing. Hence, relying only on what is stated in the text is not neutral. It would commit us to excluding certain interpretations.

Evidentiary literalism would make more sense if our subject were treatises, but we are dealing with dialogues. What is explicit here are the assumptions advanced or endorsed by interlocutors, the intermediary conclusions drawn from them and used, in turn, as premises in other arguments, and the absurd consequences drawn from both of these. Because Socrates is nearly always examining the interlocutors' views, it is questionable whether the intermediary or ultimate conclusions he states may be correctly ascribed to him; and, anyway, it is uncertain that *he* always represents the view of the author. Moreover, early dialogues end without stating a satisfactory conclusion. For all these reasons, the early dialogues invite us to seek an implicit conclusion or purpose.

This, however, literalists refuse to do. Richard Robinson, for example, identifies drawing inferences from what is written as one of five common ways of misinterpreting Plato.[6] Lacking overall doctrinal conclusions, evidentiary literalists must focus on the assumptions or the intermediary conclusions that serve as assumptions for later arguments. They identify as Socratic those that are methodological or recurring, and they pay much attention to arguments for certain intermediary conclusions. But just what is the significance of these latter if they lead inevitably into contradiction? If, on the other hand, there is some non-contradictory, ultimate conclusion that could be derived from them, it would be unstated and, so, necessarily outside the bounds of what literalists take to be the proper subject of consideration. Thus, literalism has led scholars to focus attention on the dialogues' assumptions and on claims that, though inferred from these assumptions, function as premises. Yet what is most significant and interesting about the dialogues is what, if anything, they might prove. Ironically, despite their close attention to arguments, literalists undermine the overall argument of a dialogue by focusing on its assumptions.

My aim in criticizing the literalists is not to endorse the literary approach that is often counterposed to close study of arguments.[7] Rather, I propose that there are other types of evidence that are important for understanding the arguments, namely, structural and contextual evidence. The sequence in which arguments appear could be philosophically significant if it supports a conclusion. Likewise, a single arguments, read in the context of a dialogue, could support a conclusion left to the reader to infer. It is widely recognized that the dialogues are carefully constructed; there is no good reason not to consider structure and context as philosophical evidence.

In this chapter I shall sketch how such evidence could be brought to bear on the question of an "early theory of forms." I shall be arguing that the view Plato espouses in the *Phaedo* does motivate the early dialogues. There are two main arguments supporting this conclusion. First, there are structural features common to many of the early dialogues that, when considered together, constitute a type of argument for separate forms. Second, one of these common features, the unity of virtue argument, read in the context of the dialogues, leads by itself to separate forms. Each will be treated in turn in the next two sections.

To consider all the early dialogues and to respond adequately to the literature is beyond the scope of this brief treatment. I can only hope to set out my interpretation, to show something of what supports it, and to show that it is worth considering. Besides their value in interpreting the early dialogues, the arguments to be presented are philosophically interesting in their own right.

II

Typically the early dialogues relate a conversation that is principally between Socrates and one or two other interlocutors. Usually an interlocutor has made, implicitly or explicitly, a knowledge claim that Socrates challenges with a request for a definition. Anyone who is just courageous, or moderate or who knows how to teach these or how to acquire them must know what they are. To know is to be able to give a definition. But the definitions advanced turn out, upon examination, to be inadequate, and the knowledge claim of the interlocutor is thereby discredited. The bulk of most dialogues is given over to the examination and refutation of definitions of individual virtues.

Each dialogue is unique and examines a particular set of definitions, but there are structural features that can be identified in many early dialogues. Often the definitions advanced number three or fall into three groups. The first definition is usually trivially wrong. The second seems promising, receives careful attention, and is often reformulated in the course of discussion. The third definition seems to overshoot the mark; it apparently includes too much. With all definitions refuted, the dialogue ends in *aporia*.

The *Laches* could serve as a paradigm. Laches first proposes as a definition of courage that the courageous man is someone who stands and fights (190e). Clearly, he has mentioned a behavior that would be courageous only in some situations; in others, the courageous man would do something else. The second definition Laches gives for courage is endurance (*karteria*—192b); this he quickly revises to endurance with knowledge (192d). The revised definition is rejected on the ground that someone who acted without the benefit of knowledge of an art would be more brave than someone who acted with knowledge of the art. The third definition, now given by Nicias, is that courage is wisdom or knowledge (194d–e). The most striking difficulty with this later definition is that someone possessing the knowledge which would make him courageous would have all the other virtues as well—a contradiction because it is assumed that courage is a mere part of virtue.

As a rule, the first definition is merely an example (*Hippias Major* 287e [see also 289e, 291d–e]; *Charmides* 159b,[8] *Euthyphro* 5d; *Meno* 71e; see also *Republic* I.331c–d). To us it seems like a category mistake, but Socrates does not simply dismiss the example. He treats it as a legitimate response to his question and proceeds to refute it. To do so he usually supplies circumstances in which this particular thing or act would not be desirable or good. Since the interlocutors assume that a virtue is always good or beneficial, and since there are situations in which the example would not be beneficial, the example cannot define the virtue.

The second definition is substantial and interesting, but it fails to be adequate because it misses something important. What it misses is the connection of the particular moral virtue under discussion with knowledge or with the good. To define courage as endurance, as Laches does (192b), is inadequate because endurance in a bad enterprise is not good. Since courage is always good, whatever defines courage must also always be good. To avoid the problem, Laches revises the second definition to "endurance accompanied by knowledge." But this, too, is inadequate because it does not spell out the pertinent type of knowledge. Socrates suggests that the knowledge is a military art like horsemanship or slinging. But someone who showed endurance in battle because he was skilled in the art of horsemanship would be less courageous than someone who endured without expert knowledge of this art (193a-d). So knowledge—or, at least, a certain type of knowledge—is not necessary for courage, as previously argued, but antithetical to it. In sum, knowledge is both necessary and unnecessary for endurance to be good (beneficial). The problem here is how to integrate knowledge and goodness (benefit) into the definition of courage offered by Laches. Interlocutors in other dialogues face parallel difficulties in working goodness and knowledge into their accounts.

Though it conforms to no single dialogue, we can give the problem of the second definition the following general formulation: Whatever else we are to say about courage, piety, or any other particular virtue, each must always be good and each seems to require knowledge to be such. Suppose that X is offered as a definition of a virtue; if there are circumstances in which possession of X would not be good, then X cannot define the virtue. To be the virtue X must always be good or beneficial, and what would insure this is the knowledge of how and when to use X. Consequently, we should include knowledge with whatever else characterizes the virtue. But knowledge of how to use X presupposes other types of knowledge: we cannot know when X will be beneficial unless we know what counts as benefit. Benefit is not always the achievement of what we desire; for sometimes the things we desire will, in the long run, do us harm. Possession of the virtue must somehow involve knowledge of what is good. However, those who know what is good in any particular area are those who possess the art that has that area as its subject matter. These specialists are not necessarily more virtuous than nonspecialists—indeed, they seem less virtuous just because they can rely on their knowledge. Thus, knowledge is necessary for virtue but also, in some cases, antithetical to virtue. In short, virtue requires knowledge in addition to X, but it is unclear what this knowledge is knowledge of and how it relates to X.

Considering this reasoning, we can see that the difficulty arises from identifying the knowledge necessary for a virtue with the specialist knowledge possessed by the craftsman. Since the knowledge that would be required for X always to be beneficial is just the knowledge of benefit, that is, knowledge of the good, it seems plausible simply to identify the virtue with this knowledge. So it is that the third definition often identifies virtue as a kind of knowledge. The problem is that the knowledge that would enable someone to know whether some X is beneficial is just knowledge of benefit in general, and this would be the same no matter what the X is. Thus, the knowledge required for some particular virtue would turn out to be just the knowledge required for any virtue and to have one virtue would be to have them all. Knowledge of courage, piety or any other particular good would be knowledge of the whole good. Indeed, this knowledge would have to include virtually everything that could be known.[9] Such a knowledge seems impossible for us. Besides the conclusion that virtue is one conflicts with the interlocutors' assumption that a particular virtue is—to use the language of mathematics—a proper part of the whole of virtue.

In the early dialogues all the definitions fail, but often there is, at or near the end, an ironic remark that indicates that the dialogue has not been for nought. In the *Lysis*, for example, the interlocutors are declared to have become friends in their unsuccessful inquiry into friendship (223b), an inquiry whose operating assumption is that knowledge of what friendship is is necessary in order to be friends.

These same structural elements are present, with some variations, in the *Euthyphro*, for example. The first definition of piety is an example (5d). The second definition, what is loved by the gods (7a), is modified (9e) and, then, in a difficult argument, rejected because it does not explain what sort of nature piety would have to have to cause the gods to love it (10e–11b). That piety is loved by the gods is a character (*pathos*) that belongs to it, not its nature (*ousia*). It would be necessary to know what the nature is before we could know why the gods love it, and the gods themselves must know this nature. Though the text does not speak of knowledge, it assumes that the gods know the nature of piety; that is why they love it. Once this nature comes into the discussion, it renders love inessential, a mere consequence of knowing the nature. The third definition identifies piety as just (11e), and then tries unsuccessfully to find a proper part of justice to equate it with. If piety is just but no part of justice, must we not conclude that piety is simply justice? It would seem to follow that "care of the gods" would, like other instances of justice, be much like a business transaction; but the gods have no need of anything we could give them (14c–15a). It follows that piety could not be justice, and this, in effect, refutes the third definition. Finally, at the very end of the dialogue Socrates remarks that his failure to acquire knowledge of the divine from Euthyphro will leave him unable to defend himself against Meletus' indictment (16a). But to be ignorant of divine wisdom and to recognize that ignorance would seem precisely to constitute piety. Though the differences are significant, we can recognize the same structural components we saw in the *Laches*: the example, the weak definition that is initially formulated without knowledge but turns out to include it, and the strong definition that identifies the virtue with other virtues or, here, another virtue.

This picture is, of course, too simple. Emphasizing their common structure cannot do justice to the richness of the dialogues, and even the lengthy and detailed analysis of each dialogue that would be necessary to sustain its imposition would have to acknowledge many variations and exceptions. Structure is not a universal form for the dialogues; at best we can speak of their family resemblance. But why would we want to? Part of the enduring genius of the dialogues is that they are not slave to a single, rigidly conceived paradigm. Why should we even look for common components?

Identifying a family structure is important for two reasons. First, it shows the literary hand of the author, Plato. If these conversations are not spontaneous but artfully constructed, my contention that Plato aims at a conclusion is much more probable. Second—an application of the first point—the structural components of the dialogue serve as constituents of a larger implicit argument, what I shall call the "super-argument." What is this larger argument? Let us consider the components in turn. Why is the first definition always an example? Each interlocutor, no matter how sophisticated, makes the same trivial mistake of offering an example when asked for a definition. Even literary artifice would seem to call for variation—unless, that is, the example serves some philosophical purpose. In offering the example, the interlocutor asserts that some act is an instance of moral virtue X. He affirms that (1) X exists and belongs to some individual. Of course, the interlocutor should agree to this because he typically thinks that he himself has the virtue in question. I submit that the claim that some people possess the virtue is crucial for the larger argument. The second definition typically identifies the moral virtue with some character, such as endurance or being loved; let's call it A. The refutation of this definition shows that the virtue cannot be simply A, but that (2) the virtue X ought somehow to be knowledge. However, as we saw, identifying the virtue with knowledge makes it indistinguishable it from other virtues. The refutation of the third definition shows that (3) the virtue cannot be knowledge or, at least, that it cannot be a knowledge that the interlocutor or, apparently, anyone else has. In short, what emerges from the structure are a group of contradictory claims:

1. The moral virtue X exists and can be ascribed to individuals.
2. X is knowledge.
3. No one has such knowledge.

It follows from 2. and 3. that:

4. No one has X.

The last claim is clearly inconsistent with the first. A contradiction like this one may not seem like an argument, but think of indirect proofs in mathematics: we assume the contrary of what we wish to prove and show that it leads to a contradiction. The structure I have identified contains a contradiction. Is there some hypothesis that gives rise to this contradiction, some hypothesis whose negation Plato wishes to prove? In such case, if the dialogues do contain the contradictory structure that I ascribe to them, they would be enthymematic indirect proofs. That is to say, the dialogues are not just inconclusive, but inconsistent; hence, they indirectly support the negation of some assumption. What, then, is the conclusion that the dialogues support?

What makes the contradictory structure that I have uncovered in the dialogues especially interesting is that a way out of the contradiction is indicated by the *Phaedo* passage quoted at the beginning. It is possible for virtue to be knowledge and yet not be a knowledge that anyone has if the knowledge that is the virtue is transcendent, if, that is, virtue is a knowledge that exists separately because its object exists separately. In other words, the second and third claims can both be true if we reject part of the first. There is no doubt that the moral virtue exists, but what seemed at first to be an example of it cannot be. Indeed, no action could be a perfect example of the moral virtue because no one has the knowledge requisite for possession of the virtue. If, though, no human action could exemplify the virtue, and if the virtue exists, then it must be separate from human experience. Hence, in rejecting the first claim, the super-argument supports separation.

But why should we reject the first claim? We need not rely on the authority of the *Phaedo*. The reasons for rejecting the assumption that someone has the virtue are explicit and pervasive: Socrates frequently disavows having any knowledge himself, and he questions people who seem—to themselves and to others—to have a knowledge of virtue only to find that they do not. Since whoever had the virtue could give an account of it, neither he nor his interlocutors apparently have the virtue. The spectacle of refutation depicted so often in the dialogues serves to expose pretensions to knowledge and—given the assumption that the virtuous have knowledge—pretentions to virtue. Occasionally, an interlocutor mentions someone else as possessing a particular virtue: Meno speaks of Pericles, Themistocles, and Thucydides as virtuous (*Meno* 93d-94e); Hippias speaks of a beautiful girl as beautiful (*kalon*) (*Hippias Major* 287e). But such claims are explicitly or subtly undermined. Socrates emphasizes to Meno that "you" think these men exemplars of virtue; the beautiful girl is also, in comparison with a goddess, ugly (289b–c); and in the *Gorgias* he denies that Pericles, Cimon, Miltiades, or Themistocles was virtuous (515d–516e) and concludes that "we do not know of any man who has proved a good statesman in this city" (517a, Woodhead trans.).

This passage from the *Gorgias* provides strong support for a claim that, at first glance, may seem absurd. The problem is that the method of the early dialogues is often taken to be inductive. Socrates starts with examples of a particular moral virtue and aims to find what they have in common. However, since Socrates supposes that knowledge of justice would make its possessor a good statesman, the *Gorgias'* denial that there are any good statesmen is tantamount to the denial that there are any just men in the city. It is as if in the midst of examining what a set of examples of justice have in common, we were to declare that the examples were not examples of justice at all. Questions about the validity of an example set would undermine an inductive method. Thus, so as long as we stick to the inductive picture, the denial of (1) seems absurd. But this inductive picture is not rich enough to account for what occurs in the dialogues. What we find, first of all, is that it is not Socrates but his interlocutors who propose examples of virtues and they do so in response to "What is X?" questions.[10] Typically, the example that each proposes is himself or what he is doing (e.g. *Euthyphro* 5d–e). Whether his action is indeed an example of this virtue is at issue: this is why a Socratic conversation makes interlocutors examine their own lives. In other words, in examining what X is, interlocutors are examining their own lives because each considers whether his own action is truly an instance of X. Now we cannot judge whether the action is an instance of X until we know what X is: we cannot arrive at a set of examples of X without a standard for judging them to be such (e.g. *Meno* 81e). This is the reasoning that motivates the inquiries into the virtues. On the other hand, though, it is difficult if not impossible to speak of the nature of a virtue without some examples before us, and this is why the dialogues begin with examples. We have a kind of circle here, and what we see is the dialogues playing off the supposed examples of a virtue with proposed definitions, constantly revising each in light of changes to the other. The final view should not be sought in remarks made in the course of a dialogue, but in what is reached through it. And what is reached through it? Lack of certainty about the standard and, thus, no ability to decisively determine the sample set. The supposed examples of the virtue either are not examples of it or could not be known to be such.

My contention that the first claim of the super-argument is rejected might also be challenged in at least two other ways. First, it might be asked, what is the point of Socrates' inquiry into virtue if no one has what he seeks nor likely could have it? Second, there are places where he does seem to ascribe virtues to people. For example, at the end of the *Lysis*, in a passage mentioned earlier, Socrates remarks that the interlocutors have become friends through their unsuccessful search for a definition of friendship, a search that has shown the necessity for friends to have this knowledge. Similarly, arriving at a definition of courage will, Socrates suggests in the *Laches*, require the courage to pursue an argument (194b). Again, it is suggested by Critias at the end of the *Charmides* that one could become moderate by regularly submitting to Socrates' charm, that is, to dialectic (176b).[11] Ironically, in inquiring into friendship, in seeking the knowledge necessary to be a friend and in failing to secure that knowledge, the interlocutors have become friends; in seeking an account of courage that would allow someone to become courageous, and in failing to secure such knowledge, the interlocutors have manifested courage; in the act of inquiring into moderation, interlocutors engage in an activity that could make them moderate. Is this not proof that the virtues can indeed be ascribed to people and thus a refutation of my contention that the first claim is denied? We need to look closely at the apparent ascription of virtues in these passages. What the text claims is actually, in the *Lysis*, "We believe we are friends with each other" (223b), and in the Laches, "In action, it is likely, someone might say we partake of courage, but not, I think, in words if he would now hear us discoursing" (193e). Socrates continues in the latter to encourage the interlocutor, Laches, to show courage or at least endurance in pursuing the argument (194a). The passage from the *Charmides* speaks indirectly of the importance of practicing dialectic for becoming moderate, even if the dialectic fails to define moderation; it acknowledges that the interlocutors do not have the virtue. Thus, these passages do not ascribe friendship and courage to the interlocutors without qualification. Interlocutors merely seem or appear to possess a virtue.

These ascriptions are tentative and ironic, for how could the interlocutors be friends when they lack the knowledge of friendship requisite for friendship, how can Laches be courageous when he lacks the knowledge of courage requisite for possession of this virtue? It is not the virtue itself that is ascribed but a semblance. At issue are derivative sorts of courage, moderation, and friendship that manifest themselves in the activity of dialectic. I propose that these apparent ascriptions of virtues are parallel to Socrates' claim in the *Apology* to possess human wisdom. (I shall have more to say about this disavowal of knowledge later.) Just as Socrates has a kind of wisdom, human wisdom, because he knows that he does not have genuine or divine wisdom, so too he and his interlocutors have a kind of virtue—I call it "human virtue"—through their inquiries into genuine or divine virtue. In the course of inquiring into courage, friendship and so forth, in the course of failing to arrive at them, one acquires something like them, human versions of the virtues. These are dialectical substitutes; they result not from knowledge of virtue but from ignorance of virtue and the consequent inquiry into it. That *human* virtue can come from inquiry is, I suggest, the positive lesson of the early dialogues. Acquisition of human virtue makes dialogue worthwhile even if its divine objective must remain elusive. This distinction between the human and the divine knowledge and between human and divine virtue is readily intelligible in terms of the *Phaedo* passage. It would be hard to make sense of it any other way.

Again, I acknowledge that the structure I have presented here is not found in all the early dialogues. The *Crito* and *Euthydemus* are obvious exceptions. Each of Plato's inquiries contains its own particular difficulties, its own particular version of the super-argument, and it is always instructive to explore their individual details. In this brief discussion, though, we must content ourselves with identifying structural features common to many. What I have called the "super-argument" appears in enough of the early dialogues to confirm that it is a product of their author rather than an artifact of the interpreter. The only way I see to make sense of the claims I have collected under the heading "super-argument" is that they constitute an indirect proof for the separation of the virtue, as it truly is, from human experience, precisely the doctrine asserted in the *Phaedo*.

III

A second type of evidence for ascribing separate forms to the author of the early dialogues lies—as a box within a box—in one of the common features of early dialogues, the arguments for the unity of virtue. The best-known and most frequently discussed of these arguments appear in the *Protagoras*, but if the preceding section is correct, unity arguments appear in most early dialogues. Some of these dialogues identify a virtue with the possession of a character such as knowledge and then show that the same character would enable someone to have all the virtues. Thus, the *Laches* shows knowledge of good and evil to be not only sufficient for courage but for all the virtues (198d–199e), and the *Gorgias* argues that a well-ordered man is not merely moderate but also pious, just courageous, and wise (506e–508a).[12] A second group of unity arguments define one virtue by another; for example, the argument from the *Euthyphro* discussed earlier, that defines piety as part of justice.[13]

The difference between other dialogues and the *Protagoras* is that in the latter Socrates clearly endorses unity arguments, while in the former he usually advances them as if they were unlikely consequences of an opponent's position. It is probably the rhetorical surroundings of these latter arguments that has sometimes prevented commentators from seeing fully how closely akin they are to the unity arguments in the *Protagoras*.[14] Moreover, commentators have usually taken unity arguments in dialogues other than the *Protagoras* to be simply elenctic. Just as interlocutors, faced with the conflict between unity conclusions and the assumption that a particular virtue is a mere part of all virtues, choose to preserve the latter, so too scholars have supposed that unity conclusions just could not be correct.[15] There is no compelling argument for this path. A contradiction reached in a reductio argument shows only that some premise must be mistaken; it does not show which one. It is more plausible for at least three reasons to suppose that Socrates looks instead for his interlocutors to affirm unity and reject the part hypothesis. First, the arguments of the *Protagoras* provide strong evidence that Socrates or the author of the dialogue does endorse the unity of virtues. If other early dialogues did reject unity, then we would need to charge their author with inconsistency. Second, the unity of virtue arguments are often the last arguments in a dialogue, as the preceding section maintains;

and the interlocutor's rejection of them leaves the discussion in hopeless *aporia*. Given the typical structure of early dialogues, it is likely that the interlocutors' wrong turn lies in their rejection of unity. Third, if the unity of virtue arguments support Socrates' own view, then the early dialogues are more benign and, even, positive than usually thought, for they show Socrates not merely refuting interlocutors but leading them toward what he regards as the truth. Socrates' own description of himself as a benefactor of Athens (*Apology* 36d–e) would be apt. For these reasons, it is likely that Socrates or, at least, the author of the early dialogues does endorse the unity of virtue arguments.

What sort of unity do these arguments ascribe to virtue, and what is their significance? These questions are debated widely in the literature, though attention is focused on the *Protagoras.* There Socrates asks Protagoras whether the parts of virtue are one as the parts of a face or one as the parts of gold (329d). Protagoras endorses the former unity, and he continues, "many [people] are courageous but unjust or just but not wise." Socrates argues against this type of unity by arguing that whoever has one virtue must have all the others. It is clear that he takes the different virtues to have more in common than parts of the face, but it is unclear precisely what that would be. Does unity of virtue mean only that whoever has one has the others (the extensional or referential view) or also that the virtues somehow have the same definition. Vlastos argues that the unity of virtues consists of the identity of their references.[16] Terry Penner has proposed that the virtues are one in the stronger (strict identity) sense that all virtuous actions spring from the same psychological state.[17]

The chief argument for the referential interpretation is that the alternative makes no sense; for if the virtues are a single thing, then what is said about any one of them could be said of any other.[18] Such an identity would seem to make hash of the Socratic claim that piety is a standard of pious actions because piety would also be a standard of just actions, and justice would be a standard of pious actions, etc. On the other hand, the drawback to the referential interpretation is that the text treats virtue as if it were itself a thing: Socrates speaks of it as a thing with different names (e.g., 349b).[19] Since one of these names is knowledge, and since knowledge is apparently what would make its possessor virtuous in all respects (361b), the unity of virtues must be more than referential. Moreover, if the same knowledge is responsible for all the virtues, then it makes perfectly good sense to say that the standard of piety is at once the standard of justice and all the other virtues.

For these reasons the referential interpretation should be set aside. This is not to deny identity of reference, but to recognize it as a consequence of a stronger identity. However, Penner's alternative is little better. It is conceivable that virtue is a psychic state, as he supposes, but it need not be, and there is no need to think that Socrates assumes it is. Instead, the question of the nature of virtue remains open. Why should Socrates prejudice the inquiry by assuming at the start that virtue must be a psychic state? Again, looking for assumptions implicit in the question is the wrong approach. If the inquiry is worth anything, it must assume little or nothing about the sort of entity virtue is. More important is what emerges from the inquiry. What does emerge from the *Protagoras* is that virtue is one, namely, knowledge. But there is no necessity to take knowledge as a psychic state. To be sure, if someone had this knowledge he would be virtuous, and knowledge would then be in his psyche, but there is nothing here to indicate that this antecedent is ever met: there is nothing that compels us to conclude that anyone actually possesses the knowledge that constitutes virtue.

On the contrary, there are at least three features of the text of the *Protagoras* that indicate that no one possesses knowledge or, equivalently, virtue. First, there is the refutation of the apparently wise Protagoras. Socrates argues that virtue is knowledge and, thus, one; Protagoras maintains that the virtues are diverse. But only knowledge can be taught. If, then, Protagoras is right about diversity, he is wrong to say he can teach virtue. If, on the other hand, virtue is knowledge, then it could, in principle, be taught, but clearly not by Protagoras because he does not understand its nature. In either case, Protagoras' claim to be able to teach virtue must be wrong (361a–b). Socrates looks more promising as a teacher, but he denies he has this capacity, and there is no reason to think his denial disingenuous because he does not explain the content of what one would know to be virtuous. Since no one in the dialogue is shown to have the knowledge requisite for virtue, the reader is left to infer that *no* one has genuine virtue.

A second way the dialogue indicates the absence of genuine virtue lies in its arguments against common experience. The wise coward and the courageous but stupid athlete spring to mind as obvious counterexamples to the unity of virtue doctrine. Socrates himself suggests the well-planned crime as an example of what the many might regard as an action of a moderate but unjust person (333d). Later in the dialogue, apparently accepting Socrates' earlier arguments, Protagoras claims that courage differs from the other virtues on the ground that "you can find many men who are quite unjust, unholy, intemperate, and ignorant, yet outstandingly courageous" (349d). However, in order to maintain the unity of virtue doctrine, Socrates must deny that the seemingly wise coward is truly wise, that the stupid athlete is truly courageous, and that the criminal can be moderate: our experience and our ordinary understanding of the virtues must be cast aside. Since the people we would ordinarily take to have one virtue do not manifest all of them, they cannot genuinely possess any of them. And if *they* are not virtuous, then no one would be. The virtue that is one is just not found in experience.

The third way the *Protagoras*, in particular, leads us to the conclusion that no one is truly virtuous is the analysis of Simonides' poem. According to Socrates' analysis, Simonides criticizes Pittacus for saying that to be noble is hard; to be noble is not hard, it is impossible for us. Only the gods can be noble (341e). We can become noble, at least for a time; it is *becoming* noble that can be hard. To be noble is to be virtuous, and this requires knowledge. It follows, then, that genuine virtue and knowledge belong only to the gods. They transcend our experience. We see here the key distinction of Plato's middle period, the distinction between being and becoming; and locating the human within becoming is implicit in the *Phaedo* passage quoted at the beginning. It might be proposed that this part of the literary analysis was written after the rest of the *Protagoras*.[20] This is unlikely: the distinction between being and becoming is fundamental to the entire literary analysis, and the latter is integrally related to the rest of the dialogue. (Though it would take us too far afield from our theme to defend here, I think that the connection between the literary analysis and the rest of the dialogue is much closer than has been noticed.) Rather, what we have in this literary analysis is the introduction of the Platonic doctrine of transcendence.

Poetic analysis cannot prove a claim about virtue, and this analysis, in particular, cannot be taken as a serious interpretation of the poem. Socrates is foisting an interpretation on it, just as he thinks Protagoras did; and his aim is to show that virtually any interpretation could be read into the poem. But is the interpretation his own view or just some view that his readers would realize is not

Simonides'? Either way, it is surprising that the doctrine of the *Phaedo* is present explicitly in the *Protagoras*. Can it be coincidental that just this doctrine—and nothing else explicit in the dialogue—provides a way out of the paradox of virtue's being knowledge but apparently unteachable?

That is to say, the literary analysis not only shows that no one has the knowledge that constitutes virtue, it also suggests a way to understand how virtue could still be knowledge even if it is not a knowledge that anyone has. Virtue is a knowledge that belongs to the gods; we can come to be virtuous and acquire knowledge, but only for a time. We have the semblance of knowledge and virtue, not the reality. Thus, Socrates is right to say that virtue cannot be taught—not because virtue itself is intrinsically unteachable, but because there is no person who actually possesses this knowledge. Since virtue is one, since no one can define it, and since anyone who did possess it could define it, it follows that no one is truly virtuous. Only the gods possess it. Again, the claim that virtue is one removes virtue from sensible experience. But if virtue exists apart from sense experience, if it makes possible our striving, then virtue is transcendent. In sum, the conclusion that virtue is one is tantamount to its transcendence.

How can we infer transcendence from the absence of virtue in sensible things? Does human ignorance or moral turpitude prove the existence of a nonhuman virtue? The unity of virtue argument does not deductively prove the transcendence of the forms. (Nor did the structural argument I presented earlier.) It proves only that virtue is one. Yet, because we do not experience such a unity, we are led to posit virtue as transcendent.

This latter move is presupposed by an argument of the *Phaedo:* the soul is declared to be immortal because it most resembles what is "divine, immortal, intelligible, one (*monoeidēs*), indissoluble, and what is most like to itself because it is always in the same way and possesses the same character" in contrast with what has the opposite characters, namely, the body (80b). What is one and always the same must exist apart from sensibles because they are always in flux. What the unity of virtue argument shows is that virtue, too, is just such a unity. It, too, must be separate from sensible experience where we seem to find courage without knowledge and, in general, where virtue seems to be many. There must be some one standard in respect of which to judge all these manifestations as partial realizations of virtue. Virtue must be one, on just the ground that the *Parmenides* uses to prove the existence of a form, that a plurality presupposes a unity (132a).[21] Virtue is a "one [that stands] over many" types of virtues. To be sure, neither the *Protagoras* nor other early dialogues make these arguments. Little here indicates explicitly the philosophical significance that "one" would later have for Plato and the Academy, and recent scholars writing about the unity of virtue arguments have offered less metaphysically charged interpretations. Yet, when we consider how unity of virtue is argued and what is said about it, it seems likely that the author of the *Protagoras* is leading his readers to a form of virtue much like forms he espouses elsewhere. Recall the passage from the *Phaedo* that opened this chapter. After the direct quotation, Socrates speaks of his prospects for attaining virtue after death, prospects that he declares to be favorable because virtue is knowledge and the body poses an obstacle to knowledge. This separate knowledge "makes possible courage, moderation, justice and, in a word, true virtue" (69b). That is to say, genuine virtue is one and, like genuine knowledge, it can belong to us only when we cease to be sensible beings. This passage typifies the way results of earlier dialogues are summarized in later ones. Plato expresses here what is left implicit in the *Protagoras*: transcendence and the unity of virtue go hand in hand.

If all this is right, then Socrates' frequently stated denial of knowledge (e.g. *Apol.* 21b; *Gorgias* 509a) is not disingenuous, as has often been thought.[22] It rather reflects just the conclusion intended to be drawn from the dialogues. If the forms are really transcendent, then how could anyone know them (cf. *Parm.* 133b–134e)? The most one could say of transcendent forms is that one understands that they must exist, but they are, strictly speaking, beyond human knowledge. Ironically, in saying that he does not know the forms, Socrates is expressing their nature. Indeed, the irony of Socrates' denial of knowledge is not that it is simply false, but that it is false just because it is true. This is exactly what we would expect him to say of transcendent objects of knowledge.

There are, of course, many other interpretations of Socrates' denial of knowledge. Vlastos, for example, distinguishes two types of knowledge, one elenctically supported, the other "divine" or certain.[23] According to Vlastos, Socrates denies only the latter; he affirms his possession of the former, "human" knowledge. Vlastos writes as though the two types of knowledge were distinguished solely by epistemological criteria. This is not the case. The knowledge that Socrates lacks is knowledge reputed to be possessed by statesmen and poets (*Apol.* 21b–22c). This is the knowledge he sought (through dialectic) by asking them the questions he raises in early dialogues: what is courage? what is moderation? and so forth. Thus, the knowledge Socrates lacks is the knowledge of the virtues. In contrast, the knowledge Socrates claims to have consists of maxims; for example, "to do injustice and to disobey my superiors whether god or man, these I know to be bad and shameful" (29b). Just what does one know when he knows that to do injustice is evil? As much as he knows when he knows that to do justice is good: that is, virtually nothing. Without also knowing the content of injustice, knowing that injustice is evil does not help us to make ethical decisions. I think that the author of the *Laches* says as much when he has Nicias advance Socrates' view of the definition of courage as a kind of wisdom (194c–d). Nicias is asked, a wisdom or knowledge about what? He replies: "knowledge of what is fearful and what is encouraging, both in wartime and in all other situations" (194e–195a). This "definition" tells us virtually nothing: the certainty that it is true would not *make* Socrates or anyone else courageous. Yet, in saying that courage is a kind of knowledge, Socrates does mean precisely that it would make someone who possessed it courageous. To become courageous we would need to learn what, in particular, ought to be feared and what ought to encourage us. Thus, the claim that virtue is knowledge, the various "definitions" advanced by Socrates, his unwillingness to fear what he does not know to be evil, the so-called paradoxes—all this he would put under human knowledge. Human knowledge concerns the virtues, but one who has only human knowledge does not grasp the nature of those virtues. On Vlastos' interpretation, it remains mysterious why Socrates should be so dismissive of his human knowledge.[24] But if, as I maintain, the objects of divine knowledge are transcendent, Socrates' attitude toward human knowledge is entirely appropriate. Moreover, characterizing the knowledge he lacks as "divine" is apt if its object is transcendent, correspondingly inapt if its object is anything else.[25] Divine knowledge is precisely that knowledge that Socrates and Protagoras so evidently lack at the end of the *Protagoras*.

My claim here is not that the *Phaedo* or other middle dialogues are necessary for us to understand the *Protagoras*, but that the *Phaedo* makes explicit conclusions that the reader is supposed to draw from the *Protagoras*, namely that virtue consists of a knowledge that transcends human experience. Perhaps it will be objected that the conclusions that I have drawn from the unity of virtue arguments do not follow deductively. I concede this point. The existence of separate form is merely *a* solution; nothing here proves that it must be the only solution. Socratic dialectic is open-ended and unlimited. In contrast, let me suggest that what Aristotle aims to do in his ethics is to find solutions to these and similar problems without positing transcendent forms. To understand the Socratic dialectic we must avoid reading back alternative solutions, and attempt to discern the author's solution. My aim here is not to assess Plato's unity of virtue argument nor the closely related argument from the structure of the dialogues. In the end, we may perhaps agree with Aristotle's view of Plato's arguments for the forms: "from some no inference must follow" (*Metaphysics* I.9.990b10; XIII.4.1079a6). What I have done here is to identify—to the extent that a brief treatment allows—these arguments in the early dialogues.

The early dialogues contain no explicit references to separate form, and a likely reason for this is that Plato tries to preserve the claims made by the historical Socrates. Nevertheless, when we consider (1) the way that the arguments are organized in the text and (2) one characteristic part of that organization, the unity of virtue arguments, there is good reason to suppose that Plato intends in many early dialogues to show that there must be separate forms. That this was also the view of the historical Socrates seems unlikely. But the author of the early dialogues believes that the Socratic inquiry into definitions implies the existence of separate forms. With truly Socratic irony, the dialogues show how to define the forms or, at least, an essential feature of the forms, by their failing to define the forms.

Chapter 2

PLATO AND ARISTOTLE ON FRIENDSHIP

Friendship figures prominently in the ethics of Plato and of Aristotle, far more than in modern and contemporary treatments of the subject. In the present chapter I shall be concerned only with Plato's early investigation of friendship ln the *Lysis* and with Aristotle's treatment of friendship in books VIII and IX of his *Nicomachean Ethics*. My plan here is to use these two to illustrate and illuminate each other, and in this way to cover more ground than would otherwise be possible in a brief treatment. To be sure, I will probably not be convincing on all the details; but each work is by itself subject to so many different interpretations, that having them both before us can actually serve to narrow our focus. Plus, the interpretation of each reinforces the interpretation of the other. The conclusions I shall support here are, to say the least, unusual. First, I shall argue that the *Lysis* presents us with apparently contradictory requirements for friendship, and that the aim of the dialogue is to show that these could only be met by positing a transcendent good. Second, I shall argue that Aristotle accepts Plato's paradoxical requirements for friendship but maintains that they do not demand a transcendent good. Third, I shall advance—not by argument but by illustration—a method of examining works of ancient philosophy that is unusual and unfashionable.

I

It is well-known that Aristotle distinguishes three types of friendship: friendship for pleasure, friendship for utility, and friendship for the good (VIII.3). The first two are incomplete, the last is complete and, clearly, the best sort of friendship. An example of a friendship for utility is a business deal; a friendship for pleasure exists between sex partners and, we might say, between beer buddies. We tend to regard both of these as friendships of convenience. Aristotle argues at some length that the third type of friendship is both useful (*chrēsimon*) and pleasurable (VIII.5.1157a25–36; 6.1158b7-8). I shall return to this argument shortly, but for now I want to note that the other two types of friendship arise from criteria that Aristotle thinks *complete* friendship is able to meet. Aristotle thinks that friendship should be useful *and* that it should be pleasurable, even though some types of friendship manifest only one of these characters.

With this, let me turn to Plato's *Lysis*. The question with which I begin is whether Plato shares Aristotle's view of the criteria of the best friendship.[1] To pursue this question, I must first skirt an objection. It might be objected that whereas Aristotle is concerned with the nature of friendship, Plato aims only to characterize the friends; in this case, their approaches to friendship would differ. (In a recent note David Sedley has argued that the *Lysis* is not a "dialogue of definition" because it does not seek to define friendship but to characterize the friends.[2]) But, surely, if we find out what sort of people are rightly called "friends," we will know a good deal about what friendship is. That this latter, the definition of friendship, is indeed the aim of the *Lysis* is indicated by the pattern of examination and rejection of characterizations of the friends and especially by the dialogue's last lines: "We have made ourselves rather ridiculous . . . for . . . though we conceive ourselves to be friends with each other . . . we have not been able to discover what friendship is (*hoti estin ho philos*)" (223b). Knowledge of friendship has been the aim all along, and it is assumed that without such knowledge, we would be able neither to characterize the friends nor to be friends. The motivation for the inquiry into friendship parallels exactly the motivation for the inquiry into moral virtues: knowledge of each is presupposed in actions manifesting it. The difference that Sedley notices between the *Lysis* and the so-called dialogues of definition—that the *Lysis* examines not definitions of friendship, but characterizations of the friends—can be explained in terms of the difference between friendship and the subject matters of other early dialogues, the virtues. A virtue is or is assumed to be definable independently of other things. Friendship, we will see, depends upon the virtues and on those who possess them; for, it seems, that one or both friends must be virtuous. Thus, friendship cannot be known in the same way as a virtue; it is understood in terms of the virtues. For this reason, finding who the friends are— more particularly, finding that the friends possess the virtues—is a step toward the definition of friendship. With this I can return to the question of its criteria.

What I am concerned with here is whether the criteria that Aristotle propounds enter into the *Lysis'* consideration of accounts of the friend. By my count, the dialogue explores five characterizations of who the friend is. Each of these five is itself a set of options or terms with which to characterize the friends. The first formulation relies on the distinction between the befriender and the befriended or the lover and the beloved: is it the befriender or the befriended who is properly called the friend? Socrates refutes all possible answers (212a–213d). To call either of the two the friend would leave open the possibility that the friend could be the friend of an enemy, and this is taken here to be contradictory. On the other hand, to insist that both be friends excludes the possibility of "friendships" with things that cannot reciprocate; yet horses, dogs, and children are taken to be dear to (or friends of) the happy person. What we have here are two apparently inconsistent assumptions about friendship: (a) friends should be capable of reciprocity and (b) children, dogs, and horses are appropriate objects for friendship.

The first of these, reciprocity, is a requirement for friendship, the last consists of examples that are incompatible with this requirement. It is important to see that for Plato the requirements for friendship are not clear from the start, but like treatments of the examples that serve as first proposals for definitions in other dialogues, the discussion of the first formulation here helps to clarify what the requirements for friendship ought to be. Being the friend of an enemy is inconsistent because, it would seem, some sort of reciprocity should be at least conceivable.[3] But the argument does not explain the *type* of reciprocity required of friends. Nor does the argument explain why—that is, in respect of what—dogs, children, and horses are suitable objects of friendship. Are they beneficial or do they bring pleasure? We cannot tell from the text. All we can say is that the supposition that friendship must be reciprocal is apparently foiled by examples of friendships with beings, such as dogs and children, that could not reciprocate.

The second attempt at a characterization of friends is the claim that like is friend to like (214a). The counterargument begins by distinguishing people into good and bad. The bad cannot be friends with the bad because they harm each other (214b-c). But the good cannot be friends with the good, for: "Are two such people useful (*chrēsimos*) to each other? To put it another way, what benefit could any two things which were alike hold for each other . . ." (214e, Watt trans.).[4] In other words, no two people who were alike could be friends because neither could supply the other with something he does not already have. A second argument, a bit after the quotation, excludes friendship between the good on a different ground: someone who is good is self-sufficient, and so needs nothing; such a person could not be benefited. From these arguments, it is clear that, like Aristotle, Plato's Socrates regards being beneficial as a criterion of friendship.[5] This is, apparently, a new criterion. It would seem that the relation of like to like is a good candidate with which to characterize friends because it (apparently) satisfies the reciprocity criterion from the first argument. But it fails to meet the new criterion introduced in the second argument, to be beneficial. Indeed, just because friendship between likes does meet the criterion of reciprocity, it fails to meet the criterion of benefit.

Interestingly, the dialogue's third characterization of friendship shows, in effect, the converse, that if the friendship relation be beneficial, it cannot be reciprocal. Here friendship is described as a relation of like to unlike; for example, the poor to the rich, and the sick to the doctor. Such a relationship is beneficial, at least to one party; but it fails to be reciprocal because the benefit could not extend to both parties: "is the just friend to the unjust, the self-controlled to the undisciplined or the good to the bad?" (216b). Clearly, this characterization of friends fails to meet the criterion of reciprocity. Apparently, a relationship's being beneficial excludes its being reciprocal.

If all this is right, the *Lysis*'s first three attempts at defining friends make clear that the criteria a successful definition would have to satisfy are reciprocity and benefit. But Plato takes these criteria to be incompatible.

This latter view seems, at first glance, to be unfounded: exchange relations are both reciprocal and beneficial. Consider a relationship between someone who possesses widgets and desires gadgets and someone else who has gadgets but desires widgets. They meet, and an exchange is made. The relationship is mutually beneficial. In the same way, a relationship in which a doctor and a lawyer exchange their skills benefits two people who are alike in their goodness. Even in a relationship where the doctor receives money for his services, there seems to be reciprocal benefit.

Such arrangements are excluded here because Plato assumes that each friend is entirely good or entirely bad, whereas someone who can be benefited by widgets, legal services, or money is not entirely good. Yet, even without this assumption, I do not think that Plato would grant that such relationships are genuinely reciprocal because the benefits to be enjoyed are so different for the two parties. The one who seeks widgets befriends the one who has them only for the sake of the widgets; the other party to this relationship enjoys the gadgets. In the most proper sense, one person is not dear to the other —it is the widgets or the gadgets that are dear and *they* cannot reciprocate. Consider some other cases: Is the musician the friend of the mathematician because they teach each other their arts? Is the poor doctor the friend of the rich invalid because the doctor offers him treatment in exchange for money? These are business deals, not friendships. Both sides benefit, but the relations fail to be friendship because they are not truly mutual. Genuine reciprocity requires similarity or likeness between the friends as regards what they desire. However, as we have seen, likes cannot be friends with each other because they have no benefit to offer each other.

These reflections do not appear in the *Lysis*; Plato does not elaborate the requirement of reciprocity. This is a point where I think Aristotle's treatment of friendship is helpful. He mentions two notions that resemble Plato's reciprocity. The first consists of each friend wishing the other well.[6] He terms this "reciprocal affection" (*antiphilēsis*—VIII.2.1155b28), and it might seem, at first glance, to be the same as Plato's reciprocity, particularly because Aristotle uses this criterion to exclude friendships with inanimate things. But there is no incompatibility between reciprocity, in this sense, and benefit—two people could wish each other well while benefiting each other in a mutual exchange. Indeed, Aristotle maintains that wishing each other well would belong to all three types of friendship (2.1155b31–1156a5). Since well-wishing is clearly compatible with friendship for utility, it would be surprising if well-wishing were the criterion that Plato argues to be incompatible with benefit. More importantly, well-wishing is an emotion. Since friendship is a habit or, better, an activity (5.1157b28–34; b5–11), well-wishing cannot be a key criterion of friendship. In fact, Aristotle explicitly contrasts well-wishing with friendship at least twice: (1) people who do not live together are more like well-wishers than friends, "for nothing belongs to friends as much as living together" (1157b17–19), and (2) well-wishing is the beginning of friendship, but well-wishers are not friends because they do not act together (IX.5.1167a3–10). These texts characterizing friendship as living together have an interesting consequence: even if we could somehow understand well-wishing as an activity, it would still not be the criterion of friendship, because it would be an activity of *each* friend for the other but friendship is a *joint* activity, a living together. So well-wishing should not be equated with reciprocity.

There is another Aristotelian notion that I suggest better captures what Plato means by reciprocity. If my argument as to why exchange relations are not reciprocal is correct; if, that is, in such relationships the parties do not share the same thing, then reciprocity amounts to finding pleasure in the same objects. Consider the following passage:

> Friendships endure in those cases where the same comes from each other, such as pleasure;[7] and not only this but also from the same [character], such as happens to the witty, but not to lover and beloved[8] because these do not have the same pleasure. . . . Yet many remain friends if from custom they grow fond of [each other's] characters, their characters being alike. (VIII.4.1157a3–12)

Finding pleasure in each other because of shared enjoyment of the same character defines Aristotle's friendship for pleasure, which occurs "whenever the same comes to be from both and they enjoy one another or the same things; such are the friendships of the young" (6.1158a18–20). According to this definition, you cannot have a friendship for pleasure with wine or a BMW because you cannot share a pleasure with them. Hence, Aristotle's friendship for pleasure seems to be virtually identical with the Platonic criterion of friendship that I have been calling "reciprocity."

This conclusion puts us in a position to see a striking difference between Plato's and Aristotle's accounts of friendship. Plato argues that friendship has two incompatible characteristics, reciprocity and benefit. Since he assumes that friendship is one thing, the inconsistency in the criteria poses an obstacle to the existence of any proper instance of friendship. The arguments of the *Lysis* play off the criteria against each other. Aristotle, on the other hand, does not draw our attention to this problem; he uses the two criteria to mark out two distinct types of friendship. He distinguishes a third friendship that does possess both criteria. It is just such a friendship that could satisfy both criteria that Plato seeks in the *Lysis*.

Does Plato ever get an account of friendship that satisfies both criteria? Does he ever avoid the contradiction? Since, like other early dialogues, the *Lysis* ends inconclusively, it is easy to suppose that the dialogue does not arrive at an adequate definition. Certainly, it is not stated explicitly. Nevertheless, I contend that the author of the dialogue has an answer and intends the dialogue as a kind of argument for it. In support of this claim I shall point to several details of the remainder of the *Lysis* and explain how I think that they are intended to fit together. Giving this complex portion of the dialogue the full treatment it deserves would take us too far afield; and it is well to bear in mind that my contention would, in any case, rest upon marshaling indications of an inexplicit message.

The final section of the dialogue (216c–223b) contains two significant revisions of earlier assumptions. First, the interlocutors agree that there are people who are neither good nor bad (216d–e). The earlier bipartite division was too narrow; most, if not all, people are neither entirely good nor entirely bad but somewhere between good and bad.[9] Arguments against the good being friends with the good or with the bad still obtain; but we can now see that they fail to apply to most people, perhaps, indeed, to any people.

Second, the earlier discussion of friendship is enriched with the idea of being friends "for the sake of" some other thing, a notion that leads to the positing of the "first friend." It is sometimes thought that the latter is akin to Aristotle's primary friendship, that perfect friendship in respect of which the other friendships are defined, but the argument that introduces it suggests something else. Some things are beneficial because they lead to other things; there must, though, be something else that is beneficial not for the sake of something else, but in its own right. This latter is the "first friend" (218d–220e). The dialogue argues that only the first friend is truly a friend on the ground that when we value something for the sake of something else we value the latter thing more than former. Since only the first friend is not valued for the sake of some other friend, it alone is truly a friend. Indeed, the *Lysis* identifies this first friend as the good (220b). This claim does not by itself tell us what it means to be good. The dialogue does not *assume* that the good is a transcendent Platonic form.[10] Indeed, the good is not assumed to be any character at all; it is simply the last link of a chain, that which is not for the sake of another. Nevertheless, we must still ask whether some nature of the good *emerges from* the *Lysis*.

Just what do we learn about the good here? Someone who was thoroughly good would not seek the good; nor would someone completely bad. It is the person who is neither who seeks the good. At first, it is supposed that the reason for her seeking the good is the presence of the bad (217a–218a), but Socrates argues at some length that the presence of the bad is inessential (the conclusion is stated at 221b–c). What is neither good nor bad loves the good for no other reason besides its desire for the good (221d). It is likely that this is simply a version of the Socratic doctrine that all people desire the good. To be sure, the *Lysis* does not speak of *all* people desiring the good; it maintains that only those who are neither good nor bad desire the good. But, likely, there are no people who are entirely good or entirely bad. As Socrates maintains in the *Protagoras*, "to be good is the privilege of a god alone" (344c). At one point in the *Lysis* Socrates suggests that what those who are neither good nor bad desire is knowledge, but this is never taken up again in the dialogue (218a–b). Be this as it may, the first friend of the *Lysis* stands above the people who desire it in the sense that it is truly good and they are not. It confers benefit, but could not be the recipient of any benefit in return because it needs nothing and cannot get better. Thus, the first friend satisfies only the criterion of benefit; it fails to satisfy the other criterion for friendship, reciprocity. At the very end of the dialogue this latter criterion reemerges under the guise of "akin" (*oikeion*). We are presumed to be akin to what we desire, and this is taken to mean that there is some reciprocity. But the arguments against reciprocal relations—that the good cannot be the friend of the bad, etc.—remain unanswered. Thus, the dialogue ends ostensibly in failure.

The concluding remarks, however, indicate that all has not been entirely in vain. Socrates declares that though the interlocutors have failed to find friendship, they have in the process become friends. We recognize the characteristic Socratic irony immediately, but just what sort of friendship has grown among the interlocutors? I suggest that even though the dialogue has failed to *describe* a way to avoid the contradiction in the two criteria for friendship, it has *exhibited* one. We have seen the interlocutors engaged in an inquiry into friendship. Lacking knowledge and, thus, the good, these interlocutors are not themselves good. In this respect and insofar as they work together to reach knowledge, they maintain a reciprocal relationship. It is precisely their lack of knowledge that sustains their joint inquiry and, thus, their relationship. Do they benefit each other? Not insofar as they lead each other to the truth: the dialogue is a failure in that regard. But there is mutual benefit in the sense that they help each other to recognize their ignorance of the first friend, the good. It is, thus, only insofar as they position themselves in relation to this good that the relation can be, in any sense, mutually beneficial. The "Socratic" ignorance that emerges from the dialogue consists of the ignorance of the first friend, the good; and it is only possible if the existence and significance of the good is assumed. Thus it is that the dialogue shows friendship to be possible only if there is a good that exists apart from the friends. This good is an object of knowledge, final in the sense that it is not pursued for anything else, and in need of nothing else (cf. 221e). Not only is this good distinct from the friends, but the requirements for it apparently could not be met by any other sensible thing either.

Let me reformulate these very difficult ideas. Throughout the *Lysis*, the interlocutors conceive of friendship as a dyadic relation: it involves two people. The paradox that the dialogue explores arises from the assumption that the relationship must be both beneficial and mutual: anyone who can benefit me is better than I and our relation could never be mutual; anyone with whom I can have a mutual relation is on my level and is thus of no benefit to me. The "friendship" that is reached at the very end of the *Lysis* skirts this difficulty by being a triadic relation:[11]

First Friend (Good)

(Benefit)

Friend ———— Friend   (Reciprocity)

[Bad]

The interlocutors have a mutual relation because they are ignorant; in the terms of the dialogue, they are neither good nor bad. But they are united by their joint inquiry into friendship, an inquiry that depends on identifying the first friend, the good, and is conceivable only if the existence of such a good is posited.[12] For the relationship with the good to be beneficial, the good must be better than both interlocutors. For the relationship to persist the good must *always* be better than the interlocutors: it must be and remain separate from them and on a higher level. As such, the good makes possible the friendship of the interlocutors. A entity that is separate from sensible things yet makes them possible is transcendent. Thus, though the *Lysis* does not speak of the good as transcendent, it leads reflective readers to see that the existence of the sort of friendship exhibited in the dialogue presupposes just such a transcendent good.

The assertion of the presence of a transcendent good in an early Platonic dialogue calls for comment. Is it clear from the dialogue that the ultimate good someone desires need be anything other than her happiness? Is it clear that there is *one* good that all people strive for?[13] The dialogue answers neither question. In fact, we learn very little about the first friend, the good, in the *Lysis*. None of the technical metaphysical terms that the middle dialogues typically use to describe the forms is applied to it. Its salient characteristic is just its elusiveness: no one in the dialogue has it or knows what it is. Even Socrates declares that he is so far from having a friend that he does not even know how to acquire one (212a)—he is even further from knowing the first friend. Knowledge of friendship would seem to be requisite for friendship, but in the *Lysis* it is precisely the ignorance of friendship that unites the interlocutors and, potentially, all those who are neither good nor bad. To say that the good sought in friendship is transcendent is simply to point up its crucial role in human experience and its absence from experience. The dialogue's (implicit) case for the good's being transcendent depends upon this absence.

In sum, the end of the dialogue shows a friendship that includes, besides the friends who inquire into the good, the good they seek. Friendship is the joint pursuit of the good. The message is clear: only philosophers working together can be truly friends. Though ascribing a positive doctrine to Socrates may seem to call into question his proclaimed ignorance, it does not: since the key term in the triadic relation, the good, remains unknown, the relation itself is empty—it is purely formal. Without knowledge of what the good is, to define friendship in terms of the good is not to define it at all. But just that which could, at least in principle, fill in this hole in the definition, the joint pursuit of the good, is itself an instantiation of the definition.

This "definition" of friendship has a beautiful subtlety to it, but it purchases success at a high price: all other modes of friendship must be declared illegitimate. Indeed, friendship itself is merely a mark of human inadequacy. Were we ever to discover the good (and thereby the definition of friendship) the joint pursuit of the good—that is friendship—would be unnecessary. Conversely, we can be friends only because of our ignorance. To put this point still more paradoxically: we grasp the definition of friendship only because we fail to define it. The friendship exhibited by the interlocutors at the end of the *Lysis* could be termed "human friendship" by virtue of its parallel to what Socrates calls "human knowledge" in the *Apology*: both turn on our ignorance of the good.

II

Plato's friendship invites comparison with Aristotle's friendship for virtue. As I noted earlier, Aristotle argues that this best friendship satisfies the two criteria: it is both useful and pleasurable (or reciprocal). The preceding discussion of Plato's account enables us to understand the context and significance of Aristotle's, and it focuses our attention on at least two issues: Can Aristotle avoid the paradoxes inherent in ascribing both reciprocity and utility to friendship? Can he avoid positing a transcendent good? We need to look closely at his arguments for the best friendship's being useful and pleasurable.

Aristotle's initial arguments are too brief:

Each of them is both good unconditionally and good for his friend, since good people are both unconditionally good and advantageous for each other. They are pleasant in the same ways too, since good people are pleasant both unconditionally and for each other. [They are pleasant for each other] because each person finds his own actions and actions of that kind pleasant, and the actions of good people are the same or similar. (VIII.3.1156b12–17, Irwin trans.)

At best, this passage contains a mere hint of the argument. Just why are virtuous friends advantageous for each other? Why do they enjoy each other's company? Aristotle provides answers to these questions toward the end of his treatment of friendship, in the context of a discussion of self-love. He distinguishes bad self-love from good self-love by distinguishing the "self" that is gratified: those who seek money, honors, or pleasure are motivated by the bad self-love; those who seek virtue gratify the best and "most controlling" part of the self (IX.8.1168b15-1169a6). Pursuit of this latter is, of course, the good self-love. Aristotle contends that the virtuous action that is motivated by this self-love will benefit all (1169a8–15). Apparently, this is just the character of virtue: it contributes to the common good. But this common benefit bestowed by one virtuous person would seem of only slight benefit to another virtuous person. Because two virtuous people seem to stand in little need of each other, the ability of each to contribute to the common good could hardly be the mutual benefit that is a criterion for friendship.

In fact, Aristotle has another argument: since a friend is another self, the good person is related to his friend as he is to himself (IX.9.1170b5-8). It follows that for just the reason that he chooses to benefit himself, the virtuous person would choose to benefit his friend. Normally, when we think of benefiting someone else, we think of the sacrifice that this involves for ourselves; from such a perspective, the claim that the friend is another self has little sway.[14] However, if we realize that the activities that we engage in as friends are just the joint activities of living together, then the benefit that I derive from an activity will be precisely the same as that derived by another participating in the same activity. (This is obvious if the activity is one that I could not have engaged in by myself or activities, such as pursuing knowledge, that I could only have engaged in alone less well than with another.) Thus, virtuous friends are mutually beneficial because they engage in joint activities that are beneficial in similar ways to similarly constituted people. Each friend recognizes the other as another self, and the benefit each confers upon himself is precisely the benefit he confers upon his friend; it results from his own self-love. Moreover, just as the virtuous person derives pleasure from his own activities, he will derive pleasure from the activities of his virtuous friend; it will be the pleasure conferred by choiceworthy actions (1170b8–10). Because virtuous friends are essentially alike, and because they engage in activities jointly, their actions are most properly reciprocal. In this way, virtuous friendships are both useful and pleasurable.

These arguments show that friendship for virtue should have both characters, but they do not show how to resolve the Platonic objection. Again, the latter is that in order that friendship be beneficial, one party must be better than the other, but if this is so, the relation cannot be mutual. The key move in Aristotle's resolution is the identification of friendship as an ongoing activity, the activity of living together. Each individual strives to live well, and the activity of living well Aristotle terms "happiness." Striving to live well with my friend improves my chances of succeeding. Life always presents new opportunities for being harmed or being benefited, and for virtuous or vicious actions. Undertaking the activities of life together with someone else constituted much like me improves the chances that we will each perform those functions well because our chances of overcoming the obstacles are better when we work together. Though it is possible that I might exhibit courage alone on the battlefield, it is more likely that I will act courageously when I am accompanied by my courageous friend; for the presence of my courageous friend will help to promote those conditions of engagement necessary for courageous acts—one cannot exhibit courageous action on the battlefield if the rest of the force is entirely cowardly—will help to promote the external purpose of courageous acts, victory on the battlefield, and will keep before my mind a good, namely, my friend, worth risking my life to preserve. So it is that an activity undertaken with a friend can be beneficial to both of us: joint activity differs qualitatively from similar activities undertaken alone. Furthermore, provided that the joint activity is virtuous activity and that the two friends are both constituted so as to enjoy virtue, the activity is also pleasurable to both parties. Strictly speaking, it is not the friend himself who is beneficial and pleasurable, it is the activity we engage in with our friends that satisfies both of Plato's criteria for friendship.

If this is right, Aristotle's solution to the paradox of friendship closely resembles the characterization of "human friendship" that the *Lysis* exhibits but does not discuss. Just as Plato sees the two friends working together to find knowledge of *the* good, so, too, Aristotle sees friendship as a joint striving for *some* good. The differences are: (1) Aristotle's good is not transcendent but the human good, happiness, activity in accordance with virtue; and (2) Aristotle's good does not consist simply of knowing but of activities in accordance with moral virtues as well. Whereas the Platonic friends manifest their friendship in shared philosophical inquiry, Aristotelian friends might do likewise or they might jointly pursue activity in accordance with a moral virtue like courage. Thus, Aristotle also offers a triadic account of friendship, but the third component is human happiness rather than a transcendent good. This triadic character is implicit in Aristotle's name for it, "friendship of the good." If his account does not always emphasize the three components, it is probably because, with Plato's account before him, Aristotle thinks he can take this for granted and concentrates instead on showing that this relationship satisfies the two criteria that define the two other types of friendship.

In order to allow friendship to persist, in order to insure that the two friends might always be benefited, Plato makes the third constituent transcendent. Because the good is not humanly attainable, he thinks that we remain always in the state of pursuing it: thus friendships remain viable and significant. However, Plato's move is both inadequate and unnecessary. Inadequate because Platonic friendship remains a frail affair that depends upon mutual recognition of the failure to attain genuine knowledge and that is threatened by one of the parties surpassing the other in insight into the source of the failing. Thus it is that what should be paradigmatic Platonic friendships, dialogues between Socrates and various interlocutors, are presented as single encounters—the philosophical equivalent of one-night stands—and Socrates can suggest in the *Lysis* that he has never had a friend (211d–212a). Moreover, because the two friends strive to attain knowledge, and because the attainment of that knowledge would undermine the basis for the friendship, the two friends strive to dissolve the friendship. That the friends have little or no chance of actually attaining genuine knowledge does not make it any more plausible that the friends would try to bring about and hope for the dissolution of their friendship. Friendships are valuable. Friends do not try to destroy them—they go to many lengths to preserve them. Aristotle may have Plato in mind when he asks whether we wish our friends to be gods (1159a5–12). No, he answers; that would destroy the relationship. Instead, we wish them the greatest *human* good. Plato's friends *do* wish each other to be gods. In sum, Plato's transcendent object of friendship really fails to do its job: it does not provide an adequate basis for a stable and enduring relationship.

A transcendent object is also unnecessary. Plato posits the first friend as something apart from the friends in order to make possible the joint pursuit of it. What Aristotle realizes is that there is no need for the object to be separate from human experience. Human happiness serves as well, provided only that we realize that it is not a state to be attained or preserved, but an activity. As I said, life presents constant challenges to surmount no matter what one's level of attainment. Even those who would seem to have already attained happiness could be benefited or harmed by future events. Insofar as happiness is an ongoing activity, it can always be an object of pursuit. Hence, the good need not be transcendent to make an enduring relationship possible.

Aristotle raises the question whether one who is already virtuous would need a friend: the virtuous are self-sufficient, those who are self-sufficient need nothing from others, so it would seem that the virtuous have no need of friendship (IX.9.1169b3–8). But he insists that the virtuous do need friends because happiness is a kind of activity—it does not belong as a possession; it comes to be (1169b28–30). A virtuous friend affords one more opportunities to contemplate and enjoy virtuous actions (1170a2–4), and having such a friend makes it easier to engage in the activities that constitute human happiness (1170b5–6). But even if joint activities were not qualitatively superior to the similar activities undertaken alone, friendship would still be beneficial. To possess virtue is merely to be *capable* of human activities that constitute happiness, but circumstances could prevent a person from *actually engaging* in these activities. Because even a virtuous person could be benefited or harmed by events, he could also be benefited by his friend. Because, as in Priam's case, happiness can be side-tracked by circumstances, because we cannot say whether a person is truly happy until he has died (I.9.1100a5–9; 10.1100a34–b5; 7.1098a18–20), friendship will remain beneficial throughout life. Even someone who is already virtuous must strive for future happiness. Hence, it is because happiness is an actuality, an ongoing activity, that friendship would remain beneficial even to one who was already virtuous.

My contention that Aristotle's two friends stand on the same level relative to the good they pursue is apt to seem, at first hearing, to be flatly contradicted by the text; for Aristotle has a lengthy discussion of friendship among unequals (VIII.7–14), and he maintains that there are unequal friendships of all three types. However, this treatment of unequal friendships presupposes the account of friendship among equals that he develops in the first six chapters of book VIII.

Aristotle insists that even a friendship among unequals preserves a type of equality (7.1158b27–28): the lesser of the two friends must put more into the relationship to maintain it. More of what? Whatever it is that the friendship is based upon, pleasure, utility, or virtuous acts. Thus, though a novice's contribution to a joint intellectual endeavor is of lesser value than his supervisor's, he makes up for it by increasing his contribution so that both, in effect, contribute equally. The relationship is possible here because both supervisor and novice pursue the same end and because they stand on the same level in respect of this end: both are ignorant of it. In this latter sense, the friends are qualitatively alike, and their differences in quantity are overcome through differences of effort. We need to understand the nature of the friendship relation before we can see how there can be differences in contributing to it. Hence, Aristotle's notion that in the best friendships the friends are on the same level is not only fully compatible with his treatment of friendship among unequals but necessary to understand that treatment.

III

That Plato and Aristotle differ on whether friendship is attainable is consistent with the textbook versions of their philosophies. Though this is not a decisive point in favor of my account, neither should it be held against my account. If the foregoing contributes to our understanding of the texts, it is in showing that Plato and Aristotle share the same criteria and how they differ on whether these criteria can be met. In this section I shall explore the paradox of friendship from a different perspective.

A key issue for both Plato and Aristotle is what we need to know in order to be or to have a friend. The reason that knowledge enters the analysis is that friendship is assumed to be beneficial. In order to secure the good, we need to know what the good is. If a friend is always beneficial, then to choose a friend or to be a friend requires knowledge. It is assumed that we have no problem recognizing whether a relationship is or is not pleasurable; determining whether we are benefiting or being benefited is quite another matter. How can I tell if I am getting something from a relationship? I may get the most out of relationships that I enjoy the least; such as, a relationship with a rival thinker. Suppose, on the other hand, that I genuinely want to be a friend to someone; what should I do to help him? And how will he appreciate my help unless he is already knowledgeable enough so as not to need it?

The problem is that the aim of friendship is to provide us with exactly the knowledge necessary to have already in order to find and be a friend. If we need knowledge to choose a friend and if the aim of friendship is such knowledge that would allow us to make this choice, then friendship seems to be impossible. This is, I take it, still another formulation of the dilemma of the *Lysis*. But on this version, the paradox seems not merely to point up the difficulty of understanding friendship, as Plato apparently thinks; it seems to render friendship impossible.

Genuine Platonic friendship *is* truly impossible; but there is, I have been claiming, an attainable substitute. The implicit Platonic or Socratic "solution" turns on distinguishing positive from negative knowing; that is, knowing in the genuine sense from what Socrates in the *Apology* (23a–b, 21d) calls "human wisdom," knowing that one does not know in the genuine sense. I can be a friend merely by recognizing my own ignorance and finding someone else who also recognizes his ignorance. How can I tell whether you are also ignorant? By quizzing you, as Socrates quizzes his interlocutors; indeed, it is by quizzing myself in just this way that I recognize my own ignorance. If this is right, then to choose a friend requires not knowledge in the genuine sense but Socratic "human" knowledge, knowledge of ignorance. By the same token, the outcome of such a friendship would be not knowledge in the genuine sense but more human knowledge. In short, to be a friend, we need to be aware of our own ignorance; and what we get from friendship is just more of the same, a greater recognition of our ignorance. From this point of view, the paradox is no obstacle to friendship.

On the other hand, a friendship that preserves ignorance scarcely seems worth pursuing. Why should one bother with friendship? There seems to be an assumption in the early Platonic dialogues that people would tend to think they know something unless their ignorance were constantly manifested to them. A single Socratic dialogue does not suffice to produce the profound knowledge of ignorance claimed by Socrates; elenchus must be constantly repeated. But if this is so, then another problem emerges: the profound ignorance of Socrates would not be comparable with the effect produced by a single elenchus, and he would never have even a human friendship with his interlocutors.

Even apart from this latter problem, the notion of a friendship that is based on mutual refutation is hard to swallow. Would we expect a person to feel affection for someone who did him the benefit of showing that he did not know anything? Yet the dialogues display a loyal band of Socrates' companions; surely Socrates spares none of them an elenchus when it is called for. Is the affection his companions feel toward Socrates supposed to be due to his refuting them? What would seem to be a hateful and painful act, elenctic refutation, must, if this interpretation of Socratic friendship is correct, be an act of love. This is far, far from relationships we ordinarily take to be friendships.

In fact, we can—or think we can—easily recognize the phenomenon of friendship. What we ordinarily call "friendship" is not rare among those with neither virtue nor wisdom; if anything it is more widespread. For Plato, and for Aristotle, such ordinary friendships fail to conform to the ideal; they are not always beneficial. Nevertheless, it is a good bet that they are often *believed to be beneficial*. Thus, if we replace the requirement that friends be beneficial with the stipulation that they should *seem* beneficial (cf. VIII.2.1155b25–27), we can both void the requirement for knowledge and get a description closer to the phenomenon. But to make this move would leave us open to the objection that friendship would not then always be good. Though we could "save the phenomenon" by altering the criteria in this way, to do this would require that we reject the more fundamental assumption that the best friendship is always beneficial.

So far as I can see, Aristotle does not accord the phenomena ordinarily thought to be friendships—relationships *believed* to be both beneficial and pleasurable—any more status as genuine friendships than Plato does, but neither does he suppose that the best friendships must only consist of mutual elenchus.[15] He, too, insists that the best friendships strive for what is truly good, but he regards activities other than elenchus as more important. There are at least two differences here, and they are significant because they allow Aristotle to steer clear of the Socratic paradox that to be a friend one must already have the knowledge that could be attained from friendship.

First, as I noted earlier, the scope of Aristotle's friendship for virtue can be larger than Plato's human friendship because his virtue is larger. Aristotle's virtue does not consist only of knowledge; he distinguishes the moral virtues from the intellectual. Thus, the pursuit of virtue need not be entirely intellectual. Mutually beneficial activity of two friends could involve: activity in accordance with moral virtue, activity in accordance with intellectual virtue, or activity in accordance with both. Only, the second of these resembles the joint inquiry that the *Lysis* all but identifies with the closest we can attain to friendship.

Second, Aristotle's notion of the pursuit of intellectual virtue differs significantly from Plato's because he thinks that knowledge is attainable. Aristotelian inquiry proceeds in a "scientific" way: it aims first to find the nature of the substance under investigation and then to demonstrate the per se attributes of the substance. The joint pursuit of knowledge is, therefore, not limited to elenchus.

Implicit in this notion of scientific inquiry is a sharp distinction between the starting point of the inquiry and the conclusions it is able to demonstrate. This makes it possible to distinguish the intellectual virtue that is presupposed by the inquiry from the intellectual virtue to be gained from the inquiry. Whether we seek a purely theoretical knowledge like physics or the theoretical portion of a practical science, the knowledge to be attained differs from that possessed at the beginning. Hence, we can assess our intellectual progress and the benefit of conducting the inquiry together with a friend.

Likewise, in jointly undertaken activities in accordance with moral virtue, the state from which the friends begin differs significantly from the outcome. I have already mentioned how the presence of a friend can bring about conditions favorable to the exercise of virtue and how the friend can serve to spur acts of moral virtue, such as displays of courage on the battlefield. Though one must be morally virtuous in order to be a friend of the best sort, such a friendship provides occasions to realize virtue in action. This activity in accordance with virtue has at least two dimensions: first, it is part of the activity that constitutes someone's life and, thus, crucial for his living well, his happiness; second, the activity has a goal beyond the participants, such as victory in the case of courageous acts in battle.[16] Not only does friendship increase the quality of our activity, it helps us to succeed in attaining those goals beyond our acts, such as victory, just punishment, fair exchange, and health (cf. X.7.1177b2–18). Thus, the actions that spring from friendship and the outcomes of those acts differ from the character state necessary to have friendship.

In this way Aristotle can skirt Plato's paradox that the characteristics needed to be a friend are just those that one would get in consequence of being a friend. Yet Aristotle's account can succeed only if there is some way besides friendship to acquire the virtue needed for friendship. That is to say, if friendship does not provide the friends with what they need to be friends, then where else could they acquire the requisite moral virtue? Aristotle's answer is, from their upbringing. In part upbringing occurs through "friendship" with family members, but it is also important for the young to observe the examples of virtuous citizens, to receive proper education and training, and, in general, to grow up in a good society. Aristotle even speaks as if a bad upbringing is an insurmountable obstacle to moral virtue (N.E. I.3.1094b27–1095a2). This is a disturbing claim, but the paradox of friendship shows us why he makes it. Friendship cannot itself provide the moral virtue it presupposes.

This conclusion raises, in turn, a new problem: what motivates the teachers of virtue in the state? Plato would say that there are no real teachers of virtue, only seekers after virtue who can work together. Aristotle insists that two people need to have virtue *before* they can work together. They must have acquired it as they became habituated to the practices of the *polis* in which they live. Moral virtue is, as it were, a form that is passed through habituation from one generation to the next. This explains how there could be friendship in good states. But what about those states falling short of perfection, such as the democracies of ancient Athens and modern America? If there is any possibility of acquiring virtue in such lesser states, it would be through teachers of virtue. From previous arguments we can see that Aristotle can allow no genuine friendship between teacher and student because the benefit that the teacher confers on the student is not the same as the benefit that the student will later, as a citizen, return to the teacher. The teacher's motivation is not friendship but his own, individual interest in living in a good society, a goal toward which his efforts will make the student better able to contribute. This is a self-interest that is qualitatively different from that of Sophists who seek—or are, at least, accused of seeking—their own financial benefit. Interestingly, though, it is just the motivation Socrates expresses in the *Apology* (25c–e) when he declares how foolish it would be for someone to harm his neighbors intentionally because he would risk being harmed, in turn, by them. By the same token, one who benefited his neighbors to the extent he was able, would do all he could to improve the state in which he lives. Though Plato speaks in the *Lysis* as if Socrates were simply a friend among friends, Socrates clearly stands above the other interlocutors. He does just what Aristotle thinks a good teacher should: he gets young people accustomed to virtuous pursuits that prepare them for friendship and for citizenship. Despite Plato's and Aristotle's theoretical differences, the figure of Socrates is a model for both.

IV

Though Aristotle's virtue is broader than the conception in the *Lysis*, in the end the theoretical differences between Plato and Aristotle are more substantial than their practical differences: both endorse the same sorts of activities. Both of their discussions of friendship are apt to strike us in the twentieth century as strange precisely because in them knowledge and virtue loom so large. It seems as if the friends have, in their bed, as it were, a third fellow, virtue. I conclude by proposing that it is just this notion, at first so implausible, that is the real contribution of ancient philosophy toward the understanding of friendship. Friendship, and indeed all relationships, work when there is this third thing present: friendship consists of a joint striving toward some good. It is only in this joint striving that my self-interest merges with the interest of my friend. We become friends and maintain our friendship by common activities.[17] Friends, Aristotle repeatedly insists, live together. They aim to live together well: as in the case of individual activity, the appropriate end of our common activity is just to perform that activity well. If the ends we pursue are not truly beneficial, the friendship cannot be long-lived.

All this stands in sharp contrast to the romantic notion of the friend (or more often the beloved) as some sort of end in herself. In the romantic ideal, the two friends or two lovers hold each other in the highest esteem: since each loves the other for different reasons, the relationship is not truly reciprocal. No wonder it must end in death or, more often, divorce. Plato and Aristotle describe a friendship that, though difficult to attain, is a livable, practical ideal.

Chapter 3

THE RATIONAL BASIS OF ARISTOTLE'S VIRTUE

Why is a particular act moral or immoral? Aristotle would answer this question by invoking his doctrine of the mean: an action is virtuous if it is neither excessive nor deficient. But this answer does not suffice, for it does not explain how to decide which actions are excessive and which deficient. Aristotle has quite a lot to say about particular examples of virtuous acts and excessive and deficient acts; nearly three books of his *Nicomachean Ethics* are devoted to this. He thinks that we must study these particular details in order to hone our ability to choose the mean. But when we step back and ask how we can be sure that an act is truly the mean, Aristotle seems to have no satisfactory answer. In difficult cases, we must rely on the judgment of the virtuous man; just how he decides remains mysterious. What, then, is the basis of virtue?

Two sorts of answers to this question appear in the literature. The most popular locates the basis for ethics in common opinions (*endoxa*). It is widely supposed that Aristotle sorts through and reconciles the moral perceptions, practices, and opinions of his Greek contemporaries and that he ultimately preserves the most important of them.[1] Thus, it would seem that Aristotle relies on the beliefs and practices of his society to determine what is right and that any ethics must do likewise. Some, however, maintain that a deeper basis for making ethical determinations lies in human nature or in the disciplines studying it: metaphysics, physics, or psychology. But thinkers defending such bases have not derived particular moral virtues from them. As T.H. Irwin, for example, acknowledges, what they can tell us about happiness and human functioning is "too general and imprecise to support specific and precise answers to ethical questions."[2] Thus, when it comes to deciding whether a particular act is or is not the mean, nearly all suppose that Aristotle must rely on the practices and standards of his community. Particular cases are thought to be decided by grasping "salient" features that mark them as instances of one or another character trait, much in the way that a law court extends common law to new situations.[3] There are no criteria for salience other than our agreeing that something is salient.

The purpose of this essay is to introduce a new account of the basis of virtue. I shall argue that it is reason that determines which acts are right and which wrong. Plato and Kant have rationalist accounts of ethics. Recognizing Aristotle's differences, scholars have generally thought that his ethics could not also be based upon reason. They assume that such an ethics must be rigid, universal, and incapable of adjustment to particular circumstances, and this notion probably has a hand in motivating the current emphasis on the common opinions of a community. Consequently, what needs to be done here is to show how reason could determine the content of ethical action so that it admits of variations in different circumstances. I need to carve out middle ground between rigid rationalism and fundamentally arbitrary community standards. The central issue here is to understand how a human happiness that includes acts of *moral* virtue could rightly be characterized as an activity of the soul in accordance with reason (I.7.1098a7–8; a13–14), and this has far-reaching ramifications for other philosophical and textual problems.

I

One of those other problems is the apparent inconsistency between Aristotle's endorsement in the middle books of actions in accordance with all the moral virtues and his insistence in the final book that the life of contemplation is the best and thus the happiest life. In book X Aristotle seems to abandon the balanced life for the sake of a life of pure thought. This problem has come to be called "Aristotle's intellectualism." This rubric indicates where the difficulty has been thought to lie: the endorsement of intellectual virtue in the final book is taken to be inconsistent with the better and more Aristotelian position found elsewhere in the *Nichomachean Ethics*, and commentators intent on freeing Aristotle from inconsistency have tried to soften the claims made in the final book.

A parallel difficulty is the apparent inconsistency between the account in the central books and the function argument Aristotle advances in I.7. According to the latter living well is something like playing the flute well; it consists of performing our human function well. What is our human function? It should be something distinctively human, and thus it should involve reason. On this basis, he describes the function of man as an "activity of the soul that is in accordance with reason (*logos*) or not without reason" (1098a7–8). And happiness, the human good, is the "activity of the soul in accordance with virtue or, if there are many virtues, with the best and the most complete virtue" (1098a16–18).[4] Since "the best and most complete virtue" would seem to be intellectual virtue, the conclusion of the function argument is at odds with the characterization of the moral virtues that fills much of *Nicomachean Ethics* III–V, at least as the latter is usually understood. Aiming to avoid the apparent contradiction, some commentators have proposed that "complete virtue" in the conclusion be taken "inclusively" so that the human good involves more than contemplation.[5] This approach seems to me to beg the question; for the "complete virtue" mentioned in the function argument must, however it is understood, characterize the way we perform our human function, and that function is "activity in accordance with reason." The issue here is precisely how an exercise of moral virtue could be an activity in accordance with reason; if we are to reconcile the function argument with the account of moral virtue, it is this that needs to be explained. The inclusivist's claim that "complete virtue" includes the moral virtues would, if true, avoid the problem; but by itself it does not explain just what needs to be explained, how the exercise of moral virtue could be a rational activity. Moreover, this latter would seem to be particularly difficult for inclusivists who also adhere to the view that the moral virtues are based upon common opinion. To say that an act manifests virtue because it conforms to a community's standards for action (even if it be a community of philosophers) is difficult to reconcile with what is implied by the function argument, that an act is virtuous if it is in accordance with reason.[6] In short, the naturalism of the function argument seems inconsistent with Aristotle's account of the moral virtues, especially if what counts as a moral virtue does so because of the standards of some community.[7]

In sum, the account of the moral virtues in books III–V would seem to be at odds with the arguments or doctrines of books I and X. Scholars typically try to avoid the difficulties by reinterpreting the latter books. Instead, I shall reconsider the former. I propose that the source of both difficulties lies in a mistaken view of the account of the moral virtues, the view that certain habits are virtuous only because of the dictates of common opinion. The problems would vanish if we could reinterpret the account of these virtues in such a way that they manifest reason. This is just what the function argument would lead us to expect, and it would narrow the gap between moral and intellectual virtue. Let us suppose for the moment that there is some rational justification for the moral virtues; in other words, suppose that (1) we could give reasons why a particular action is an instance of courage and that (2) these reasons somehow concern the furtherance of the faculty of reason.[8] Doubtless this is a lot to grant at this point; but if it were true, there would be arguments showing particular acts to be right, and choosing to perform them would be an exercise of reason. In this case acts of moral virtue would manifest reason, and it would be reasonable to think that they are inherently valuable insofar as they are acts in accordance with our nature. (More on this latter shortly.) If acts of moral virtue derived their worth from the reason they manifested, then the life of contemplation would not be opposed to the life of moral virtue; it would be the fulfillment of such a life.

In short, a rational basis for moral virtue would, at one fell swoop, resolve the apparent contradiction of books I and X with the account of the moral virtues in-between, and resolve the controversy between inclusivist and exclusivist accounts of happiness.

II

The benefits would be large, but how could I possibly show that the virtues are rationally justifiable? It seems that Aristotle specifically denies this. The reason that the science of ethics does not admit the precision of theoretical sciences is that it contains a degree of randomness (I.2.1094b11–17). There is no rule which determines virtuous

action in all cases. It is always necessary to examine the particular circumstances, and even then the only sure way to determine what is
right in any set of circumstances is to see what the virtuous man
would do. It seems that we cannot appeal *only* to reason to guide us
in our moral decisions. A Kantian set of rational rules is out of the
question. If, on the other hand, virtuous action were entirely rational,
we could rely on rules or arguments to determine precisely what we
should do in any set of circumstances.

This line of reasoning shows only that Aristotle's virtues are not
determined by what Kant would have called "pure reason"; it does
not show that they have no rational foundation. Were the virtues
completely devoid of reason, it would scarcely make sense for Aristotle to give us a *science* of ethics. Indeed, Aristotle states clearly that
there is a rational component to ethical action; he calls it practical wisdom and ties it closely to moral virtue (VI.13.1144b30–32). Though he
denies the Socratic view that the virtues simply are rational principles, he maintains that the virtues are "with reason" (1144b28–30).
Concerned to distinguish his own position from that of Plato, Aristotle may, perhaps, emphasize the nonrational elements in his account.
He just *assumes* that ethical activity is rational: "that we must act in
accordance with right reason (*orthos logos*) is generally conceded and
may be assumed as the basis of our discussion" (II.2.1103b31–32).

Just what does it mean to "act in accordance with right reason"?
Given the inapplicability of the Kantian notion of moral rules legislat-
ed by pure reason, we might be tempted to take "reason" as simply a
capacity to reflect on alternative courses of action and to justify our
decisions. In this case, rational justification would be identical with
giving reasons, and there need be no inconsistency in contrary actions
provided that we could give reasons for each. To say that the virtues
are rational in this very weak sense would not take us far toward justifying their content.

To see that Aristotle has a stronger sense of reason in mind we
need to turn, at last, to the text. Let me begin with his account of moderation (III.10–12). Moderation is a mean in respect of the pleasures of
taste and touch (1117b24–25; 1118a26). There are at least two questions that we would like Aristotle to answer: What is wrong with too
much pleasure? How can we determine the amount of pleasure that is
neither too much nor too little? Aristotle has several answers to the
first question. (1) First, the pleasures we should moderate are those
that we share with other animals (1118a23–25). To indulge in these
pleasures is not properly human but bestial (1118b1–3). This reason-

ing assumes the function argument: we live well when we perform uniquely human activities well. Since the pleasures that would be indulged are not uniquely human, they cannot be the main component of living well. (2) Second, Aristotle claims that immoderate people take more than nature dictates they need (1118b16–19). They "fill their stomachs beyond what they ought" (1118b19–20). The thought here is that immoderate behavior is destructive to the body (cf. 1119a16–18). Since happiness consists of performing our proper function well, and since the body is necessary for this function, immoderate behavior is, in the long run, destructive of happiness. Besides this immoderate indulging of common, physical desires, Aristotle also mentions immoderate enjoyment of desires that are peculiar to individuals (1118b21–27; cf. 1118b8–9). Though he says that we err here by desiring the wrong things (hateful things), by desiring more than other people, and by desiring in the wrong way, he does not explain here what makes such desires excessive or wrong.[9]

Aristotle does explain this near the end of the discussion of moderation in what I take to be a third explanation of what is wrong with excess pleasure. (3) The assumption is that the exercise of an appetite increases it. Aristotle cannot have in mind an increase in physically caused desire; eating does not make us physically more hungry. What he means is that someone used to always getting what he wants finds it difficult, even painful, to constrain his desires (1119a1–5). Over indulgence increases our psychological desire; the more we eat, the more we wish to savor the pleasure of the food. This is the desire that is insatiable (1119b8–9). So far from being bestial, this desire is uniquely human and, in a way, even depends upon reason. What, then, is wrong with it? "If the appetites are great and intense, they push aside the power of reasoning (logismon)" (1119b10, Ostwald trans.). That is, lack of moderation interferes with reasoning: strong desire for food makes it difficult to assess its value or to assess the relative values of other things. Aristotle makes a similar point elsewhere in this discussion: "The immoderate man loves pleasures more than they are worth. The moderate man is not of this sort, he loves them as right reason (orthos logos) prescribes" (1119a18–20). In loving pleasures more than they are worth, the immoderate person has not evaluated them as reason prescribes. Immoderation goes hand in hand with a failure of reason, moderation with its proper use. The faculty of reason at issue here is later termed "practical reason," and Aristotle claims that moderation is called by its name (sophrōsunē) because it preserves (*sōzousa*) practical reason (*phronēsis*) (VI.5.1140b11–16). Since practical reason is an intellectual virtue, moderation preserves and immoderation destroys intellectual virtue. In short, what is wrong with an excess of pleasure is that it interferes with the exercise of intellectual virtue.

These three explanations of what is wrong with too much pleasure provide an indirect way of answering the other question raised about moderation, how can we determine the mean? Insofar as we share the capacity for taste and touch with animals, and insofar as we must exercise these capacities in order to survive and to exercise our more properly human capacities, pleasures of taste and touch must somehow be included in happiness. However, they should be included only to the extent that they are necessary to replenish the body: the body sets its own limits. Additional indulgence will interfere with reason.

Aristotle expresses this harmony between the rational and non-rational parts of the soul in the final lines of the treatment of moderation:

> Consequently, the appetitive element of the self-controlled man must be in harmony with the guidance of reason. For the aim of both his appetite and his reason is to do what is noble. The appetite of the self-controlled man is directed at the right objects, in the right way, and at the right time; and this is what reason prescribes. (1119b15–18, Ostwald trans.)

The point is that the appetitive part should work with the rational part to attain a rational end, what is noble.[10] Notice that there are two senses of reason here: (1) the noble end is rational—this is the exercise of practical reason, but moderate action also contributes to theoretical knowledge and contemplation; (2) the appetites are in accordance with reason when they contribute toward this end. In an immoderate person, the appetites are not in accordance with reason, nor consequently can his rational part attain its end. Likewise, moderate actions could be called rational in a double sense: they are rational because they contribute to the further exercise of reason, and they are rational because they are in accordance with what reason dictates.

The virtue of justice is rational in much the same way. First, justice is properly concerned with the distribution to a community of honors, things, or whatever can be divided, or with the rectification of transactions (V.2.1130b30–1131a1). Both types of justice are defined by a proportion: distributory justice lies in a geometrical proportion—giving to each what is in accordance with his worth (1131a24–b13); rectificatory justice lies in an arithmetic proportion— taking a portion from the aggressor and giving it to the injured, that is, splitting the difference (1132a30–b6). Since proportion is a type of ratio or formula (*logos*), it is obvious that justice is in accordance with reason (*logismos*).

The basic notion of justice is that each person should have what is due to him. The crucial question here is how to decide the basis on which to assess worth. Rather than answering it, Aristotle acknowledges different standards: "for democrats [worth] is freedom, for oligarchs wealth (or, for some, good birth), for aristocrats virtue" (1131a27–29). If, though, standards of worth vary with the type of government, then so too does justice. That is, what counts as a just act depends upon the type of society in which one lives. Indeed, distributory and rectificatory justice are, as Aristotle describes them, the justice of the ruler and the judge. Acts of justice thus serve to preserve society. Since Aristotle assumes that it is only in society that we have the opportunity to develop our capacities and so to live a fully human life, justice serves a higher good. This fully human life is the happy life we learned about in the function argument: it consists of activity in accordance with reason.

In short, we can see in the discussion the same two dimensions we saw in the treatment of moderation: justice is itself rational in the sense that it follows the dictates of reason; justice is also rational in the sense that it promotes reason. In particular, justice promotes reason because it is essential for the existence of the state, and the state is in turn essential for the development of the arts and sciences.

These arguments about moderation and justice provide the basis for understanding the rational foundation of courage. Courage, in fact, is the test case for my analysis, for it is often doubted that a rational person would be courageous. Courage is manifested most of all in battle, but should someone intent on a contemplative life jeopardize his life on the battlefield for the sake of others less virtuous or less rational than himself? On the surface, the moral virtue of courage seems incompatible with intellectual virtue.[11]

The first point to make is that Aristotle states clearly that the courageous person does act in accordance with reason: "A courageous man endures and fears the right things, for the right motive, in the right manner, and at the right time . . . [for he] feels and acts according to the merits of each case as reason guides him" (III.7.1115b17–20, Ostwald trans.). What are the right things to fear and why is it in accordance with reason to fear them? Most properly, the courageous man is someone who is fearless in the face of a noble death, such as death in battle (1115a32–34). Why would someone acting "as reason guides" him be fearless in battle? Not because he wishes to die. Quite the contrary, Aristotle maintains that it is just those who are virtuous to whom life is most pleasant and who, consequently, have the most to lose (9.1117b11–13). Rather, he is fearless because he recognizes that acts of courage are noble (1117b13–15) and that it would be worse to act ignobly than to die. The courageous man fears not death but being ignoble. Though this conclusion explains something of what are the right things to fear, it does not go far toward explaining why it is right to fear them. The issue here is, just why are acts of courage noble? Why would someone acting "as reason guides" be courageous?

Though Aristotle does not answer these questions explicitly, he does supply us with enough material to be reasonably confident of what he would say. First, it is clear that life is not unconditionally valuable; what is unconditionally valuable is to live well. This view is reminiscent of the Socratic dictum that the unexamined life is not worth living. Only certain kinds of life would be worth living, lives that realize moral and intellectual virtue. Second, near the beginning of the *Nicomachean Ethics*, Aristotle claims that politics is the master science and that its end, like that of ethics, is the good for man, but that its end is greater and more complete "to attain and to preserve" (I.2.1094b7–9). The reason that politics is the "master science" is that someone intent on virtue needs to live in a good state before he can acquire and exercise it. It is a truism for Aristotle that the arts and sciences can flourish because of society. Hence, only someone who lives as a citizen in a state can lead a life that is worth living.

The rational person would recognize that his activities require the existence of a society, and he would be willing to risk his life to defend his society. Like the philosopher king of the *Republic*, he would realize the need to occupy himself with nonintellectual matters, at least for a time. And life would indeed be worth risking if losing the war meant slavery; one needs freedom to lead a contemplative life. A philosopher who displays courage on the battlefield is very much acting in his own interest. In short, the case of courage closely resembles moderation and justice. Just as overindulgence prevents us from using reason, so too lack of courage could indirectly prevent us from the exercise of reason. Not always, perhaps, but for the most part; and the importance of a particular individual in battle would be all the greater in a small *polis*. Courage, like justice, contributes to the preservation of the state. Thus, it *is*, under some circumstances, rational to risk one's life to preserve society.[12]

Like the other two virtues, there is a dual sense of rationality at work here. First, courage preserves the rational in the sense that it preserves the state, and the state is, in turn, necessary for the activity of reason. Second, because courage is rational in this way, an act of courage is itself rational in another way: it is an act that is appropriate under the circumstances. Thus, in the case of all three virtues, a rational principle gives the virtues their meaning and value.

III

That the virtues have some sort of rational foundation should be clear even from this cursory survey. What remains important to explain is the peculiar type of rational foundation they have. In particular, I need to show how Aristotle's rational foundation can steer clear of the equivalent of Scylla and Charybdis. Scylla is pure rationalism, the position of Plato and, later, Kant. On this view reason by itself can define the virtues: it is possible, at least in principle, to demonstrate rationally which actions count as virtuous ones.[13] Charybdis is the view that the moral virtues are simply means to intellectual virtue, the view that Aristotle's moral virtue has merely instrumental value. I have already explained why Aristotle's position is not purely rationalistic, and I have explained why this does not exclude a lesser type of rationalism. For Aristotle the right action is always relative to the particular circumstances at hand, and there are always an indefinite number of factors of which to take account. Moreover, the right action inevitably involves an irrational element in the soul. Under the circumstances there is no way to spell out rules for right action that would be universally applicable: the Kantian project is doomed from the start. This is one reason that we need to rely on habit. To decide a difficult case we need to see what someone with good habits would do, and even he may be unable to articulate thoroughly compelling reasons for a unique course of action. In short, reason cannot completely determine the content of virtue. At best it can provide a general guide. But this does not imply that the virtues lack a rational basis. We saw that courage, moderation, and justice all aim at preserving reason. Risking one's life to preserve the state is an act of courage just because the state is good, and the state is good because it enables its citizens to realize their rational potential in arts and sciences. Hence, to choose to act courageously is rational just because it amounts to choosing to preserve reason.

Still, reason does not tell us precisely how to behave in a given set of circumstances. It supplies us with an end, and a general guide for the type of actions that would under most circumstances contribute toward this end. This is what we find in the *Nicomachean Ethics*. Because ethical generalizations are true only for the most part, Aristotle provides an account that is true only for the most part. There are instances where even moral virtue might be harmful: "some were destroyed through wealth, others through courage" (1094b18–22). Given the character of the subject matter, Aristotle relies heavily on examples. They are not meant to displace reason but to sharpen it, for particular acts are recognized to be in accord with virtue by considering the circumstances in which they occur. Studying these examples hones our ability to choose the appropriate mean. It is not that the examples show us what most people regard as virtuous action, but that they enable us better to choose the path that would, under most circumstances promote reason. Virtue is not dictated by reason as Plato and Kant would have it, but it is rational, nevertheless.

The opposite objection to my account, Charybdis, is that it seems to make the moral virtues into mere means for attaining intellectual virtues.[14] There is no doubt that Aristotle thinks that acts manifesting moral virtue are valuable for their own sake. How can these acts be intrinsically valuable if, as I have argued, their ultimate aim is to preserve intellectual virtue?

The first point to notice is that Aristotle recognizes that intrinsically valuable acts can also serve further ends. He says as much in the opening chapter of the *Nicomachean Ethics*. There he distinguishes between the master science and subordinate science: the ends of the latter contribute toward the end of the former, for which they are pursued (I.1.1094a14–16). He adds that it makes no difference whether the subordinate sciences have as their end something beyond their activities, as, for example, shipbuilding or medicine, or whether the ends of those subordinate sciences are simply the activities themselves (1094a16–18). Thus, it is possible that a subordinate science have as its end its own activity and, yet, also contribute to the end of a master science.[15]

The same thought appears in book X's arguments that contemplation is the highest good. Aristotle claims that nothing else comes from theoretical activity, whereas from practice we do obtain something else (7.1177b2–4). In speaking about practice, Aristotle means to include actions in accordance with moral virtue. Just what these produce becomes clear in subsequent lines. He claims: "We are busy in order that we may have leisure, and we make war in order that we may live in peace. The realization of the practical virtues occurs in politics or in wars, but these are unleisurely" (1177b4–7; see also *Politics* VII.14.1333a33–b3). Neither politics nor war is done for its own sake, nor only so as to act justly or courageously (1177b7–18). The point here is not to deny that just or courageous acts are done for their own sakes, but to maintain that such acts are done when the tense circumstances calling for them arise and that they aim *also* at some end beyond themselves, such as victory or peace or the preservation of the state. It would be foolhardy to go into battle for no other end than to act with courage; rather, courageous actions are called for when the security of the state is threatened. Indeed, being fearless in the face of an enemy attack is only truly courageous when one is defending one's state; only then would one have something worse to fear than the loss of one's life. Thus, acts of moral virtue are at once their own end and aim at some other end apart from them. A third passage where Aristotle recognizes that things themselves intrinsically valuable are also useful for other ends appears in his discussion of practical wisdom. Practical wisdom is the intellectual component of moral virtue, but it is itself an intellectual virtue and, thus, valuable in its own right. Yet practical wisdom acts to secure theoretical wisdom:

> Practical wisdom does not rule [theoretical] wisdom or the better part of our soul, any more than medicine rules health; for practical wisdom does not use theoretical wisdom but it sees to its coming to being. It issues commands not to wisdom, but for the sake of wisdom. Saying that practical wisdom controls theoretical wisdom would be like saying that politics rules the gods because it issues commands about everything in the city. (VI.13.1145a6–11)

Though practical wisdom is itself valuable, it also contributes toward attaining another end, theoretical wisdom.

These texts show that there need be no inconsistency between saying that acts of moral virtue are their own ends and that they serve higher ends. They, especially the last two texts, also help to show why moral virtues are both instrumentally and intrinsically valuable. Ultimately it is theoretical wisdom that makes an act morally virtuous, though only indirectly; for morally virtuous acts are those that tend for the most part to secure and to preserve intellectual virtue—this we have seen in courage, moderation, and justice. But, for two reasons, to say this is not to make moral virtue merely instrumental. First, in order to know which actions will tend to foster intellectual virtue, we need practical reason. But in exercising practical reason, we are realizing an intellectual capacity. Since the exercise of moral virtue involves the exercise of practical reason, the exercise of moral virtue is to some extent an intellectual act. Thus, in performing acts of moral virtue, one is realizing his rational capacities. Insofar as they manifest practical reason, acts of moral virtue are acts of the soul in accordance with reason.[16] A second reason moral virtue is not instrumental is that it exercises other human faculties. Courage, for example, involves not only practical reason but also fear. By itself, fear is an emotion, not a virtue (cf. II.5.1105b28–1106a6). But fear can become a virtue when it is a disposition to fear the right things, at the right time, etc.; when, that is, fear is habitually determined by reason. In exercising the capacity for fear, we are realizing our natural capacities and, thus, performing our human function. What reason does is set the proper limits and appropriate objects for this capacity: it makes fearing not just part of our functioning but part of our functioning well because it determines the object feared, when it is feared, and so forth. Reason sets these limits and controls by means of habituation; fear becomes rational in the process. It is thus that one part of the soul is rational by obeying reason (*logos*), the other part by having it and thinking (I.7.1098a3–5). (The same distinction appears in the closing lines of Aristotle's account of moderation, quoted earlier—1119b15–18.) The point is that the moral virtues involve an exercise of faculties that is part of our proper human functioning, faculties like practical reason, fear, desire, and so forth. Insofar as life is itself intrinsically valuable, exercising those faculties is intrinsically worthwhile. But most of those faculties happen to have ends beyond themselves. The ultimate end, Aristotle argues, is contemplation. Those uses of our faculties that contribute to this end constitute functioning well. In this way, the function of theoretical reason determines the proper functioning of other faculties which latter both contribute to theoretical reason and are themselves the ends of their own activity. To be sure, we also exercise reason and, perhaps, fear in playing football, but this would not usually be moral activity because it does not generally contribute to contemplation. Activity in accordance with moral virtue, on the other hand, is necessary for contemplation (X.8.1178b33–1179a13).

Among the peculiarities of this account is that morally virtuous actions often fail to promote the end in reference to which they are defined. They need not lead one to contemplation. Someone who acts virtuously does what should, under the circumstances, make contemplation possible, but no one can fully guard against his efforts being derailed by the "slings and arrows of outrageous fortune." Besides such failures due to external circumstances, there are other, internal failures: moderate behavior will not promote contemplation in someone who lacks the natural capacity for it (the man Aristotle calls the "natural slave"); acts of courage may promote contemplation only in someone else or, perhaps, in no one at all if there is no person in the state fitted for it. Particular acts of moral virtue may not be instrumentally good for their agent or for anyone else. This conclusion is troubling. To put the problem concretely, suppose that I accept Aristotle's contention that what is wrong with immoderate behavior is that it obstructs practical reason and, ultimately, theoretical reason as well. But suppose that I also know that I will never be a philosopher. Should I still pass up that tempting chocolate eclair?

If the interpretation advanced here is correct, Aristotle's answer must be yes. The reason is that what counts as an act of moderation is defined by what would, under ideal circumstances, promote contemplation, and this definition is taken to express the properly human uses of the faculties of taste and touch. Once proper uses of these faculties are defined, then to exercise the faculties in these ways is to perform human functions well—and this itself is intrinsically valuable, regardless of whether such activities do actually lead to contemplation. To put the point another way: moderation is not defined by its actually achieving contemplation—then it really would be merely instrumental—but by what would ideally achieve contemplation. The acts of moderation so defined are their own ends: they constitute a proper human use of the body. To behave immoderately would be to use the body for something for which it is not suited, for pleasure that is not properly human. An inability to attain, even under the best of circumstances, the best human life is no justification for leading a bestial life; for the life of moral virtue is itself uniquely human—involving practical reason and our other faculties—and open to nearly all. To be sure, this reasoning is not likely to persuade the person unable to contemplate, nor is likely to deter the person who is strongly attracted to the chocolate eclair. Consequently, good habits are often practically necessary; they enable one to live well without fully grasping the ultimate end, and they enable reason to be effective in controlling nonrational elements in our souls.

IV

Still, moral reasoning is an essential part of moral virtue. Because it is so often tied to contemporary accounts of virtue, it is important to understand what it is. Aristotle does not think it consists of following rules, the traditional Kantian paradigm of rational thinking. However, it would be an instance of the fallacy of false dichotomy to infer from this—as I think McDowell and others have done—that ethical reasoning must instead be a matter of pointing to salient features of particulars.[17] Aristotle thinks that moral reasoning differs from either alternative. To understand it, we need to realize first that he typically describes a process of reasoning as the securing of an end. The doctor aiming to relieve a fever works backward from the end:

> The healthy subject is produced as the result of the following train of thought:—since *this* is health, if the subject is to be healthy *this* must first be present, e.g. a uniform state of body, and if this is to be present, there must be heat; and the physician goes on thinking thus until he reduces the matter to a final something which he himself can produce. (*Metaphysics* VII.7.1032b6–9, Oxford trans.)

What the doctor produces is rubbing (1032b26). His action here could be described as finding and following a rule linking rubbing and fever.

The morally virtuous person also aims at an end, living well or activity in accordance with reason, and, like the doctor, he seeks a chain of events that would produce this result and that he can initiate (*N.E.* III.3.1112b12–31). However, he finds nothing analogous with rubbing that will nearly always produce this end. Instead, he is confronted with a variety of circumstances potentially relevant for his aim. His task is to sort through them and to assess them. One and the same thing could be counted differently—the sweet, for example, is both pleasant and harmful (cf. VII.3.1147a25–34). Its assessment will depend on other circumstances and on the particular aims of the moment. Acting in accordance with virtue is more like formulating a rule than following one, but even this will not do because the act of making the assessment is itself part of action in accordance with virtue. Nevertheless, given any particular set of circumstances, there *is* a right assessment and a right action, namely, the judgment and action that would in most cases be expected to promote intellectual virtue.

The point is that the process of moral reasoning, as Aristotle describes it, makes no sense without an end, and that end is—to judge not only from book X but also from indications in the accounts of moral virtues—contemplation. Good moral reasoning is correct deliberation that achieves a good (VI.9.1142b7–22). Hence, moral reasoning does not consist of pointing out significant features of particulars; being rational is not simply offering reasons. Rather, moral reasoning is a process of securing an end, and we can, at least sometimes, evaluate it by its success in achieving its end. That moral reasoning is also its own end may induce some to suppose that any type of moral reasoning, no matter how wayward, must be valuable. But this is no more the case than that any realization of, say, fear would be valuable insofar as it is an actualization of a human capacity. Rather, moral reasoning is valuable when it does its job of properly pursuing the highest human ends. Moral reasoning is a normative activity.

In this way practical reason serves as a kind of bridge between theoretical reason and the emotions, and following its dictates imparts a kind of rationality to the nonrational portion of the soul, as stated earlier. This thought allows us to resolve at one swoop the scholarly problems mentioned at the beginning of this chapter. The question whether happiness lies only in the intellect or in some mixture of the intellectual and the emotional is a false dichotomy.[18] Aristotle denies that the emotions are virtues (1105b28–1106a6), but when the emotions are trained and directed by reason, they manifest an entirely different character: in itself, fear is not good, but the disposition to fear the right things, at the right time, in the right way is courage. What makes an emotion morally good is its accord with reason, its obeying reason (cf. 1098a3–5). The moral virtues are not distinct from reason; they are defined by it, manifestations of it, and are valuable in part because they manifest it. The emotions are the matter for reason, and the task of moral education is to train them to work in harmony with reason.[19] Hence, the life of contemplation is not opposed to the life of moral virtue; it differs from the life of moral virtue only in degree. And with this conclusion the supposed conflict of books I and X with the account of the moral virtues vanishes.

Aristotle's ethics is one of the few treatments of the subject that takes account of the richness and diversity of our moral lives. The interpretation that I have presented here attempts to show that moral virtue is based upon reason without reducing the diversity of moral experience. Though Aristotle realizes that much of the rich detail of our lives escapes reason, he remains an intellectualist through and through.

Chapter 4

Two Problems in Aristotelian Ethics

This chapter addresses two particularly thorny problems that have exercised recent commentators on Aristotle's ethical writings. Both concern Aristotle's account of *eudaimonia*, happiness. A thorough treatment of either could well be a lengthy undertaking. It may, then, seem foolhardy to tackle both here. However, I shall try to address them by playing them off against each other. The problems are, I think, mirror images of each other. Simply to show that my account can avoid either problem will serve to support that account. In particular, I shall explain how the problems arise from the tendency of current thinkers to think of Aristotle as either a utilitarian or a deontologist. I sketch my own account of happiness while showing how to avoid these two problems.

I

The first problem might be termed the problem of maximum happiness. On one formulation, it is the question of whether an increase in the number of external goods or acts of moral virtue will make a happy life happier. Since in *Nicomachean Ethics* I.7 Aristotle characterizes happiness as complete or final (*teleion*) and as self-sufficient (1097b20–21), it does not appear to admit of increase (1097b16–20). Nothing could make it better; it seems to be inherently maximal. Yet this maximal conception seems inconsistent with our ordinary views of happiness: we usually think that even a happy life could have been better if, for example, the subject had only had more money, more or better children, more opportunities for virtuous actions, or whatever. Still worse, the maximal conception of happiness seems inconsistent with Aristotle's own apparent endorsement of some lives as better (and thus happier) than others. How could the politician's life really have been happy if it could have been better? However good Solon's life was, would it not have been better if he had been able to devote more time to contemplation? If the life of contemplation is indeed happier, is it right to say that Solon's is complete?[1]

The standard interpretations of Aristotle's account of happiness in I.7 suggest answers to these questions. On one hand, there are those who take "complete" in this account to characterize a life that includes all the actions that are desirable in themselves; in this case, happiness would lie in the life that is most full of what is valuable and it would not admit of increase.[2] On the other hand, there are those who insist that a life is truly complete only when it consists of activity in accordance with complete virtue, contemplation. Other lives are happy by reference to this dominant end.[3] In this case, too, an increase in external goods will not improve the best life because they play virtually no part in that life; nor would an increase in acts of moral virtue improve such a life—they would just take time away from a better activity.

Neither view is very plausible. It is hard to see how an inclusive happiness could be conceived, much less attained. Could there be a life that includes all the virtues in the greatest degree? Is the political life of Solon compatible with the wisdom of Socrates, or vice versa? In what sense would either include all the desirable political acts or all the desirable contemplative acts?[4] If, on the other hand, happiness is identified with contemplation, then neither Solon nor those who live lives in accordance with moral virtues are happy.[5] Again, Aristotle's claim that Solon is truly happy speaks against both interpretations of the account of happiness.

In fact, there is no doubt that Aristotle regards some types of happiness as better than others—contemplative lives are better than political lives—but that he regards lives where moral virtues are exercised in politics as properly happy ones (X.7). This is a case where Aristotle's answer to a problem is perfectly clear. What is difficult is to make sense of that answer.

What I want to propose here is that the question of how happiness can be complete and self-sufficient and still admit of increase is a problem that has its source in the way that scholars typically think of happiness. They take the Aristotelian good to be a collection of constituents and then try to quantify them. It does not matter whether we take these constituents to be virtues, virtuous acts, or external goods. We can ask the same type of questions of each: Just how much justice does a virtuous man need for happiness, and will more justice increase his happiness? Just how much money or good looks does someone need for happiness, and will having more of either increase happiness?

Such questions are inappropriate. The mistake is to ask a quantitative question about something that Aristotle takes to be nonquantitative. In calling happiness self-sufficient and complete, Aristotle is applying to it his own technical terminology. These characteristics describe any *energeia* or *entelechia*, and Aristotle gives them a definite sense in the final book of the *Nicomachean Ethics* (X.4) and in *Metaphysics IX* (6.1048b18–35): an *energeia* is something whose end lies within itself. Both characteristics of happiness follow from this description. A happy life is (1) self-sufficient because it "rules itself": the happy person acts from his own principle, namely his own virtue, and he acts for the sake of his own virtue. Happiness is (2) final or complete (*teleion*) because it is not for the sake of some further end but for the sake of itself: it needs nothing else. Thus, happiness is complete not because it includes everything, but because insofar as it is its own end, it lacks nothing outside of itself. Completeness describes the character of an actuality, not its quantity.

To ask of happiness whether it gets better when its quantity is increased is to misunderstand its nature. It is a type of category mistake. It is also anachronistic, for this question would be appropriate for a utilitarian. Scholars who ask whether happiness can be improved by adding something to it, scholars who think of happiness as a collection of goods, even a hierarchical collection, are all working from a utilitarian framework. This is particularly unfortunate because they miss what is unique and interesting about Aristotle's account.

To see how Aristotle could (or should) deal with the problem of maximum happiness we need only compare happiness to other Aristotelian *energeiai*. Seeing and contemplating are *energeiai*, Aristotle tells us, because each is its own end (*Met.* IX.6.1048b22–28). A sign of this is that neither takes place over time, for we see and have seen at once. That is to say, these actions are complete because they always have their end. Now try to raise the analogues of the problem of maxima: in saying that seeing or contemplating is complete, is Aristotle saying that we cannot see or contemplate more than we do at any one time? Not at all. Any act of seeing is complete because it is its own end. Nothing prevents some acts of seeing from being more inclusive than others. After studying art for some time I would no doubt see more in a painting of Picasso than one untutored, but my act of seeing is not thereby more complete than his. Seeing is an *energeia* not because of how much it includes but because of the way it is executed, the *quality* it has as an act. Analogously, a life is not happy by virtue of the amount of virtue or external goods it contains, but by its being its own end. Only a life that is its own end could be chosen for its own sake.[6]

To say that one happy life is better than another is to say that one actuality is better than another. What makes one actuality better than another? The better actuality should be more of an actuality—it should be more complete and self-sufficient than a lesser actuality. This, in fact, is precisely the criterion Aristotle uses to compare lives. He does not scale the happiness of a life by the *quantity* of virtue or goods it contains. On the contrary, its *quality* is what counts: he argues that contemplation is more properly an actuality than the political life because insofar as the latter seeks ends beyond itself, it is less complete (X.7.1177b6–26). A life that is chosen for its own sake *and* for the sake of something outside of it is less complete than a life that is chosen *only* for its own sake because the end of a life chosen only for its own sake is simply itself.[7] Contemplation is the best life because it is the most complete, and it is most complete because it has no end beyond itself.

In short, it is not inconsistent to say that happiness is "not made more choiceworthy by the addition of even the smallest good" (1097b16–21) and also to say that some lives are happier than others. The former claim describes the nonquantitative character of happiness; the latter distinguishes differences in the degree to which happy lives possess a quality. With this result we need no longer be troubled by Aristotle's endorsement of two apparently incompatible lives, the political and the contemplative lives, as complete. Each can be complete without including the content of the other; indeed, it is a mistake to consider a life by looking at the constituents of its content. Again, this is the perspective of the utilitarian. A life is not better because it has more of something, even if that something is contemplation. When it comes to happiness, it is quality not quantity that counts.

Aristotle's central metaphor in this discussion is that the whole of life is an act. This comes through quite clearly in the function argument (I.7.1098a18–20). The analogy is obviously strained. Life consists of many acts. It is a rare life indeed that has the degree of coherence that Aristotle supposes. He leaves no room for mid-life crises or career changes. Although it may seem that Aristotle also leaves out the affective part of life, that is, experiences, feelings, and so forth, he actually treats them as parts of action. Yet this inclusion implies that life consists of many acts; for as our experiences vary, so too must our acts. Indeed, Aristotle himself speaks often of particular acts of moral virtue. How can such particular *energeiai* be reconciled with the notion that life is one *energeia*, a single act? It seems that Aristotle's analysis itself forces us to divide happiness into distinct acts of virtue. If happiness is so divisible, then would it not be important to inquire about its constituent parts? Those questions that I have argued in this section are inappropriate now seem to arise from Aristotle's account of distinct acts of virtue.

This line of thought, however, stems from the tendency to separate acts of moral virtue from other aspects of life. It is this mistake that I address in the next section.

II

The second problem concerns the status of external goods. By "external goods" Aristotle means human goods that do not belong to the soul.[8] He maintains that they are necessary for happiness (I.8.1099a31–32; VII.13.1153b17–19; X.8.1178b33–35). Some he refers to specifically as instruments of action; namely, friends, wealth, and political power (I.8.1099a33–b2; *Politics* VII.1.1323a38–b1, esp. b7–8).

Others he mentions simply as things whose absence would spoil happiness: good birth, good children, and good looks (I.8.1099b2–3). In this latter context he mentions friends as well, and he appears to have in mind good (= virtuous) friends (1099b3–6). In another passage, he includes health, food, and care under the heading "external prosperity" (X.8.1178b33–35; cf. 1099b6–8). The second problem is just how these external goods are necessary for happiness. Are they means for that end or are they, or the enjoyment of them, somehow parts of happiness?

In support of the former position is Aristotle's reference to some external goods as instruments of action. To appreciate the significance of this reference we need to recall that happiness is an activity; it is the activity of the soul in accordance with virtue (I.7.1098a16–18). Because happiness is an activity of the soul, and because the external goods are, by definition, outside the soul, there seems to be no other alternative than to declare them accessories of some sort. Moreover, Aristotle denies that happiness is identical with virtue: someone possessing virtue is not happy unless it is exercised (8.1098b31–1099a7). External circumstances could prevent or allow virtue to realize itself in action. Like the acorn that by nature develops into an oak, virtue should express itself as happiness; but just as the acorn also requires water, soil, and so forth, a virtuous person would seem to need good looks, health, money, and the like in order to perform virtuous acts. External goods provide opportunities for the exercise of virtue, opportunities without which the exercise would be impeded (cf. VII.13.1153b17–19). The external goods that Aristotle calls "instruments," namely, wealth, power, and friends, readily fit this picture. Yet Aristotle lumps all external goods together when he claims that the absence of goods of the body, external goods, or goods of fortune—apparently, the absence of *any* external good—would impede our activity (1153b17–19). From this last passage, John Cooper concludes that *all* external goods are instruments. He proposes that without children a person will lack the opportunities to exercise virtue in their rearing and in subsequent common pursuits with them and that without at least normal good looks someone would lack opportunities for moderation in the exercise of sexual appetites.[9]

The implausibility of this purely instrumental account supports the notion that at least some external goods are intrinsically valuable. It seems more plausible to say that health is good in its own right rather than good because it enables us to act justly, and that good looks are good in their own right rather than good because of the increased opportunities they afford us to exercise the virtue of moderation. Eating fine food seems part of happiness whether or not it increases our opportunities for restraint. Are we to say that children and close friends are only valuable to us as instruments of virtue? Would we mourn their loss only because our opportunities for virtuous actions would be decreased? Any account that makes children and friends mere instruments of happiness is not simply implausible; it is immoral.[10] If, on the other hand, children, friends, health, and so forth are worthwhile for their own sakes, then part of happiness would seem to consist of our enjoying them. Moreover, it is plausible to suppose that enjoying children, friends, and health is an intrinsically valuable part of happiness because the accidental loss of any of these could destroy happiness, and happiness is thought to depend upon chance.[11] Were these external goods merely instrumental, their loss need not be devastating: we might achieve our ends without them or with others like them. Thus, Aristotle's acceptance of the ordinary view of the importance of chance would apparently lend support to the view that external goods are intrinsically valuable.

The problem, in short, is that there are grounds for saying that external goods are mere means to happiness, but it seems to be more plausible and more in line with Aristotle's other views to say that they are intrinsically valuable.

In fact, there are very few pertinent texts and none is decisive. The single text that Cooper relies upon to support his instrumental account is the claim that the absence of external goods would impede our activities (1153b17–19), a point Aristotle makes to show that happiness is pleasurable. However, this passage says neither that happiness consists solely of acts of virtue nor that it is such acts that the absence of external goods would impede. It is reasonable to suppose, as Cooper's opponents do, that at least some of the activities that the absence of external goods impedes are acts of enjoying external goods.[12] So Aristotle's claim that the absence of external goods impedes our activities is compatible not only with external goods' being instruments but also with the enjoyment of them being part of happiness. Indeed, this claim is compatible with other positions as well. The absence of sunny weather impedes my tennis game, but this fact does not imply that weather is an instrument in the game. Phlebitis might impede a display of courage, but not because a healthy vein, or even the whole body, is an instrument of virtue. Aristotle's claim that the absence of external goods impedes virtuous action tells us little about the role they play when present. On the other side, I suggested earlier that support for the second position lies in its making happiness partly dependent on chance. However, someone who thinks that external goods are instruments for acts of virtue and denies that these acts—either all or some that are essential for happiness—can occur without the instruments also recognizes happiness as dependent on chance. Thus, the second position is no more compatible with chance than the first. In short, there is no real textual evidence for either position.

The difficulty about the external goods seems intractable, but it is, I propose, an artifact of assumptions that scholars bring to the text. Whereas the first problem had its source in a utilitarian view of happiness, the problem of external goods stems from a Stoic or Kantian view of virtue.[13] The assumption that generates the issue is that the external goods must be either means to happiness or intrinsically valuable themselves. The problem is that they fit squarely under neither head. If they were intrinsically valuable constituents of happiness, then happiness would not lie only in virtuous activity. If they were mere means, then the loss of children, defeat in battle, and other misfortunes, would be unfortunate only insofar as they deprived us of future opportunities for virtuous actions.

Could external goods be neither means to virtue nor themselves intrinsically valuable? Christine Korsgaard has argued convincingly that these two terms belong to different distinctions: means are opposed to ends, and what is intrinsically valuable to what is extrinsically valuable.[14] External goods are ends but they derive their value from something else, virtuous acts. Hence, they are neither intrinsically valuable nor means; they are extrinsically valuable ends. These distinctions are Kant's, and he uses them to locate external goods as parts of happiness but outside the sphere of virtuous actions. At issue in the present chapter, though, is just whether there is anything to Aristotelian happiness besides virtuous actions. If there is not, as Cooper would have it, then friends and children must be mere means; if there is, then they would be extrinsic ends and Aristotle would seem to be some sort of Kantian. The Kantian distinctions do not by themselves decide the nature of happiness.

On the contrary, both positions on external goods *are motivated* by a Kantian perspective, despite the efforts of recent commentators to rid themselves of this alien baggage. Kant sees man struggling against desires; virtue lies in overcoming them. While we know very well that Aristotle's virtuous man has trained his desires so that they aim at the right things to just the right degree, the Kantian picture of virtue as restraint of desire is often terribly difficult to overcome. Consider a standard Philosophy 101 illustration of moderation: the moderate person is someone who is able to go to a dinner party and neither eat nor drink too much. The moderate person is someone who knows when to say no. We seem to be virtuous by restraining desire, but to think this way is to invoke a Kantian separation between virtue and desire. The Stoics make a parallel distinction between what belongs to ourselves and what belongs to our bodies. Like Peripatetics eager to defend Aristotle against Stoic accounts of virtue, some current commentators on Aristotelian ethics do not dispute the character of moderation and other acts of virtue; they seek instead to add to this another constituent of happiness, a nonmoral physical good. There is, they suppose, first, the good that lies in the satisfaction of desire for food or drink and, then, the good that comes from the restraint of this desire. It is as if two acts were involved here, one physical, the other moral. Likewise, the pleasure someone gets from children and friends would be distinguished from the exercise of virtue with them.

Some such thought stands behind the debate over external goods. Cooper thinks that an external good, like good looks, puts one in a position to exercise a virtuous restraint of desires; he thinks that children and friends are instruments for virtuous acts. The opposing side agrees with Cooper about virtue, but they deny that it is the only constituent of happiness. They insist that happiness consists of both the exercise of virtue *and* the enjoyment of external goods. Both sides implicitly recognize two distinct acts; the issue between them is whether one or both constitute happiness.

Aristotelian happiness is not simply a combination of external goods and goods of the soul, nor is it appropriate to think of the external goods as simply presenting means or opportunities for virtuous acts. The connection between most so-called external goods and the goods of the soul is much closer. Aristotle's account of moderation (III.10–12), for example, is remarkably free from any idea of restraining desires. On the contrary, he takes feeling pain when desires are not satisfied as a mark of immoderation (1118b30–1119a5). A person is moderate when his desires are in accord with reason (1119b15–18). To be sure, Aristotle does distinguish two parts of the soul, one that obeys reason and the other that possesses reason (I.7.1098a3–5). But, unlike Kant, he does not think these two parts engage in two distinct activities, unless a person is incontinent, in which case practical reason will not be in accord with the appetites. In a moderate person, the two work together as two constituents of a single act. There is no moral act that exists over and against the physical act of enjoying food; there is no way to distinguish the act of restraint from the act of enjoyment it is supposed to restrain. Aristotle sees no bifurcation: the act of moderation *is* also the act of enjoyment. It is a single action that is "in accordance with reason." Food is worthwhile, and eating it is naturally enjoyable. Moderation lies in the appropriate amount of this enjoyment, the amount that is in accordance with reason. It is the amount that is best for *both* body and soul. (In the preceding chapter I discussed what determines what amount is appropriate.) It makes no sense to speak as if the pleasure of eating were different from the pleasure of moderation—moderation here consists of the consumption of food. The pleasure of moderation *is* the pleasure of eating in a certain way. Much the same could be said about moderation of sexual activity. Likewise, the enjoyment of friends and children is not distinct from the activities we undertake with them. Acts of virtue are in accordance with reason, but they are not, in general, only acts of reason.

It is a consequence of this account that Aristotle's virtuous man has none of the grim seriousness of Kant's or of the Stoic's. A fine meal or even a beer bust may well be the appropriate action under certain, possibly rare, circumstances. But in such cases the food or the alcohol is valuable neither as means to the action nor as distinct constituents of a happy life. They are valuable for their own sakes *as a part of the act of moderation*. Again, moderation is not something that we exercise in addition to eating; it is what we exercise *by* eating, and involved in its exercise is the appropriate enjoyment of pleasurable things.

If this analysis is right, food is a part of the act of moderate eating. To regard it as merely an instrument for moderation or, as the glutton does, merely an object of enjoyment is equally perverse. By the same token, it would be wrong to regard a person as either a means for sexual activity (or restraint) or an object of enjoyment—wrong not merely in that it would amount to treating her as a thing, but wrong in the quality of the act, much in the way that a glutton perverts the act of nourishing the body into an unwholesome act of savoring food. The Romantic identification of virtue with restrained desires has no place in Aristotle. If it is to be moderate, sexual activity or abstinence must be a single act where desires are in conformity with what reason dictates under the circumstances.

It may, then, seem wrong to call food and sex partners external goods. To be sure, they are less external than, say, the money used to buy the food. Nonetheless, they count as external goods because they are not entirely under our control; they depend to some extent on fortune. A famine or flood might make moderate eating impossible. Aristotle's marking out certain goods as external serves as a guide for action. Since a person could never have fortune under his control, he ought to focus attention on the portion of happiness that he could influence, that is, he ought to cultivate the virtues. To call a good external is not to say that it stands outside of an act of virtue, but that it is beyond our control. Again, it would be nonsensical to think of food eaten as being outside the act of eating moderately.

Good looks, on the other hand, are not a part of moderate action; Aristotle does not connect appearance with moderation in any way. Besides his identification of good looks as external goods, the only passage where he seems to speak about good looks is his claim that the goods of fortune can make a person more magnanimous because people honor their possessors (IV.3.1124a20–24). Aristotle mentions wealth, power, and noble birth here, but he may have in mind physical beauty as well because he had mentioned it earlier with these (I.8.1099b2–3). In fact, he thinks that none of these external goods by itself makes a person truly worthy of honor (1124a25). Aristotle's point would seem to be that a person used to being honored can come to behave in a magnanimous way; he takes pride in features, such as good looks, that others honor. Good looks are as intrinsic a part of this pride as food is a part of moderate eating. Aristotle thinks it far better to take pride in and be honored for genuine goodness, but one who has external goods in addition to goodness is still more worthy of honor and pride (1124a25–26). His thought seems to be that someone who was extremely ugly would find it difficult to take pride in himself.

The most difficult external goods to make sense of are children and friends. Clearly, we cannot be happy without at least some of either. Just as clearly, we cannot justly regard them as mere means to our own activity. The first point to notice is that Aristotle mentions friends among the external goods that are instruments for action and also among the external goods whose absence mars happiness (I.8.1099a33–b6). This need not be an inconsistency: he probably has in mind two different types of friendship or two different aspects of one type. Friendship for advantage is clearly an instrument (VIII.3.1156a10–31). Since friendship for virtue is also beneficial, it has some instrumental value; but it is also pleasant and, most important- ly, a joint activity in pursuit of virtue (1157b7–33). Because this activi- ty is essential for happiness, it is friendship for virtue whose absence would mar happiness. Aristotle includes the parent-child relation among friendships for virtue (VIII.7.1158b11–28). That may be why after mentioning the absence of good children as marring happiness, he illustrates the point by speaking not of one who is merely childless but of one who is "alone and childless" and someone whose children and friends are worthless or dead (I.8.1099b2–6). Neither would be able to engage in the joint pursuit of virtue that constitutes friend- ships for virtue.

We saw (in chapter 2) that friendship for virtue is a joint activity. Examples include pursuing knowledge together in mutual inquiry and fighting together on the battlefield. In each case, the joint activity is qualitatively better than the same activity would be were it engaged in alone. That is what makes friendship so valuable. It would be a mistake to think that a friend simply provides an opportunity for the exercise of friendship or for the exercise of some virtue: the two friends are intrinsic parts of a joint activity that could not exist as such apart from them both. This is as true of mutual inquiry as it is of the training and education that occur in family life. Thus, a friend (for virtue) or a child is neither an instrument nor an object of pleasure to be enjoyed. Both are external goods in that they are not entirely under our control, but each is properly a partner in the pursuit of virtue. That friends are intrinsically valuable does not entail that taking plea- sure in friendship is an element of happiness distinct from activity in accordance with virtue. Taking pleasure in friends is just what we do in the process of the shared pursuit of virtue. The case of friendship shows clearly that acts of virtue need not be divorced from the enjoy- ment of external goods. Though our friends remain to some extent beyond our control, they are not external to our happiness.

Besides his treatment of friendship, Aristotle also speaks of our interactions with friends and children as instances of the exercise of the virtue of justice. He recognizes a "household justice" that includes the justice of a father toward a child, a master toward a slave, and a husband toward his wife, though his aim in the *Nicomachean Ethics* is not to examine it but to distinguish it from political justice (V.7.1134b8–17). Elsewhere, he mentions as an example of an unjust person the man who would "destroy his dearest friends for a fourth [of an obol]" (*Politics* VII.1.1323a31–32). In contrast, the just person gives each his due: he gives his friends what is their due and his children what is due them. Initially, this latter claim appears cruel. Should he give children *only* what is their due? Does the virtuous person value his children only as objects to be cared for? Is Priam unhappy because his has lost opportunities to exercise his virtue or is he unhappy because he has lost children whom he loved? These questions betray, once again, an implicit Kantianism. They assume that we can distinguish what a parent feels for his children from what he owes to them, and that only the moral duties could count as part of justice. Nonsense. What is due to children is the love parents naturally feel for them, and it is because of this feeling that parents care for them. There is surely a moral deficiency in a person who does his duty towards his children without any feelings for them. We may be reluctant to use the term "feelings" for an aspect of justice because Aristotle distinguishes feelings from virtues in the course of defining the latter (*N. E.* II.5.1105b28–1106a6). But the feelings he has in mind in that passage are momentary—nothing like the more habitual concern that a parent feels for a child; and virtue amounts to a tendency to have the right feeling at the right time. Perhaps a worse obstacle to speaking of "feelings" here is the recognition that feelings can—and often, probably, do—lead parents astray. But is not this what distinguishes a just from an unjust person? The just person has appropriate feelings for the appropriate things and is not led astray.

Perhaps some of the implausibility of saying that parent–child relations manifest justice is mitigated by recalling that Plato also treats family relations as part of the treatment of justice, though of course with scarcely a shred of natural feeling. That Aristotle treats family relations as an origin of the *polis* and devotes some attention to them in the first book of the *Politics* is an indication that he regards them, more than external goods, as a proper sphere of justice.

To conclude, once we understand how external goods are involved in acts of virtue, the second problem in Aristotelian ethics vanishes. There are indeed external goods—such as useful friends, political power, and wealth—that Aristotle speaks of as instrumental to virtuous activity. But a distinct and more interesting group of external goods are those that are intrinsic constituents of virtuous acts. Near the beginning of this section I proposed that external goods stand to virtuous activity as water stands to the acorn; the former are necessary for the development of the latter but not part of its nature. I suggested that instrumental external goods conform to this picture. We can now see that another group of external goods—food, children, and friends—more closely resemble the physical matter that Aristotle includes in the definition of a nature (*Met.* VI.1.1025b31–1026a6);[15] they belong to the act that is in accordance with virtue. Besides these two groups, there is another class of circumstances figuring in the exercise of virtue that Aristotle does not discuss in the context of external goods. Courage in battle requires war; rectificatory justice requires injustice, etc. These circumstances we could call external evils. Ironically, the worst of circumstances can also promote virtuous action. Yet such circumstances ought not to be desired, for they interfere with the exercise of reason that is the highest expression of our nature, an exercise that employs no external goods.

PART II

METAPHYSICS

The preceding essays on ethics show us the nature of actuality, how it functions in ethics, and why it comes to be important. In order to make the right choices, there needs to be a standard. Plato argues, albeit indirectly, for the transcendence of the standard. Aristotle shows that the requirements for the standard can be met by a different sort of entity, an entity that can be understood as an activity that is its own end, an actuality. If living well is such an activity, then the end of living well is nothing more than living well. Though some modes of living well may be better than others, they are not better because they contain more of something or because they possess a different qualitative attribute. Instead, modes of living well are better than others when they are more of the nature of actualities and, thus, more self-sufficient and complete. That living well is an actuality to a high degree does not imply that it is eternal. Insofar as it is an activity that uses various physical substances, it can be sidetracked and fail. Thus, living well is an activity that is self-subsistent without existing apart from everything else, an activity that is independent of time without being eternal.

The first essay of this part, "Aristotle on Knowledge of Nature," accomplishes for physics what all the papers of the preceding part together accomplish for ethics. One important Platonic motivation for positing transcendent forms is the supposition that they alone could be objects of knowledge because everything else is in motion. What Aristotle realizes is that even things in motion could be objects of knowledge provided that their motions are regular and orderly, like the circular motions ascribed to the heavens. Though entities with regular motions are always changing, they are also always the same because they are always changing in the same ways. These regular changes are precisely what Aristotle identifies as actualities. Plato supposes that nothing could remain true of things that change; hence, he posits unchanging, eternal objects of knowledge. Aristotle's actualities are not eternal but they are atemporal, and this suffices to meet the objection against the existence of knowledge of changing things.

Once we grasp the notion of an actuality, we can see the poverty of the prevailing analytic or linguistic interpretations of Aristotle. These interpretations do not and cannot deal adequately with actualities. In "Ackrill, Aristotle, and Analytic Philosophy," I argue against the notion that Aristotle uses linguistic hints to arrive at metaphysical conclusions and the notion upon which this is based, that Aristotle assumes that language simply reflects the world. On the contrary, the vagaries of language are themselves phenomena, and Aristotle looks to essences to explain them. Thus, he argues against the Eleatics by drawing on the distinction between essences and accidents, and he supports claims that terms like "being" are said in many ways not by analyzing usage but by finding a plurality of essences. It is only the contemporary view that an essence must be a linguistic entity that makes us want to ascribe this view to Aristotle. It is clear that he takes them to be something else, namely, forms or actualities, as we can see from earlier essays.

The last two chapters in this part consider problems that arise when we try to use actualities or substances as principles that account for everything. If all attributes must always inhere in some substance, it is hard to see how numbers could exist. A number is not a substance, nor would it seem able to inhere in any (single) substance. "Some Problems in Aristotle's Mathematical Ontology" argues for a solution. Still another problem that arises from taking individual actualities as fundamental is that there seems to be no way to account adequately for interactions of two or more substances. As a result,

Aristotle must recognize accidents. Thus, the last paper in this group explains how accidents are possible.

Taken together the essays in this part show how natures can be substances, how those substances can have attributes, and how they can interact with one another. So the studies of particular topics work together to yield a reasonably rounded picture. This treatment is not and does not emerge from an analysis of language: it aims to come to grips with the regularities and structures that must exist for there to be language.

Chapter 5

ARISTOTLE ON KNOWLEDGE
OF NATURE

It is well-known that Plato and Aristotle disagree on the possibility of knowledge of nature. Plato maintains that knowledge, in contrast with belief, is never mistaken (*Republic* 477e–478a), that the objects of knowledge are always the same and never becoming, and that what we sense is always becoming (*Rep.* 508d; *Timaeus* 27e–28a).[1] He concludes that knowledge is possible only of objects that are unchanging and separate from sensibles, i.e., the forms (*Timaeus* 28b–29c, 52d–e; see also *Rep.* 529b–c). Aristotle rejects this conclusion and recognizes knowledge of sensibles. Surprisingly, though, he accepts Plato's assumptions. He too maintains that knowledge is not sometimes true and sometimes false, but always true (*An. Po.* II.19.100b5–8; *Met.* VII.15.1039b32–33); he distinguishes the sensibles from the unchanging eternal beings (*Met.* XII.1.1069a30–34); and he asserts that the objects of knowledge "always are or are for the most part" (*Met.* VI.2.1027a20–21; XI.8.1065a4–5) and occasionally he even claims that they cannot be otherwise (e.g., *N.E.* VI.3.1139b19–21). The problem is, how can Aristotle accept Plato's assumptions about the nature and objects of knowledge and still maintain that knowledge of nature is possible?

There is another formulation of this question. Both Plato and Aristotle agree that the objects of knowledge are forms. These forms can be known because they do not change and because they are each one (cf. *Phaedo* 78c–79a; *Rep.* 585c). Both also agree that the sensible world is changing. Plato concludes that the forms must be supersensible. But Aristotle denies the forms of sensibles can be separate from them and insists that they exist with matter in the sensible world. The problem is, how can Aristotle accept nonseparate forms of changing sensibles?

The goal of this chapter is to explain Aristotle's answer to these questions. It ought to be apparent that both questions turn on the same issue. Aside from the intrinsic philosophical interest of this issue, an examination of it will give us a handle on another well-known question that initially seems unrelated, the interpretation of actuality.

Before I proceed any further, it is worth pointing out that Aristotle does not justify knowledge of nature by softening his rigid criteria for knowledge. Current philosophers and scientists often speak "scientific knowledge" even though reflection on scientific method shows that theories are never proven but, at best, well supported. Our use of the term "knowledge" is looser than Plato's and Aristotle's. Aristotle could have justified knowledge of nature by allowing "well-supported beliefs accepted by most people with recognized competence to judge" to be called by the term "knowledge." Since he recognizes equivocal senses of terms, he surely has the conceptual apparatus available to make this move. But Aristotle still rigidly adheres to the same view of knowledge as Plato: knowledge, unlike belief, must always be true. Indeed, when Aristotle affirms this character of knowledge in *Metaphysics* VII.15, it is of the sensibles that he speaks. His reluctance to use his doctrine of equivocal terms to introduce a loose sense of "knowledge" makes Aristotle's acceptance of knowledge of nature all the more surprising.

Still, the possibility of knowledge of what changes is not apt to strike us as a philosophically significant problem. We can, after all, give a formula that describes the motion of, for example, a frisbee or an automobile. Why would Aristotle not count possession of this formula as knowledge of the frisbee or the automobile? According to Jaakko Hintikka, the Greeks formulate knowledge claims in temporally indefinite sentences.[2] A formula describing the motion of a frisbee would have to refer to time. On the other hand, any temporally indefinite claim about the frisbee could be falsified by its motion. This explanation is fine as far as it goes, but it does not make Aristotle's insistence on temporally indefinite knowledge claims very plausible. A more Greek explanation of why a formula of what changes is not knowledge is that to be known as a definition a formula must be the formula of one thing (cf. *Met.* VII.4.1030b5–10). Change, though, is the ceasing to be of something and the coming to be of something else (cf. *Phys.* I.8). Thus, any formula that described a change would not be the formula of one thing. This is the reason that what changes does not admit of being known. Of course, this is reasoning that Aristotle discredits, but not because he thinks that possession of any formula counts as knowledge. Again, what is puzzling is that Aristotle disputes the conclusion of Plato and Parmenides while still accepting their assumptions that the object of knowledge is one and that knowledge claims are temporally indefinite. How he could accomplish this is the story we have to tell.

I

Surprisingly, Aristotle never specifically addresses the problem of the possibility of knowledge of nature. He was doubtless aware of the issue. In the first two books of the *Physics* he attacks both Eleatic arguments against the possibility of motion (I.2–3, 8) and also the view that all motion arises from chance (II.4–8). In each case his analysis amounts to a defense of the possibility of nature. Further, he criticizes Plato's separate forms on the ground that they do not enable us to have knowledge of sensibles nor do they account for the being and becoming of the sensibles (*Met.* I.9.991a10–14; 991b3–9). Clearly, Aristotle thinks that his own forms do provide knowledge of sensibles. How can he avoid the Platonic contentions that there are no forms of sensibles and that knowledge of what changes is impossible? We must speculate on Aristotle's answer, but there is ample material to go on. Indeed, considering the text with this question in mind enables us to tie some seemingly scattered remarks together, especially in *Physics* II.

Most discussions of how Aristotle's treatment of motion differs from that of his predecessors focus attention on the substrate that persists through change, the corresponding denial of unqualified change, and the three principles of motion. These topics are important to explain why a substance like Socrates remains unaltered by accidental changes, but they do not really explain how essential change and the thing that changes essentially can be known. How can we have knowledge of what a human being is if change is an essential feature of human nature? What Aristotle needs to explain is how, *pace* Plato, we can have knowledge of changing things.

Briefly stated, Aristotle's account of the possibility of knowledge of changing things relies on recognizing regularities in the changes. If Plato were right that the sensible world is *always* changing, his conclusion that sensibles do not admit of knowledge would be correct. Aristotle's insight is that even though the sensible world does constantly change, the changes are regular. Constantly changing in the same way, the sensible world is always the same. In a sense it is unchanging. As such, sensibles are knowable and the Platonic arguments vanish.

The key move in Aristotle's solution is the doctrine of actuality (*energeia* or *entelechia*). One of the ironies of Aristotelian scholarship is that this doctrine is so successful in transforming the terms of the problem of knowledge of what changes that scholars fail to recognize that that is its purpose. In order to resolve the problem of knowledge, Aristotle introduces a sharp distinction between actualities and motions. Yet the only way to understand how this doctrine does resolve the problem is to recognize that what Aristotle calls "actualities" would be termed "motions" by other Greek philosophers. First, let us be clear that despite his distinction of motion (*kinēsis*) and actuality in *Metaphysics* IX.6.1048b18–35 and *Nicomachean Ethics* X.4.1174a14–23, he often uses these terms as if they were closely connected. In some passages he calls actualities motions (*Rhetoric* III.11.1412a10); in others motions are types of actualities, e.g., the *Physics* and the *De Anima* call motion an incomplete actuality (*Phys.* III.2.201b31–32; see also III.1.201a9–11; VIII.5.257b7–9; *De Anima* II.2.417a14–17; cf. III.7.431a6–7). Sometimes Aristotle even uses the terms interchangeably (*Gen. Anim.* II.6.743a28; *E.E.* II.1.1218b37; *Met.* V.14.1020b20). Particularly significant among these passages is Aristotle's definition of motion in terms of actuality. At *Metaphysics* IX.3.1047a30–b2 Aristotle declares that "actuality seems to be most properly motion." He may intend to assert that actualities are motions. Yet, regardless of the significance of this passage, it is clear that what appears to be a sharp distinction between actuality and motion masks their close connection.

For other Greek philosophers there is no distinction.[3] The Atomists account for thought and sensation by referring to the motions and shapes of atoms. And three of Aristotle's paradigm actualities, life, thought (*nous*), and soul (*Met.* IX.6.1048b23–27; *De Anima* II.1.412a27–28) are mentioned as examples of motion in Plato's *Sophist* (249a).[4] Aristotle's distinction between actuality and motion represents a radical departure that enables him to explain how what moves can be known and have forms. To grasp how the distinction resolves this problem it is necessary to realize that what he calls actualities would ordinarily be termed motions. The first step of his argument is to show that actualities are not subject to the difficulties raised by Plato. This forms the basis on which he can show that other motions can also be known by tracing them to actualities. In addition to actualities Aristotle must consider two other types of motions, natural motions and accidental motions. The difference between these two groups is the difference between what we and other natural beings do in virtue of our nature, e.g., grow, decay, eat, etc.,[5] and those motions of natural beings that are not consequences of their natures, such as throwing a frisbee or playing chess.

Aristotle's distinction of actualities from other motions is important because they can be known in a different way and on different grounds than other motions. Accordingly, we should look for those features of actuality that enable it to be known in passages where Aristotle distinguishes it from motion. The fullest discussion occurs at *Metaphysics* IX.6.1048b18–35. There Aristotle describes motions as incomplete because their ends do not belong to them. In contrast actualities have their ends present within them.[6] The passage illustrates this claim by noting that we see at the same time that we have seen, we think at the same time that we have thought, and that we live well at the same time we have lived well; for otherwise "it would be necessary that (these actualities) stop at some time." *Nicomachean Ethics* X.4.1174a14–23 draws the distinction in substantially the same terms. While motions are always incomplete until they attain their ends, actualities are complete at any time.

The text from the *Metaphysics* is corrupt and there are difficulties in interpreting this distinction, but Aristotle's point is not nearly so obscure as the literature on these passages suggests. According to Gilbert Ryle, Aristotle uses "actuality" to refer to verbs that "declare a terminus" of action, like "to start," "to launch," and "to stop." Such instantaneous termini cannot continue through time.[7] J.L. Ackrill objects that actualities like thinking do go on through time. He draws attention to Aristotle's justification of the claim that one lives well and has lived well at the same time: "otherwise it would have to stop at some time." This suggests that actualities do occur through time, but differ from motions in that they do not contain temporal limits.[8] Ackrill maintains that what distinguishes actuality and motion is that in the case of actualities, but not in the case of motions, "he is Xing" entails "he has Xed."[9] The consequences of this interpretation—of which Ackrill is well aware—are that (1) he must reinterpret *Nicomachean Ethics* X.4.1174a17–20, which says, on the surface, that pleasures are not motions but actualities because motions are in time while pleasures are not; and (2) whether a process is an actuality or motion depends on the description we give of it, and under variant description motions like walking seem to be actualities and actualities like enjoyment seem to be motions.[10] Ackrill himself makes clear these difficulties with his linguistic interpretation. What is even worse is that his analysis does nothing to explain why actuality is so important in the *Metaphysics*: what does the linguistic fact Ackrill points to—or any other linguistic fact for that matter—have to do with the identification of form as actuality *(Met.* VIII.6.1045a29–33), with the identification of actuality as the highest cause (XII.7.1072b4–8), or with the problem of this chapter, the possibility of knowledge of sensibles?

Both Ackrill and Ryle err in supposing that Aristotle's distinction of motions from actualities depends on analyzing linguistic usage. Aristotle does not consider different verbs but different processes. Some of these processes have their ends within themselves, like seeing and thinking, and other processes have their ends outside of themselves, like walking or building. There is nothing in this distinction that derives from language, and attempts to make it a linguistic distinction merely introduce obscurity.

What, though, about Aristotle's discussion of present and perfect verbs? Is this not a linguistic point? It is, but Aristotle introduces it as an illustration *(hoion* [1048b23]) of the distinction he has already drawn. He does not use this linguistic point to distinguish between motion and actuality, as Ackrill supposes. Quite the contrary; he intends the distinction to account for the linguistic point. The perfect tense signifies completion. Because actualities contain their ends within themselves and are thus complete, any actuality can be designated with the perfect tense. Since the actuality of seeing contains its own end, it is true at any time that to see is to have seen. In contrast, the end of walking lies outside of the process of walking and this is true no matter how we describe walking. For the purpose of walking is to get somewhere or to get exercise, and once we attain the end we stop walking. The end of walking lies outside of the process of walking; walking remains incomplete until we stop walking (cf. *N.E.* X.4.1174a32–b2). This is the reason that to walk is not he same as to have walked.

Although Ackrill accords too much significance to Aristotle's linguistic point, he is correct in insisting, contra Ryle, on the possibility of actualities persisting through time. Yet it still does not follow that actualities are temporally defined. Seeing, thinking, and feeling pleasure can persist through time, but time plays no role in their defintions because each act is always complete. As Aristotle puts it in the *Nicomachean Ethics:* "Seeing seems to be at any moment complete, for it does not lack anything which coming into being later will complete its form; and pleasure also seems to be of this nature. For it is whole and at no time can one find a pleasure whose form will be completed if the pleasure lasts longer" (X.4.1174a14–19, Oxford trans.). Actualities last through time, but they are not temporal because they are complete at all times. The passage goes on to explain how motions remain incomplete until they attain their ends: "all motions are in time and are for an end" (1174a19–20). Time is inevitably a part of motion because it is only with time that they attain their ends. It is no accident that Aristotle's analysis of time occurs in the *Physics* rather than the *Metaphysics*. While motions necessarily involve time, actualities are intelligible without time.

There is another way of expressing this point, a way that allows us to see why actualities can be known. Consider a motion like housebuilding. Someone who builds a house engages in a step-by-step process. First, he lays the foundation, then sets up the walls and roof, installs wiring and plumbing, and finishes the interior. The housebuilder is himself changing. In contrast, someone who sees or who feels pleasure is not changing. Actualities like these may exist or not exist, but they are never partially or incompletely realized. They are *always* complete. Hence, someone could never be in the process of coming to see. Sight and other such actualities preclude change. They are unchanging in the sense that what possesses them is unchanging in respect of them.

These unchanging and atemporal characters of actualities are what allow them to be known. Because of these characters, actualities are exempt from the Platonic arguments against knowledge of what changes and satisfy the assumptions about the character of knowledge that I mentioned at the beginning of this chapter. Plato points to the discrepancy between unchanging knowledge and a world that is always becoming. But actualities are never in the process of change; they never alter. Hence, there is no objection to unchanging knowledge of them. Further, because each actuality is unchanging, there is no possibility that an actuality might become something else. Thus, there are no objections to ascribing unity to an actuality. It follows that there are no objections to identifying actualities as forms. With similar reasoning we can see that actualities satisfy Plato's and Aristotle's criteria of knowledge: since actualities are unchanging, they "always are or are for the most part" and are thus suitable objects of knowledge; since they are atemporal, knowledge claims about them can never be falsified by their changing, that is, claims about them are not sometimes true and sometimes false, but always one or the other.

What is interesting about Aristotle's use of actualities is that they can be present in the sensible world. Plato's attempt to justify knowledge by positing separate forms is not only unsuccessful, it is also unnecessary. To insure that knowledge is unchanging, Plato posits forms that are eternal. But this condition is too strong. An object does not falsify a claim that expresses what it is if it ceases to exist, unless in the process the object becomes something else. An actuality might cease to exist, but it is never in the process of ceasing to exist and thus never partially existent. The object of knowledge need not be eternal; it must merely be incapable of engaging in change over time.

Accordingly, Aristotle accounts for the possibility of knowledge of the changing sensible world by focusing on one group of these changes, changes that contain their own ends within themselves. Because they are complete, they do not alter and are thus atemporal. Aristotle calls this group of motions "actualities" and distinguishes them from other motions.

To argue that we can have knowledge of actualities is not yet to show that a science of nature is possible. What we need to know is that there are actualities in nature. This is the significance of Aristotle's identification of the form, essence and actuality of sensible substances in *Metaphysics* VII–VIII (see VIII.6.1045a29–33). The form of a

sensible substance is an actuality. Since there is no difficulty in knowing an actuality, there is no difficulty in knowing the essence of a
nature. Because the forms of sensibles are actualities, the Platonic
objections to knowledge of them vanish.

In fact, the central books of the *Metaphysics* provide strong support for my analysis of Aristotle's solution to the problem of knowledge of what changes. They do not explicitly address the problem,
but they connect change with matter and show that form does not
change. Consider, for example, Aristotle's discussion of generation
and destruction in VII.7–9. His chief contention is that forms persist
unaltered in generation and destruction. These latter involve a form
that comes to be or ceases to be present in a matter, but the form persists unchanged. Similarly, VII.10 excludes the parts of matter from
the form on the ground that things with material parts are destructible (1035a17–22). In so doing, it eliminates a reason to think form is
destructible. In short, these passages effectively answer objections to
knowledge of sensibles by showing that some part of sensibles, form,
does not change.

The location of forms that are actualities in sensibles has an
important consequence for the *Physics*. In the *Metaphysics* actualities
are complete motions because they have their ends within themselves. The *Physics* expresses the same condition when it asserts that
in a nature the formal cause is identical with the final cause
(II.7.198a22–26). Since the form of a nature is also its end or final
cause, the nature has its end within itself: it is complete. I think that
the identity of formal and final causes in the *Physics* draws on the
identification of form as actuality established in the *Metaphysics*. But
whether or not this is the case, the former doctrine supports my interpretation of the actuality in the *Metaphysics* and its role in the problem
of knowledge of sensibles.

The identification of formal and final causes in the *Physics* also
ties together the actualities that are forms of sensible natures and the
actualities that are Aristotle's paradigms in the *Metaphysics*, thinking,
seeing, and living. The form of human being is an actuality; and, since
it is complete, the end of a human being is just to be a human being.
There is no need to look for an end of human life beyond the fulfilling
of those human functions that constitute our nature. If thinking or the
capacity for thinking is the function which is our essence, then the
end of human life for each of us is just to exercise this capacity for

thought. Thinking serves no higher end. It is, to use Wittgenstein's phrase, a "form of life."

In short, the possibility of knowledge of sensibles rests on the identification of motions that are proper to and characteristic of each nature and that are complete in the sense that they are their own end. Both the *Physics* and the *Metaphysics* share this view of the forms of sensibles. The sensibles are known through their forms, but their forms are actualities. Thus they are known as actualities; they are known as complete motions. These complete motions escape the arguments against knowledge of what moves because they are atemporal.

As we might expect, there are difficulties with this account of the possibility of knowledge of sensibles, but I think that they are difficulties that Aristotle recognizes and is willing to accept to preserve a central plank of his philosophy, the possibility of a science of nature. First, there is the practical problem of identifying a complete motion that defines each species. There is some doubt whether his biological works succeed in this ambitious goal—or, for that matter, whether they even come close. However, I want to set this problem aside and focus on the conceptual difficulties. Aristotle's standard example of the form of human being in *Metaphysics* VII–VIII is "two-footed animal." The actuality this formula is meant to signify must be walking on two feet; but, as we saw, IX.6 specifically rejects walking as an actuality. Perhaps Aristotle's intention in this passage is to dismiss "two-footed animal" as a poor definition of man, but the problem will not vanish so easily. Aristotle suggests that the defining actualities of animals are their modes of sensation and local motion. Let us suppose that the actuality of some type of bird is a particular mode of flying. (I am intentionally leaving this definition vague in order to focus on the conceptual problem rather than the interpretation of the biology.) Aristotle's reasons for rejecting walking as an actuality (*N.E.* X.4.1174a19–23) apply equally to flying: flying necessarily involves traversing a distance over a period of time and is therefore incomplete during the time before it reaches its end. Neither motion, flying, nor any other mode of local motion can be an actuality. How then can Aristotle define a bird by flying or any other animal by its mode of local motion?

Let me suggest that despite this argument it may still make sense to define animals in this way. To say, for example, that the actuality of a particular type of bird is flying is to assert that the bird does not fly merely to get somewhere; it flies for the sake of flying. The fact that the bird happens to traverse a distance in the course of flying is incidental. The bird flies for the sake of flying just as we, perhaps, value seeing not merely on utilitarian grounds but for its own sake (See *Met.* I.1.980a21–27).

If this analysis is correct, then whether or not a mode of flying is the essence or actuality of a bird depends on whether the flying is done for its own sake; that is, on whether flying is also the final cause of the bird. How could we decide whether this is the case? It seems to me that someone who examined flying or any of those "actualities" that are supposed to define natures would likely not arrive at the conclusion that they are their own ends. It is not clear that flying is any more its own end than other motions that birds engage in. I want to suggest that there is an element of arbitrariness in Aristotle's choice of the actuality that defines a nature. This choice is arbitrary in the sense that there is often no way to tell from the examination of a motion by itself that it is complete. On the surface it seems just as plausible to focus on flying and to assert that it is the nature of a bird because birds fly for the sake of flying as it is to focus on eating worms and to assert that birds do this for its own sake.

We can understand this arbitrariness better if we recognize that it is also present in Aristotle's paradigm examples of actuality. Neither seeing nor thinking is obviously done for its own sake, and both seem to be processes. As Hume claims, we think in order to satisfy our passions. And whether we are solving a mathematics problem or designing a cathedral, our thought seems to occur sequentially in time. If Aristotle is to maintain that thinking is an actuality, he must also insist that (1) thinking is its own end and any additional end is merely accidental, and that (2) thinking is complete and any change or development of the content of thought through time is accidental. Neither of these requirements is obvious. Both ought to cast doubt on Aristotle's claim that thinking is an actuality.

Nearly the same could be said of seeing. It too can be done for other ends, and it is sequential in the sense that the content of sight alters in the course of time. For example, as we look at an object, what we see develops and changes, particularly in the case of art objects. Surely seeing and thinking have a better claim to be called actualities than do flying and walking, but none of these seems to be without a degree of arbitrariness. Only Aristotle's highest cause, the unmoved mover that is thinking about thinking and pure actuality, indubitably has its end within itself.

Why does Aristotle insist that (human) thinking is an actuality? And why does he insist that each nature can be defined by an actuality? Aristotle's works contain no examination of thinking that would justify his assertion that it is an actuality. Nor does he examine individual natures in order to determine whether their essences really are actualities. Instead, his view of actuality is motivated by the insight that the doctrine of actuality will resolve the metaphysical problems of how sensibles can have forms and how they can be known. It is this metaphysical solution that comes first. Thus, the reason that Aristotle's identifications of some motions as actualities seem arbitrary is that he has first decided that each nature must have a defining actuality and then proceeded to identify the most likely candidate. It is the recognition that actuality can account for knowledge that motivates Aristotle to choose one of what we would usually term the thing's motions and designate it as the actuality of the thing, the character that is its own end and the end of all the thing's other motions.

Let me suggest that Aristotle's choice of a motion to identify as the form or actuality of a nature is motivated by the motion's explanatory power. The most likely candidate for a nature's actuality is that one of its motions which cannot be explained in terms of its other motions and which in turn can be used to explain these other motions. In the *Physics*, for example, Aristotle advances arguments for identifying nature as matter and as form on the ground that each of these can account for the other motions possessed by natures (II.1.193a9–b21). (I will consider two of them in the next section.)

Let us consider some other examples. The reason that thinking is a likely candidate for human actuality is that it is easier to explain human activities like eating in terms of thinking than the reverse. (Aristotle would say eating is for the sake of thinking; but thinking, especially abstract thinking, is not for the sake of eating.) Similarly, if flying is the actuality of a bird, it is partly because the bird's other motions can be explained as leading to the end of flying. The suggestion that the choice of actuality in a nature is motivated by explanatory power is contrary to the view of actualities that Aristotle usually expresses, the view according to which they are recognizable as actualities independently of motions. The latter view is more true of the pure actualities that are Aristotle's first principles than it is of the actualities that define natures. This is not the place to examine the question of how Aristotle arrives at actualities in any detail. Let me only note that I think my view is confirmed by Aristotle's lengthy discussion of definition in *Posterior Analytics* II and also by his use of actuality and essence in his physical and biological works.

The role of actualities in the *Metaphysics* is mirrored in the *Nicomachean Ethics*. Just as the identification of forms of natures as actualities helps to explain how they can be known, so too the identification of happiness and virtuous acts as actualities (I.7.1098a16–18) also explains how they can be known. If happiness is an actuality and if a just act is also an actuality, the Platonic arguments against knowledge of what changes do not pose an obstacle to knowing them. As actualities, virtuous acts are atemporal and thus not subject to change through time. It should come as no surprise that Aristotle shows that happiness is an actuality by showing it is complete, self-sufficient, and an end (I.7.1097b20–21; 1098a16–17). The recognition of happiness and virtuous action as actualities is the key move in Aristotle's location of them in the sensible world and formulation of a "science" of ethics. Pursuing the question of how Aristotle determines that particular acts are virtuous would lead to results just as troubling as the question I raised about how Aristotle determines that particular natural functions are actualities. (For example, is playing handball any less complete than exhibiting courage under fire?) But there is no need to develop this argument here.

In sum, Aristotle is able to justify knowledge of nature by recognizing that some of what are usually called motions have a completeness that renders them atemporal. As such they escape the arguments against knowledge of nature and satisfy Plato's and Aristotle's criteria for knowledge. By identifying these actualities with the forms of sensibles, Aristotle at once explains how form can be present in nature and also how nature can be known despite its changes. By further identifying ethical actions as actualities, Aristotle locates the good in the sensible world and explains how a science of ethics is possible.

II

The analysis presented so far accounts for the possibility of knowledge of natures because their essences are actualities, complete motions. What about the things with incomplete motions? Can they be objects of knowledge, or does Aristotle accept the arguments against knowledge of what moves in their case? It is well-known that Aristotle recognizes knowledge of things with incomplete motions and knowledge of their motions. Without these he could have no science of physics. However, commentators do not generally consider how he avoids the arguments against the possibility of this science. As I interpret Aristotle, he offers two different ways of avoiding these arguments. The first applies to what he terms "natural changes" (*Phys.* II.3.194b21–22). These include motions like growth and decay, and they are the primary concern in the *Physics.*[11] The second applies to "accidental changes" (V.1.224b26–27), like throwing a frisbee and playing chess; I will consider it in the next section.

The central text for a discussion of natural motions is *Physics* II. Indeed, once we consider this text with this question in mind, Aristotle's account of the possibility of knowledge is easy to see. In a word, it depends on recognizing that, in a way, natural motions are also unchanging. These motions are attributes that belong to natures per se, that is, in respect of their essence. Since the natures are knowable, their attributes are knowable through them. The main moves appear in the first chapter of book II.

Book II opens with the assertion "some beings are by nature; others through other causes" (192b8–9). Clearly, nature is a cause. Thus, when Aristotle offers his well-known description of nature as an internal principle of motion a few lines later (192b13–14), there is no doubt that "principle of motion" means "cause of motion" (cf. *Met.* V.1.1013a17).[12] These claims are part of a discussion of what is "by nature" (*phusei*) and "according to nature" (*kata phusin*). Both expressions apply to substances such as plants, animals, their parts, and the "simple bodies" like earth and fire (192a9–11). But they also apply to what belongs to these substances per se, and Aristotle illustrates this assertion by mentioning the upward motion that belongs to fire (192a35–36). The Oxford translation rightly calls upward motion a "property" of fire. Upward motion belongs to fire in respect of the nature of fire; it belongs to fire per se.

This example of a motion that is a per se attribute of a nature is not unusual. Other examples are stated or implicit throughout book II. References to generation and corruption as "natural changes" at 3.194b21–23 imply that they are attributes of natures. Later in the book, Aristotle speaks of growth as "by nature" (8.198b23–27 with 199a5–6); and he and offers as an example the growth of teeth in animals (198b24–25 with b34–35). Plants growing leaves and roots (199a27–30), the swallow making a nest, and the spider producing its web are also examples of motions that are by nature (199a26–27).

Some arguments in II.1 implicitly assume motions are per se attributes. They are worth examining because they also show the relation of nature and natural motion. Consider, for example, Antiphon's argument (193a12–14): If a bed were planted and acquired the power of sending up shoots, it would generate not a bed but wood. It follows that the form of the bed is a mere artistic arrangement and that the nature of the bed lies in the wood, its matter. The argument assumes that whatever causes the motion of generation is nature. Since what persists through motion is, in one sense, its cause, Antiphon identifies nature as matter.

These same assumptions, however, also lead to the opposite conclusion (193b8–12). Even if a bed does not come from a bed, man comes from man. In general, things generate other things with the same form. Thus, assuming that nature is the cause of generation, nature is form. Generation is a per se attribute of natures; since form seems to be a cause of this attribute, it is nature.

Another argument for the same conclusion appears in an obscure passage near the end of the chapter. Aristotle declares, "further, what is called nature is a path into nature" (193b12–13). Whereas art is a process that leads to something else, nature is a process that produces itself. A growing thing comes from something and goes into something *qua* nature. What it becomes is its nature (193b13–18). As I interpret this passage it treats growth as a natural motion, a motion that belongs to something in virtue of its nature. The process of growth is the process through which a form comes to be manifest in a matter. It is caused by what it brings about, the form. Since form is the principle of growth, and since this natural motion is caused by nature, Aristotle infers that nature is form.

These arguments show Aristotle using the assumption that nature is a cause of motion to determine what nature is. Since motions like growth and generation are "according to nature," something that can account for them is a strong candidate for nature. Whatever nature is it must be able to cause those motions that are "by nature."

Once we recognize the way that Aristotle traces natural motions to natures, the other, seemingly scattered topics of book II fall into place. The second chapter makes the point that unlike mathematicians, physicists must treat both the form and the matter to account for motion. Likewise the discussion of causes in the third chapter elucidates the ways that natures can cause motion, and this is Aristotle's intention: "Since the investigation is for the sake of knowledge and we do not believe we know something until we grasp the 'why' in regard to it (this is to grasp the first cause), clearly we must do this in regard to generation, decay and all natural changes" (194b17–22). Further, Aristotle needs to consider whether chance and luck are also causes of natural motion (II.4–7). He argues that whatever happens always or for the most part cannot be due to chance or luck. A regularly occurring motion must be caused by a nature (8.198b34–36). The book ends with a discussion of necessity, the relevance of which will be apparent shortly. Thus, book II is a treatment of natural motion.

There should be no doubt that Aristotle regards natures as the causes of motions like growth and generation. The question is, how? How do natures cause natural motions and how can we know natural motions through natures? Does tracing motions to nature allow Aristotle to avoid the Platonic arguments against knowledge of what moves?

While book II provides ample evidence that Aristotle regards natures as the key to knowledge of natural motions, when we come to the details we are forced to speculate. Just as in the preceding section, I am going to offer an analysis that I believe is Aristotelian and support it with frequent textual references. Still, the most I can argue is that my solution is consistent with what Aristotle does say and that it gets him out of the difficulty.

The first point to notice is that natural changes do not prevent us from knowing a nature. The reason that change seems to be an obstacle to knowledge is that things are different after they change and putative knowledge claims may no longer be true. Natural changes, however, are according to nature: they do not result in a different nature. It is nature that causes natural change, and this change is a reflection of nature. Growth clearly does not alter nature; generation is from nature and the result is a nature of the same sort. The only natural motion that might seem to alter nature is decay or destruction. But Aristotle argues that in decay and in generation, form or essence is neither created nor destroyed; it comes to be or ceases to be present with matter in a composite (*Met.* VII.10.1035a28–30; 8.1033b16–18). Hence, no natural change alters a nature. It follows that they pose no obstacles to knowledge of a nature.

To show that natural motions do not interfere with knowledge of natures is not yet to show how natural motions themselves can be known. In order for natural motions to be known they must escape the Platonic objections to knowledge of change and satisfy those rigid criteria of knowledge that I sketched in the beginning of this chapter.

There are, in fact, two ways that natural motions can be known. First, they can be known insofar as they themselves have a nature. Earlier, I mentioned that Aristotle calls motions "incomplete actualities." This phrase seems to contradict the sharp distinction between actuality and motion at *Metaphysics* IX.6 and *Nicomachean Ethics* X.4, but it is easy to see that Aristotle's contrast is between processes that have their ends within themselves and processes whose ends lie outside themselves. To speak of motion as a kind of actuality is to assert that motions have their own forms and essences. If the idea of an essence of a motion surprises, we have only to recall that natural motions are per se attributes of substances and in the *Metaphysics* Aristotle speaks of secondary essences of the attributes of substances (VII.4.1030a28–32). Insofar as motions are actualities, they are unchanging. In fact, Aristotle argues at some length that changes cannot themselves change (*Phys.* V.2.225b33–226a23), and these arguments also support the claim that motion is a kind of actuality and form. As unchanging actualities, motions can be known for much the same reasons that physical natures can be known. Because motions have a kind of nature, they can be known in themselves as motions. I will come back to this way of knowing motions in the next section. It is not of primary concern to the *Physics*.

What is more important for Aristotle's physical and biological sciences is to know natural motions through the natures of which they are essential attributes. This second way of knowing natural motions is possible only if a grasp of the attributes in respect of nature escapes the Platonic arguments against knowledge of what moves and meets Aristotle's strict criteria of knowledge. I will reconstruct an Aristotelian explanation of how motions can be known in this way.

Let me begin with a claim Aristotle makes in *Physics* II.9: "It is clear that the necessary in natures is what we call 'matter' and its motions" (200a30–32). The necessity here is hypothetical: if nature is to exist, matter and its motions must be present. Understood in this way, nature is the end of matter and motion, and Aristotle claims that it determines what they are. For example, in order to have a saw, it is necessary to use material as hard as iron; wool will not do (200a11–13; *Met.* VIII.4.1044a29). Similarly, in order to see, it is necessary to have an organ capable of this function, a transparent covering for it, eyebrows, eyelids, etc. The nature of sight determines the material necessary for it to be realized.

In the same way, nature determines the natural motions through which it is realized. The nature or essence of a polar bear determines the particular processes of its growth and development. Its development of reserves of fat is necessary for its mode of life, and a different nature would not develop them. Analogously, there are definite steps in the growth and development of a human being and what they are is dictated by the nature that is realized. In this way natural motions like growth are "necessary" to their natures.

We can understand why matter and motion are necessary to realize a nature if we consider the actualities that exist in the physical world. In both the *Metaphysics* and *Physics*, Aristotle asserts that matter is part of the essence of a nature in the same way that matter is part of the essence of snubness (*Phys.* II.2.194a6–7 with a12–15; *Met.* VI.1.1025b30–1026a6). Just as snubness refers to a curvature that necessarily belongs to a nose, so too the actualities that are the essences of natures exist in matters.[13] Seeing must include matter in some way because it does not take place apart from matter. Similarly, the essences of physical natures are actualities that always occur with matter, actualities like modes of flying or of sensation.

Since physical actualities always exist in matter, they require natural motions. Natural motions are just those motions by which an actuality comes to be realized in a matter or those motions that result from the presence of the actuality in matter. Since the essence of an animal occurs in matter, it is necessary that the essence come to be present in matter by a process of generation, that the matter develop through growth, that the composite decay, and thus that the composite reproduce to preserve the essence. Growth, generation, decay, and all the other natural motions consist of an essence or form coming to be or ceasing to be present in a matter. They are all changes in the category of substance; and, as I mentioned earlier, *Metaphysics* VII.7–9 argues that the form remains unchanged when the composite is generated or destroyed. Because the forms or actualities found in sensibles occur with matter, they cause natural motions.

This analysis gives some depth to the claim in *Physics* II.9 that matter and its motions are necessary to realize natures. Once we recognize that natural motions involve the realization of a form in a matter, it is easy to see the way this form determines natural motion. The course of any natural motion depends on the form that comes to be or ceases to be in matter. The processes of growth, decay, and so forth are not random changes. They are regular changes that proceed along fixed paths, paths that are determined by the forms or actualities that come to be present or cease to be present in matter. It is in this way that nature is an internal cause of motion. Since, as we saw in the last section, a nature or actuality does not alter, the motions that it causes are also unchanging. Things that are generated, grow and decay, do, of course, change; but because these motions occur in a fixed and regular way in virtue of the nature they possess, there is a sense in which things with natural motions are unchanging. The natural motions of each instance of a nature are always the same and always proceed in the same way.

It is clear from this analysis why natural motions satisfy Aristotle's criteria for knowledge and escape the Platonic arguments. Just as the actualities that constitute the essence of sensibles are unchanging because they are complete, the natural motions that inevitably accompany these actualities are also unchanging, albeit to a lesser extent than the actualities. All human beings are born, follow much the same course of development, and decay in much the same way. And the same could be said of the natural motions of other species. To be sure, some children develop faster than others, and some people die prematurely. To claim knowledge of natural motions Aristotle must relegate such events to the status of accidents. The natural motions that we can know through the science of physics are not the particular movements of individual substances but what all substances of a particular sort do. Knowledge is of the universal, of what is always or for the most part. Understood through the nature that is their cause, natural motions are universal in the sense that they belong to nearly all such natures.

The foregoing analysis seems so familiar that we are apt to overlook how different Aristotle's notion of attribution is from that of current logic. We usually think of an essential attribute as a character that always inheres in a nature. But natural motions like growth and decay are primarily confined to specific periods of a nature's life. For Aristotle to say that something grows in virtue of its nature is not to say that it always grows; nor is what reproduces by nature always reproducing. The nature may not even possess a disposition for growth or for reproduction at all times during its life. Instead, Aristotle's per se attributes are such because, barring impediments, a nature will (at some time) possess them. Aristotle's attribution is atemporal in a way that modern attribution is not. I think recognition of this fact has important consequences for interpretations of both Aristotle's logic and his biology, but pursuing these claims would take us too far afield. For our purposes what is important to recognize is that the attribution of a motion to a nature carries no temporal content. Since to ascribe the motion of growth to human nature is not to assert that human beings are always growing, such an ascription cannot be falsified if a human being stops growing. Growth is an attribute of human nature because it belongs to human nature in a nontemporal way.

A paradigm natural motion is the circular motion of the heavenly spheres. They are always changing; but, because they always change in the same way, they are always the same. Even though this motion is in time, the change is atemporal because it is unchanging. In a similar way, the natural motions of other natures can also be known because even though the motions are in time, the changes are always the same and the same changes always belong to the same natures.

III

The account that I have given of the possibility of knowledge of natural changes relies on recognizing them as per se attributes of natures, and to support it I have mined *Physics* II. Since accidental motions are not per se attributes of natures, the same account will not work to justify knowledge of them. Nevertheless, they can be known; and in this section I will propose an explanation of how they satisfy Aristotle's criteria for knowledge. My discussion here draws on an analogy between natural and accidental motions that I think Aristotle has in mind in *Physics* I and III.1–2.

Any attempt to explain knowledge of accidental motions ought to begin with Aristotle's denial that there is knowledge of what is accidental (*Met.*VI.2.1027a19–21). What Aristotle means to deny here is that accidents can be known through the substrates in which they inhere. "Walking to the agora" is an accident of Socrates; there is no way to determine whether Socrates possesses this accident by examining his essence. In contrast, generation and growth belong to things in virtue of their essences, as we saw in the last section. However, the consequence of these remarks is only that accidents cannot be known as attributes of substances. There is nothing here to exclude the possibility of knowing accidental motions in themselves as motions. As I noted earlier, all accidents have essences of a sort, and their essences are actualities of a sort. Since accidental motions are accidents, they are actualities and thus admit of some type of knowledge.

That motions are actualities is also clear from the definition of motion: motion is the actuality of what is potential *qua* potential (201a10–11).[14] This definition does not explicitly distinguish accidental from natural motions, and I think we can understand why if we recall the discussion of motion in book I. There Aristotle addresses the question, how many principles do we need to account for motion? His answer is three: form, its privation, and matter (7.191a7–15). These principles apply to change in the categorial genus of substance and also to changes in other categories. In the preceding section I explained how Aristotle uses these principles (especially form) to account for change in the genus of substance, "natural motions." In the first chapter of book III, Aristotle claims that the equivalent of these principles, actuality and potentiality, are present in each category (200b26–29). Further, he identifies form and privation as principles of substance in contrast with principles in other genera, such as white and black in the category of quality and up and down in the category of place (201a3–9).

What we have here is an analogy between the principles of change in substance and the principles of change in the other categories. It is this analogy that the definition of motion expresses. Just as natural changes consist of a form coming to be present or ceasing to be present in a matter, so too accidental changes (i.e., changes in the accidental genera) consist of an accidental form coming to be present or ceasing to be present in a matter, a substance. Becoming white and building a house resemble generation and growth because they consist of a form coming to be present in a matter or, in other words, of a potentiality that is actualized. Becoming black or the collapse of a house consists of a form ceasing to be present in a matter. (The rough edge of the analogy is that while the privation of substantial form is not an identifiable character, the privation of an accidental form can often be used to describe motion; we can speak of becoming black as well as becoming white. But Aristotle insists that pairs of contraries like white and black consist of positive and privative terms, cf. *Met.* X.4.1055b26–27.)

The really significant point that emerged from the discussion of natural changes in the preceding section was that the course of motion is determined by the substantial form that is acquired or lost. For this reason, natural motions are unchanging and can be known. Since accidental motions are analogous to natural motions, they too should be unchanging in the same way. Just as the course of generation is determined by the form that comes to be present in matter, so too the course of becoming white or of building a house is also determined by the (accidental) form that come to be present in the matter. Accidental motions are like natural motions in that they follow a determinate path. In this sense they too are unchanging, and therefore can be known.

It is this unchanging character that I think Aristotle has in mind when he defines motion as a type of actuality. Motions are incomplete and thus not actualities in the most proper sense, but they are regular and unchanging in the sense that each type of motion always occurs in the same way. The sensible world is always changing, just as Plato said, but since it always changes in the same way, it is always the same.

A passage that both supports and elucidates my interpretation of the definition of motion is the following: "For example, if a house were among what is generated by nature, it would come to be in the same way as it now does by art. And if what is generated by nature were to be not only generated by nature but also by art, it would be generated in the same way as it is generated by nature" (*Phys.* II.8.199a12–15). Apparently, just as the form of a human being determines the process of generation and growth of an individual, so too the form of a house determines the process by which it comes to be present in building materials. To say that it makes no difference whether generation is by art or by nature is to assert that the processes that occur in natural motions could also occur in accidental motions. But the processes of natural motions are regular and always occur with the same sequence of steps. So accidental motions must also occur with a determinate sequence of steps. The art of housebuilding imitates nature. In both cases the motion is determined by the end to be realized, the form that comes to be present in matter.

For the same reasons that we can have knowledge of the natural motions that belong to natures, it is possible to have knowledge of accidental motions, like how to build a house. In each case, the motion can be known because it is unchanging. In a way they can even be said to be atemporal. As such they escape the Platonic arguments and satisfy Aristotle's criteria for knowledge.

This treatment of accidental motions is based on the existence of forms of accidents that come to be present in substances. While there are forms of accidental composites like a house, they are not forms or actualities in the most proper sense (see *Met.* VIII.2.1043a2–7,14–19). It follows that the accidental motions known through them are known in a lesser way than we know natural motions. In the case of natural motions, we have knowledge through the nature of which they are per se attributes; in the case of accidental motions, we can know the motion in respect of the accident that is acquired or lost. While I earlier raised some questions about designating forms of natures as actualities, they are surely actualities in a more proper sense than accidents like the form of a house are actualities. If it is actuality that makes knowledge possible, then natures are more knowable than motions and natural motions are more knowable than accidental motions.

To summarize, Aristotle shows that nature can be the object of knowledge despite its changes by arguing that it contains unchanging actualities or forms. Substances, accidents, natural motions, and accidental motions are all sorts of actualities. As such they are atemporal, unchanging, and not subject to the Platonic objections to knowledge of what changes. In addition, we can know natural motions through their causes, the actualities that are their natures. Only the inherence of accidents and accidental motions in substances remains beyond knowledge.

If my interpretation is correct, Aristotle's remarks on actuality and motion in the *Metaphysics* and the *Physics* reflect an intelligible and coherent response to the Platonic problem of the possibility of knowledge of the sensible world. In a word, Aristotle's solution is to notice that the motions of the sensible world are regular and unchanging and thus satisfy his criteria for knowledge and escape Plato's arguments.

This solution will very likely not make Aristotle palatable to most current thinkers. The idea of unchanging natures is antithetical to evolutionary biology and to modern physics. Further, while the idea that motion is unchanging explains how we can have knowledge of motion, it also excludes motion of motion (*Phys.* V.2.225b14 ff.).

Thus, the notion of acceleration which proved so fruitful for physics is inconsistent with Aristotle's explanation of the possibility of knowledge of motion. Perhaps still more disconcerting for the physicist is Aristotle's method. If my analysis is correct, Aristotle justifies some of his most important doctrines of nature by showing that they are able to resolve the problem of the possibility of knowledge of nature. For modern science, to presume that the problem has a solution and that the solution has a particular form seems hopelessly prejudicial.

Many commentators pass quickly over such differences and emphasize Aristotle's similarities with current problems and ideas. It seems to me more important to recognize the differences. If we are unwilling to resolve the problem of knowledge of nature by positing unchanging essences and unchanging motions as Aristotle did, we face the necessity of accounting for the possibility of knowledge of what changes in some other way.

Chapter 6

ACKRILL, ARISTOTLE, AND ANALYTIC PHILOSOPHY

Why is Aristotle still interesting? While Continental philosophers often regard Greek philosophy as a stage in the development of contemporary thought, Anglo-American philosophers tend to view the Greeks in terms of contemporary problems. J.L. Ackrill's *Aristotle the Philosopher*[1] is squarely in the latter tradition. To Ackrill, Aristotle is not interesting for his doctrines but for his arguments. Aristotle the philosopher—as opposed to Aristotle the knower or Aristotle the dogmatist—poses perennially significant problems in crisp, simple terms and then argues for theories that will resolve the problems by carefully examining Greek linguistic usage. Because Aristotle pursues philosophical problems by means of linguistic or conceptual analysis, his work is thought-provoking and contemporary. Although Ackrill accepts the use of developmental hypotheses to account for Aristotle's apparent inconsistencies, he interprets development as Aristotle's reconsideration of problems in the light of different linguistic idioms. Far from being a single rigid system, Aristotle's philosophy exhibits the sort of doctrinal vicissitudes common in the work of many contemporary linguistic philosophers. Since the Aristotelian texts are assemblages of his notes made by later editors, we ought not to view them as finished products but direct our attention to the "strata" pertinent to contemporary problems. In short, Aristotle is interesting because he is an ordinary language philosopher.

This view of Aristotle is not new. It has been stated or assumed in a number of well-known papers by Professor Ackrill and others, and *Aristotle the Philosopher* draws on this work freely. The authors of the Clarendon Aristotle series which Ackrill edits share the same view. Indeed, this book could well serve as an introduction to the series and to much current work. Like the Clarendon series, this book is more concerned with applying an interpretation than with justifying it; and, also like the series, it makes no attempt to be comprehensive.

Though he devotes at least a chapter to most of the major works, Ackrill actually picks out one or two issues from each and considers only small portions of the texts. These issues include: teleology in scientific explanations, the mind-body problem, scientific method, proof of the existence of an unmoved mover, responsibility and *akrasia*. In each case Ackrill presents Aristotle's analysis by means of lengthy quotations and afterwards engages the philosopher by confronting him with contemporary alternatives. His translation of the text is extremely readable; it is so readable that there is often no need of explication. Indeed, since these quotations are set off from the text by only a slight indentation, careless readers will easily confuse a lengthy quotation with Ackrill's own words. (I should add that some quotations fail to indicate ellipses in the text and that, at least once, a paraphrase stands in place of a translation.) Whenever possible Ackrill links Aristotle's analyses to contemporary analogues. Often he attempts to defend Aristotle from criticism, but even where he is unable to do so, he shows Aristotle to be a formidable thinker with something to teach us. In these critical sections Ackrill eschews history in order to engage Aristotle as a philosopher because he feels certain that Aristotle would sanction the use of everything at our disposal to solve the problems.[2]

On the whole *Aristotle the Philosopher* is an extremely lucid development of a view of Aristotle that has become important through the efforts of its author and others. It presents recent scholarship straightforwardly and accessibly; and Ackrill's style has the same qualities he ascribes to Aristotle's: it is clear, crisp, and thought-provoking The book will be most appreciated by its intended audience, philosophers and students trained in analytic philosophy. Unlike other introductory works, it does not attempt to provide a compendium of Aristotle's doctrine; instead, Ackrill wants to stimulate interest. In this goal, even those like myself who disagree with his overall perspective will surely agree that he succeeds admirably.

The thesis of *Aristotle the Philosopher* is that Aristotle engages in philosophic inquiry through analysis of language. Although Ackrill never specifically marshalls the evidence in support of this interpretation, he makes a strong case for it by extracting it from and applying it to particular texts. Lengthy quotations of passages which are easily interpreted as examinations of language seem to provide strong support. Further, Ackrill convincingly presents these texts as treatments of problems pertinent to contemporary thought. In both problems and methods Aristotle seems in accord with current linguistic analysts. Because Ackrill's book addresses a general audience and because it is likely to be influential, I shall consider the merits of Ackrill's case for interpreting Aristotle as a linguistic philosopher.

Let me begin by delimiting Ackrill's position further. Precisely what use does he see Aristotle making of language? In the wake of Wittgenstein many philosophers and scholars have accepted the conclusion that philosophical problems must be approached through analysis of language. For them, knowledge about the world comes from observation and experimentation; philosophy can only analyze the language that we use to talk about the world or, equivalently, the concepts through which we think of the world. It follows that Aristotle must be analyzing language whether he knows it or not. Ackrill apparently shares these philosophical views but he approaches Aristotle a bit differently. First (I), he maintains that Aristotle self-consciously analyzes language in a way that is similar to current linguistic philosophy. Although he does not explicitly distinguish among them, Ackrill mentions three uses of language: (1) Aristotle examines what other philosophers say about a topic; (2) he examines how people ordinarily speak about a subject and (3) he analyzes concepts without specifically referring to usage. Though the last of these predominates, Ackrill emphasizes the second. Later, I shall deal with both at length. The second (II) key claim in Ackrill's linguistic interpretation is that Aristotle assumes his conceptual and linguistic analysis accurately reflects objective reality. Here current science and philosophy show Aristotle to be largely mistaken for two reasons: (1) he often looks to an analysis of language to resolve factual questions that call for observation and experimentation;[3] (2) he assumes that Greek linguistic usage indicates the nature of the world because he lacks sufficient acquaintance with languages other than his own.[4]

There are obviously points of tension in the two main elements of Ackrill's interpretation (I and II). On one hand, Ackrill maintains that Aristotle's interest in ordinary usage stems from the supposition that it provides "essential clues" for conceptual clarification.[5] On the other, he accuses Aristotle of examining language in order to infer empirical facts. Ackrill propounds two divergent motives for Aristotle's analysis of language, conceptual clarification and the determination of facts. Could Aristotle have had both motives?

Ackrill seems unaware of the problem. Yet I think his considered view would be that, though Aristotle's motive for examining language is to find the nature of the world, we stand to profit from Aristotle most if we interpret him as undertaking conceptual analyses. The problem with this is that it undercuts the claim that Aristotle is an ordinary language philosopher. If Aristotle accords language a different status than a means to conceptual clarification, he is no ordinary language philosopher. In short, the two general points of Ackrill's interpretation are inconsistent.

Ackrill will likely remain undaunted by this point. He passes the inconsistency on to Aristotle. Hence, it is necessary to consider his interpretation more carefully. Does Aristotle analyze language in the way Ackrill claims? To answer this question I shall closely examine his analysis of a particular passage. I have chosen chapter 3's treatment of *Physics* I because it is representative and because it is the first place where Ackrill attempts to extract his interpretation from a text. My first question will be whether *Physics* I is a self-conscious examination of linguistic usage. Next, I will consider whether we should regard it as conceptual or linguistic analysis. In neither case, I argue, is *Physics* I an example of linguistic philosophy. These considerations also show what part of Aristotle one must criticize or ignore in order to insist that he is a linguistic analyst. I shall argue that Ackrill's criticism of Aristotle often springs from his own interpretation and thus indicates its inadequacy. Finally, while considering some of Ackrill's suggestions about physical laws, I suggest an alternative explanation of why Aristotle is still interesting. The linguistic interpretation of Aristotle is widely accepted, and I do not expect to dislodge it in the brief compass of a single discussion. I hope, however, to stimulate thought, and since this is also Ackrill's goal, whatever success I attain is a tribute to the success of his book.

According to Ackrill, *Physics* I examines the ways we speak about change in order to understand this phenomenon and why other philosophers were mistaken about it. In I.2–3 Aristotle criticizes the Eleatics whose hypothesis that all is one implies there is no change. For Ackrill, Aristotle points out linguistic errors: "Here in book I, he makes two simple but central points about the verb 'to be' in order to explode the thesis that what is is one."[6] Aristotle's first point, Ackrill continues, is that things are said to be in many ways; that is, that qualities, quantities, and so on exist in different senses. In none of these senses is the Eleatic claim even intelligible. Ackrill sees Aristotle's second point as the claim that "is" not only identifies subject and predicate, as the Eleatics think, but also functions as a copula. While the "is" of identity excludes assertions of change, use of the copula allows us to ascribe attributes and changes to subjects.[7]

If this interpretation of Aristotle's criticism of the Eleatics is correct, Aristotle's arguments are surely ineffective. The Eleatics are making a substantial claim about the nature of being. To show that they are violating ordinary usage accomplishes nothing. We might just as well show that quantum mechanics or atheism violates ordinary usage. Analysis of usage just does not provide the sort of evidence that could refute the Eleatics' claim. The only way this type of linguistic analysis could be effective is by showing that the Eleatic thesis is nonsensical and unintelligible. This, I take it, is Ackrill's view in the first point he mentions. Yet Aristotle himself does not regard the thesis as unintelligible for he goes on to attack it with other arguments that presuppose the thesis has a definite sense. By understanding what this sense is, we can see why Ackrill is mistaken about Aristotle's first point. Aristotle takes the Eleatic thesis to be equivalent to the claim that only a single nature is said to be; that is, that all beings have the common character of being (186a24–27). This claim does make sense, but Aristotle argues that it is false. The problem is that the Eleatics are unable to spell out just what character all beings share. If the nature they intend is substance, then their claim is false because there is more than one substance. Nor are the Eleatics right if the nature is quantity, quality, or any of the other characters said to be. Though this argument is not conclusive, it does cast doubt on the Eleatic thesis. In any event, it does not rely on analysis of ordinary usage as Ackrill supposes.

After this argument Aristotle goes on to show that, analogously, the Eleatics are unable to indicate the kind of unity that they claim all beings possess. He argues that "all things" are not one in the way that any particular thing is called one. The response that the Eleatics would make to both arguments is to insist that the character all things share is "just being" (*hoper on*) or "just one" (*hoper hen*). Aristotle's refutation of this in I.3 seems to be what Ackrill describes in his second point to which I referred earlier, though he mixes in some details about change from I.8. In fact, neither chapter contains anything about copulas and identity statements. Ackrill's version of this second point is incorrect. What, then, is Aristotle's analysis? In I.3 Aristotle maintains that the Eleatics confuse a character and the thing to which the character belongs, for example, white and what is white. (In Greek, phrases like *to leukon* may refer to both, see e.g. *Met.* VII.6.1031b22–25.) Hence, they do not distinguish the character of "being" from that to which it belongs. That this is no mere linguistic slip is apparent from the arguments Aristotle mentions here (186a32–187a10). They begin with the claim that "being" signifies a single nature. Suppose that that substrate to which "being" belongs is different from it. Then, the substrate is a nonbeing, and calling it "being" amounts to an absurd ascription of "being" to a nonbeing. Hence, "being" can belong to nothing else besides a being. By similar reasoning, Aristotle shows that nothing besides "being" can belong to the substrate being. His criticism of the Eleatics is that they are inconsistent in ascribing magnitude and other characters to being. The problem is not so much the kind of reasoning they use, but their application of this reasoning to being.

Part of Ackrill's error in his interpretation of this argument as well as the preceding one is his supposition that Aristotle uses "*to on*" to indicate the verb "to be." Grammatically, this participial form could refer to the verb; perhaps Aristotle uses it this way in other passages. However, in *Physics* I.2–3's discussion of the Eleatic thesis *to on* signifies the common character that all things possess or the things that possess this character. Here *to on* is a noun. Ackrill's error is not, however, a mere oversight. We do not ordinarily use the noun "being"; and even when we do, it is not to indicate a character common to all things. If Ackrill is to maintain that *Physics* I.2–3 analyzes ordinary usage, he must insist that *to on* indicates a verb. His presuppositions about the character of Aristotle's analyses have misled him here.

The two arguments that Ackrill claims to find in I.2-3 are not contained in these chapters, and what is there does not show Aristotle to be self-consciously engaged in an examination of ordinary usage. Perhaps someone will still maintain that these chapters *can* be construed linguistically or that what Aristotle does *really* is conceptual analysis. I shall have more to say about these sorts of responses shortly. For now, suffice it to say that Ackrill's claim that *Physics* I.2-3 self-consciously examines linguistic usage is not borne out by the text.

After considering chapters 2-3, Ackrill goes on to present Aristotle's analysis of change in I.7. Again, Ackrill maintains that Aristotle draws inferences from the way we speak about change. Lengthy quotations that frequently repeat expressions like "we say" (*legōmen, phamen*) and "it is said" (*legetai*) enhance his case. According to Ackrill, Aristotle distinguishes two locutions: (1) something comes to be something else, and (2) something comes to be from something else. Examples of (1) include both a man coming to be musical and an unmusical (*scil.* man) coming to be musical; examples of (2) include the musical (man) coming to be from the unmusical (man) but *not* the musical (man) coming to be from man. I presume that Ackrill regards the difference between these two locutions as suggesting the difference between man and the quality unmusical as principles of change: the former is a substrate and the latter a privation. Although they are numerically one composite, language indicates that they are distinct principles of change. Apparently, Ackrill sees the doctrine that there are three principles of change as emerging from the analysis of language; Aristotle assumes that "how we speak will be a good guide to how things are."[8]

Does Aristotle's doctrine of change in I.7 result from the analysis of linguistic usage? As the discussion of this argument continues, Ackrill mentions the "important" distinction between what remains after change (the man) and what does not remain after change, the quality (unmusical).[9] Whether he regards this distinction as factual or conceptual is unclear, but Ackrill never suggests that Aristotle derives it from analysis of ordinary usage. It is this distinction that plays the major role in I.7. An important conclusion of the chapter is that all change requires a substrate that persists. But this does not follow from the way we speak. At the beginning of I.7 Aristotle does make the seemingly linguistic distinction that I described earlier, but he never refers to it again in the chapter. In fact, he ignores it and speaks of characters coming to be from substrates (190b9-10). Once again, the text fails to show Aristotle self-consciously examining linguistic usage in the way that Ackrill asserts.

There are more reasons to doubt Ackrill's interpretation of I.7. Aristotle's primary argument for the three principles doctrine runs throughout *Physics* I . His motive for criticizing the Eleatics in I.2–3 is that the single principle they posit fails to account for change; in fact, it excludes change. In chapters 4–6 he examines attempts to explain motion by two contrary principles. They too prove insufficient; for, among other difficulties, one contrary cannot act on another contrary (6.189a22–24; *Met.* XII.10.1075a30–31). It follows that there must be at least three principles. Thus, Aristotle begins I.7 with the knowledge that the principles consist of two contraries and a substrate. In a remark near the end of the chapter, he claims that he had already shown that these three are the principles of change, but that "now" (I.7 as usually interpreted) he has "made clear what the *differentiae* of the contraries are, how they are related to each other, and what the substrate is" (191a15–19). These are exactly the topics that we would expect as a sequel to I.6. While the latter chapter argues that contraries require a third thing to act upon, I.7 explains that this third thing is the substrate that persists through change and that all change requires such a substrate (190a14–21). This chapter is not arriving at principles of change but identifying them with attributes and substrate. As I noted earlier, the necessity for a substrate does not follow from analysis of linguistic usage. For I.7, the ideas of matter persisting through change, the dependence of accidents on substance, and the analogy of natures and artifacts are more important. Not only does Aristotle fail to exploit ordinary usage to derive his doctrine of change, but in some respects that doctrine is inconsistent with ordinary usage. Greek ordinary usage has it that the unmusical (*to amousikon*) comes to be musical; yet Aristotle maintains that there must be a substrate involved in all changes. Nevertheless, Aristotle's analysis does account for the ordinary way of speaking. The principles of change are three in formula but only two in number because, in a way, the privation and the substrate are numerically one. Hence, we are justified in speaking of changes without mentioning the substrates or the privations. Ordinary language, though inaccurate, is preserved. However, it has a role quite opposite to the one Ackrill assigns it. Aristotle is not using ordinary usage to arrive at a philosophic point. To the extent that ordinary usage is involved in I.7, Aristotle uses a doctrine derived from different considerations to explain it. In short, Ackrill puts the cart before the horse. In I.7, as elsewhere, linguistic usage is subsidiary.

The reason that Ackrill's linguistic interpretation often seems so compelling is that, as I have mentioned, Aristotle frequently uses locutions such as "we say" and "it is said" (*legōmen, legetai, phamen, eipomen*). Mere citation of these phrases appears to support claims that Aristotle does analyze linguistic usage. Yet we must be wary. Does Aristotle really describe ordinary usage when he lists the ways something is said? Is, for example, "being is said in many ways" a claim about ordinary usage? In neither this claim nor others like it does Aristotle suppose that he is merely reporting usage. Despite appearances these assertions are not about linguistic practice but about objective reality. An indication that this is so comes when Aristotle interprets the Eleatics as maintaining that being is said in one way or, equivalently, that all beings share a common nature. The contrary assertion, that being is said in many ways, amounts to the denial that there is a nature common to all beings. "Being is said in many ways" because there are *in fact* many beings, and this is exactly what the sentence asserts. The basis for this assertion lies not in analysis of linguistic usage but in the recognition of a plurality of different essential natures. Each of these essences somehow contains being immediately (*Met.* IV.2.1003b32–33; VIII.6.1045b3–4). A parallel point could be made for other instances of the "it is said" and similar locutions. Aristotle uses such expressions to report claims about the world much as we might give an account of contemporary geology by recounting what it is that geologists say.

Doubtless many philosophers will disagree with Aristotle and insist that claims about the plurality of beings and the like are not factual but result from Aristotle's conceptual analysis. My point so far has been to show only that, *contra* Ackrill, Aristotle does not regard himself as analyzing linguistic usage. In the course of this discussion, I have also indicated a reason for rejecting one of the other ways in which Ackrill sees Aristotle using language. If my interpretation of the "it is said" locutions is correct, Aristotle is not self-consciously engaged in an analysis of terms or concepts either. Rightly or wrongly, he thinks that he is making claims about the world.

Let us consider conceptual analysis in more detail. If Aristotle does not examine ordinary linguistic usage for hints about the nature of the world, can we not at least agree with Ackrill that he analyzes concepts or language? Ackrill does not explicitly distinguish the

analysis of usage from the analysis of concepts, but this is a distinction that he may wish to fall back on if he cannot maintain that the
Physics analyzes usage. Indeed, in most of the arguments he presents,
he does not refer to ordinary usage; and since he would reject the
notion that these arguments are factual, he must regard them as
involving some sort of conceptual or linguistic analysis. This expedi-
ent, however, fares no better than the claim that Aristotle analyzes
usage.

According to Ackrill Aristotle examines language or concepts
for hints about the nature of the world. If this assessment were true,
we would expect to find Aristotle first analyzing language and then
applying the results to the world. Instead, we find no such separation
between language and the world. Aristotle speaks as if he were examining the world. He does not see himself as analyzing concepts or language.

Ackrill is well aware of this fact, and he accounts for it by
describing Aristotle as a linguistic philosopher with a mistaken view
of the connection of language and the world. As Ackrill would have
it, Aristotle simply assumes that language accurately reflects the
world and that an analysis of language is an analysis of the world
because he lacks close acquaintance with languages and cultures
other than his own. This account is scarcely credible. Aristotle was a
Stagirite who lived and worked in both Athens and Asia Minor.
Could he have been as provincial as Ackrill supposes? More importantly, if Aristotle does think language reflects the world, it is because
he maintains that things are named in respect of their essences. In the
De Intepretatione he asserts that words are symbols of things in the
soul; though they differ among different races, the things of the soul
are the same. Why? In the *De Anima* he explains that knowledge consists of having a form (somehow) in the soul without its matter
(429b13 ff.). All human beings are capable of knowledge, and knowledge consists of having the form or essence of the thing known in the
soul. Hence, though languages be different, the essences in the souls
of people with knowledge are the same. An essence can exist in a
thing or in a soul, or be symbolized in language. Whatever we think
of these doctrines, it is clear that Aristotle's view of language and the
world is not merely the assumption of a linguistic philosopher with
insufficient experience. It results from Aristotle's notions of the character of knowledge and of essences.

Ackrill may still wish to insist that Aristotle's analysis of essences and his supposition that the essences we know are in things *amounts to* analyzing language and supposing that it reflects the world. However, to say this is to admit that Aristotle does not self-consciously analyze language for hints about the nature of the world.

In sum, Ackrill's position that Aristotle consciously engages in linguistic analysis and simply assumes that it reflects the world is difficult to maintain. While Ackrill presents Aristotle as recognizing the importance of linguistic analysis and making an unwarranted application of it to the world, the reverse is closer to the truth. Aristotle sees himself as examining the world and his doctrine of essences is the basis for this view. What seem to be remarks about our conceptual framework are really claims about essences and, thus, the nature of the world.

It is still possible to contend that Aristotle does analyze language, but not without accusing him of prominent errors. For one, he seems to confuse the scientist's explanation of physical facts and the philosopher's conceptual analysis of common opinions, for he makes both instances of "saving the phenomena."[10] Ackrill attempts to defend Aristotle from this well-known difficulty by praising his insight into the close connection between science and philosophy,[11] but such a distinction between science and philosophy occurs nowhere in the Aristotelian corpus. On the contrary, Aristotle's "confusion" results from foisting upon him the distinction between physical facts and concepts (or language) implicit in linguistic analysis and in the claim that Aristotle is a linguistic analyst. According to Aristotle, beliefs or opinions consist in a grasp of an attribute as inhering in a subject but not inhering in respect of the subject's essence (*An. Po.* I.33.89a19–21). Though they are not knowledge, common opinions are generally true because they are based on sensation. The task of the philosopher is to find the essence that causes the attribute. This essence is at once the cause of both the phenomenon and the common opinion of it. Only if we reject or ignore this view of essence can we maintain that Aristotle analyzes language and also that he confuses facts and opinions.

Thus far I have focused my attention on refuting the claims that Aristotle examines linguistic usage and analyzes language. A by-product of this discussion is the recognition of the price Ackrill must pay to maintain that Aristotle is an analytic philosopher. First, he is forced to accuse Aristotle of the mistaken view that ordinary usage reflects reality. Second, he must deemphasize or dismiss Aristotle's doctrine of essences and treat it as an analysis of language. Third, he must reject Aristotle's epistemological claims about the possibility of knowledge of essences and attributes. Fourth, he must accept the view that Aristotle is unsystematic in order to justify focusing attention on some facts and ignoring others. All of this is a high price to pay. At issue here is not whether Aristotle is right or wrong. My point is simply that an interpretation of Aristotle which omits his central doctrines is mistaken. If, in order to maintain that Aristotle is a linguistic analyst it is necessary to ignore many of his major claims, it ought to follow that Aristotle is no linguistic analyst.

The author of *Aristotle the Philosopher* has a keen sense of the Aristotelian texts and I doubt that anything I have said here will either surprise or sway him, for the basis of his interpretation lies more in current philosophy than the texts. As I mentioned earlier, many philosophers and scholars under the influence of Wittgenstein and Austin maintain that we inevitably approach philosophical problems through language. They infer that Aristotle must be analyzing language whether he knows it or not. Convinced by recent philosophy, they attempt to salvage at least some part of his philosophy by treating him as if he were analyzing language. In short behind the linguistic interpretation lies the desire to make Aristotle relevant. If he is indeed using language, then, despite apparent errors, his concerns and methods are intelligible and pertinent.

It scarcely needs to be said that Aristotle did not have the benefit of reading Wittgenstein and Austin, and that he did not recognize the primacy of language that is the cornerstone of their work. To suppose otherwise is historically inaccurate. *Aristole the Philosopher* does not, however, purport to be history, and my chief objection is not historical. On the contrary, I fully agree that it is Aristotle's arguments that are most important and that we ought to examine them with everything at our disposal. The question is whether viewing Aristotle as a linguistic philosopher allows us to examine his arguments. I have argued that a number of the mistakes Ackrill ascribes to Aristotle arise from his own interpretation. If so, then Ackrill does not really confront Aristotle; he confronts himself. All too often Ackrill's critical assessment of Aristotle merely points up the inadequacy of supposing Aristotle to be analyzing language in a contemporary way. It is possible to force Aristotle into the linguistic mold, but the fit is not good. What hangs out of the mold is not due to Aristotle's mistakes but to the defects of the mold. If we really intend to engage Aristotle the philosopher, we must recognize the fundamental differences between his philosophical perspective and more current perspectives and consider how he might respond to current views.

How can this be done? Does the denial that Aristotle is a linguistic philosopher leave him a mere museum piece? Part of the motive for the linguistic interpretation is that it makes Aristotle interesting. I intend to undercut this motive by showing a different reason for interest in Aristotle.

Let me begin by considering another of Ackrill's criticisms of Aristotle. In response to the claim that everything happens for an end, Ackrill wonders how Aristotle can ignore what happens simply according to law without any purpose.[12] Further on, Ackrill suggests that teleology might be dispensed with if we had laws.[13]

These and other remarks about laws presume that it makes sense to speak of laws in the context of Aristotle's philosophy. Of course, if Aristotle were a linguistic philosopher, he would have no difficulty in accepting laws as statements or regularities in experience. In fact, neither this nor other modern conceptions of physical law are to be found in Aristotle. Instead, his primary mode of explanation is to trace an attribute or a phenomenon to an essential nature, often the nature of the thing that possesses the attribute. Logic is designed to find such essential causes. Ackrill sometimes speaks as if the necessary connections sought in logic were laws, but Aristotle emphasizes the nature that causes rather than the connection. To explain the being of all things he does not produce laws but a group of self-subsistent beings.

Once we grasp Aristotle's mode of explanation it is easy to understand his emphasis on teleology. Any regular occurrence must be traced to some nature. There are relatively few possibilities. The occurrence could be a part of the nature, a necessary requirement for the nature, brought about by a nature, or for the sake of a nature. Since the nature of a thing is its end, all four possibilities presuppose some end. Hence, the reason that a regular occurrence always indicates a *telos* is rooted in Aristotle's mode of explanation.

Rather than pointing out Aristotle's failure to recognize other modes of explanation, it seems to me more fruitful and interesting to focus on the character of Aristotle's mode of explanation. In understanding what Aristotle is doing, we can easily see the metaphysical difficulties inherent in something we often take for granted, the idea of physical law: What is the connection of the law and what the law explains? Where is the law? A study of these difficulties would be a history of modern philosophy. Even if we are unwilling to accept solutions such as the rationalists proposed, that laws are ideas in the mind of God, we are in a position to understand what motivates them. That questions about the status of laws are very much alive is indicated by difficulties about the interpretation of quantum mechanics and by recent attempts to connect the laws of physics with the events in the first microseconds after the big bang. The latter even suggests the Aristotelian mode of explanation in terms of things, though in a distinctly material vein. I am not, however, claiming that the significance of Aristotle's philosophy lies in its similarity to recent thinking. I am proposing that the contrast of Aristotelian and contemporary thinking provides an insight into significant problems, problems we too often ignore because we blindly accept assumptions, such as the existence of laws, without considering what is involved. Awareness of the profound differences between Aristotelian and current thinking forces us to rethink our fundamental assumptions. This is, of course, what we expect of philosophy.

To conclude, let me return to the question with which I began, why is Aristotle interesting? Aristotle does not use contemporary methods, nor does he arrive at conclusions consonant with current thinking. Rather, he is interesting because his profound differences challenge our basic assumptions and perspectives and suggest alternative paths. Contemporary philosophy stands to gain more from Aristotle through his differences with it, than through his similarities. Aristotle is interesting because, to borrow a slogan, he offers a choice not an echo.

Chapter 7

SOME PROBLEMS IN ARISTOTLE'S MATHEMATICAL ONTOLOGY

Aristotle is not usually thought to be much of a mathematician. While Plato is credited with mathematical genius, Aristotle is supposed to incline more toward biology.[1] This mathematical ill-repute could hardly stem from a lack of references to the discipline. Aristotle often supplies mathematical examples, and the science figures prominently in his discussions of scientific method in the *Posterior Analytics*.[2] It is true that there is no extant work devoted to mathematics and that Aristotle did not do creative mathematical work so far as we know, but the same could be said of Plato. One source of Aristotle's supposed lack of mathematical ability is that Greek mathematical proofs cannot, in general, be formulated as syllogisms.[3] Another source, equally important, is his mathematical ontology. Aristotle's mathematical ontology can be stated, in broad terms, quite simply: mathematical objects exist as attributes of sensible things. One difficulty with this ontology is its apparent inconsistency with the mathematical practice of both Aristotle's contemporaries and present mathematicians. I want to mention this problem at the outset in order to indicate why I am not going to be concerned with it here.

The problem is that since Aristotle maintains that the universe is finite, he is committed to recognizing a maximum length; whereas his mathematical contemporaries were in all likelihood employing claims about infinite lines that he could not countenance. Claims about infinite lines appear in Euclid, and Euclid was drawing on earlier sources some of which, it is supposed, would have been available to Aristotle.[4] It seems to me that the presumption is that if Aristotle's ontology is at odds with mathematical practice, he must have been either unacquainted with that practice or inept at it. But Aristotle insists repeatedly that mathematicians treat mathematical entities as things that are quite different from what they really are: mathematicians treat them as separate, self-subsistent entities, though they are, properly, merely attributes of substances. This liberty on the part of mathematicians does not lead to mistakes, Aristotle maintains (XIII.3.1078a21). Though the claims of mathematicians fail to be ontologically precise, they can, it would seem, be expressed in an ontologically precise way. In short, Aristotle recognizes a distinction between the ontology implicit in mathematical practice and metaphysical treatments of mathematicals.[5] It is not obvious that Aristotle is right to make this distinction or to suppose that a mathematical result could always be given a proper ontological formulation, but I shall not undertake to defend Aristotle on these points here. Let me simply note, on the one hand, the inappropriateness of criticizing Aristotle's ontology for its failure to be consistent with mathematical practice when Aristotle recognizes that mathematical practice presupposes its own distinct ontology, and, on the other hand, how a particular problem that occupies many present-day philosophers or mathematics, the problem of describing mathematical practice, has no place in Aristotle's properly philosophical treatment of mathematical entities.[6]

If it is a mistake to assess Aristotle's mathematical ontology by comparing it with the practice of mathematicians, how ought it to be evaluated? It ought to be considered like any other ontological or metaphysical doctrine, in terms of its inner consistency. My concern here is with a cluster of problems that arise from Aristotle's characterization of numbers and his treatment of substance. These problems are quite simple to formulate, and they arise almost immediately. We could, perhaps, forgive Aristotle if his ontology could not accommodate the complex mathematical entities examined by current mathematicians, but what could we say if it failed to accommodate even the simplest mathematicals, like number and figure? The following two problems stem from Aristotle's claim that mathematicals exist as attributes of substances:

1. The first problem is how mathematicals can be attributes.[7] According to the *Categories* anything besides substance is either present in or said of primary substance (5.2a34–35). Aristotle makes clear that this means that everything else is present in or said of some *particular individual*: "Animal is predicated of man, thus of some individual man; for if [it were predicated] of no individual man, neither would it be predicated of man in general. Again, color is in body; accordingly, it is in some body; for if it were not in some individual, neither would it be in body in general" (2a36–b3). This doctrine makes it difficult to grasp how number could possibly be an attribute, for a number would need to belong to a particular individual. By definition, a number is a plurality of units: the Greeks do not regard one as a number. So five, for example, cannot be conceived simply as an attribute of a group of five things; there must be some one thing of which it is an attribute. But how could one thing be five? Insofar as it is one, it does not admit of plurality as its attribute.

In his *Hippias Major* Plato distinguishes terms that apply to all of their instances *and* to each of their instances, such as, "beautiful" and "good," from terms like "both" that apply to all but not to each, terms that apply collectively but not individually (303a–b). All numbers clearly belong under the latter heading. So it seems unlikely that Aristotle would have simply failed to notice the difficulty. Indeed, there is an entire group of apparently relational and collective characters that do not readily fall under the Aristotelian scheme that can only accommodate attributes of individuals. The present problem about numbers is merely part of a larger problem of how Aristotle understands nondistributive properties. At any rate, several obvious ways of assimilating numbers to the categories can be quickly discounted. First, we might be inclined to take numbers as generic attributes. Aristotle does accord a place to generic attributes; but, so far as I can see, he always traces such attributes back to individuals: a universal can be both white and black, he admits, but only because at least one of its instances is black and one white or because one is white at one time and black at another (*Met.* X.10.1058b32–35). So even though Aristotle can admit generic attributes, his adherence to the doctrine of the *Categories* leaves them unable to resolve his problem. Sometimes

Aristotle speaks of numbers as measuring genera (e.g., X.1.1052b16–35). I shall have something to say about this shortly, but to anticipate my argument, let me simply note that these measures are not generic attributes either.

A second, related approach to the problem was popular in the Middle Ages: numbers are second intentional. While man is a concept that signifies a particular thing, numbers are concepts that signify man and other first intentional concepts. It is clear that this is a medieval development—it probably originated with Avicenna—that represents an attempt to introduce generic attributes. It could not have been adopted by Aristotle, for it implies that numbers are primarily mental constructs: it makes numbers attributes of our concepts. But Aristotle includes numbers in the categorial genus of quantity, and quantities are attributes of substances. Thus, the only way that the doctrine that numbers are second intentional could solve the problem is if Aristotle gave up his mathematical ontology; but, of course, if he did that we would not have a problem to worry about. The difficulty we face is to understand how numbers can be attributes of individuals.

Recently, a third way of avoiding the problem has been advanced by Jonathan Barnes. He credits Aristotle with making numbers properties of sets. Barnes does not advance any evidence for the unlikely suggestion that Aristotle was aware of set theory, nor is any to be found, so far as I can see. Besides, the supposed "sets" in the passage that Barnes cites (X.1.1053a20) and in similar passages (V.13.1020a13; X.6.1057a3–4) are not pluralities of substances, as his view requires, but pluralities of units.[8] And if Aristotle did regard sets of substances as individuals capable of receiving attributes, it would be hard to imagine why he insists on treating other apparently collective attributes, such as relatives, as if each belonged to some individual (cf. V.15.1021b6–11). To be sure, Aristotle does ascribe attributes to artifacts (such as houses and plays), cities, and other entities that are not strictly substantial, but in each case he does so in virtue of what he takes to be a quasi-substantial character (*Metaphysics* VIII.3.1043a4–7; *Poetics* 6.1449b22–24; *Politics* I.2.1252b27–1253a29; III.1.1274b32–34[9]). Since Barnes's groups have no such character, there is no basis for ascribing attributes to them. Again, such an ascription would be inconsistent with *Categories* 2a34–35. Aristotle's number is a plurality, but each such plurality should be an attribute of some individual substance.

This leads to the second problem:

2. How can mathematicals be attributes if the aim of the mathematical sciences is to find the attributes of mathematicals? The problem is that attributes cannot themselves have attributes. This follows directly from the doctrine of the *Categories* that I mentioned earlier. There Aristotle distinguishes those beings that are primary substances from what is said of them or is present in them. Assuming that what is present in a substance is an attribute, we can see that this division excludes the possibility that an attribute will itself have an attribute, for the latter attribute would have to be present in the former attribute but not in the underlying substance. Attributes of attributes would, it would seem, be neither present in nor said of a primary substance.[10] That Aristotle himself not only drew this inference but continued to endorse it is clear from a claim he makes in the *Metaphysics*: "An attribute (*sumbebēkos*) is not an attribute of an attribute unless both are attributes of the same thing; I mean, for example, that white is musical and this is white because both belong to Socrates" (IV.4.1007b2–5). Though the term Aristotle uses for attribute in this passage is not limited to accidental attributes (see V.30.1025a30–34), here it apparently does refer to accidental attributes. That the doctrine ought to apply to per se attributes as well follows from the *pros hen* doctrine of being: "Each [way being is said] is related to one principle [substance] . . ." (IV.2.1003b5–10). If *each* being is related to some substance, then there could be no attribute of an attribute—whether accidental or per se. Every attribute could only be an attribute of a substance. Since mathematicals are attributes of substances, they should not have their own attributes, except accidentally. Nevertheless, Aristotle describes mathematics as demonstrating the per se attributes of mathematical entities. How could the existence of per se attributes of per se attributes be consistent with Aristotle's insistence that everything else be present in or said of—or related to—some substance? Can we make any sense of mathematics?

Since I have referred to the *Categories* in formulating these problems, it may seem as though they could be skirted simply by recalling that the *Categories* is an early work; could Aristotle perhaps have changed his mind when he developed the mathematical ontology we find the *Metaphysics*? This standard developmental move will not work here, for all that my account of the problem really requires is just what we find in the *Metaphysics*, the contention that mathematicals are attributes of substances (VII.3.1029a14–16), the presumption that an attribute belongs to an individual substance,[11] the claim that mathematicals have attributes (IV.2.1004b10–15), and the apparent impossibility of one attribute's belonging to another attribute in any but an accidental way.

Thus far, I have described two problems that Aristotle should have dealt with in advancing a mathematical ontology. Both are so straightforward and obvious that it would be hard to imagine that he had not resolved them somehow in his own mind—even if not in texts that have come down to us. We will soon see that the solutions are fairly simple—perhaps the reader has guessed them already. But to prolong suspense and to boost the plausibility of the interpretation I shall offer, I want to look at some prominent accounts of Aristotle's mathematics first. My plan is to use the two problems as touchstones to evaluate the competing accounts. If the accounts cannot resolve these two problems, then they are likely to be inadequate or, at least, less adequate than an account that can resolve the problems. As we see why these accounts fail, we will also see the sort of account that could solve the problems. Thus, the refutation of the alternatives helps to establish my own interpretation. The failure of these alternatives will also, I hope, do something to show that the problems ought to be taken seriously. Despite their easy formulation, they are significant. A caveat: what have been proposed as accounts of Aristotle's mathematics are accounts mainly of how we come to know mathematicals and only derivatively accounts of how mathematicals exist in sensibles. Scholars who discuss Aristotle's mathematics tend to be more interested in epistemology than ontology.

The first account is sometimes called the "abstractionist account." Its exponents refer to *Metaphysics* XIII.3 and to other discussions of how numbers are abstracted from sensibles. It is well known that the process that Aristotle calls "abstraction" differs from what is usually understood by this term. Aristotelian abstraction is not the result of collecting individuals and finding common properties. It is rather a process of disregarding certain characteristics: indeed, the Greek term usually rendered as "abstraction" could be rendered, equally well or better, as "subtraction."[12]

To find mathematicals, we begin with sensible things and subtract or leave out all characteristics except for quantitative ones. We arrive at a particular solid, or figure, or magnitude. This is what it means to treat Socrates *as* a quantity, the tack that the mathematician is supposed to take. The first mathematical that we would come to as we removed the sensible characteristics would be a solid. Further abstractions yield, in turn, planes, lines, and points. Finally, we arrive at the unit. Socrates *qua* indivisible is one unit. This much Aristotle describes clearly in the text. The problem is how to get number. There is widespread agreement among commentators on the process of abstraction that yields number. If removing in thought Socrates' non-quantitative sensible characteristics yields the unit, the way to arrive at a plurality through abstraction is to start with a group of sub-stances. Thus, Gottfried Martin, for example, speaks of starting from the planets, removing their sensible characteristics, and so abstracting the number nine.[13]

Aristotle does not require that the mathematicians themselves be the ones who extract number from things. Metaphysicians may perform that initial labor and then hand the mathematicians their subject matter. Leaving aside whatever uneasiness we might feel at this division of labor, we need to ask whether this account resolves the two problems. It is obvious that it does not answer the first problem. It does not explain how the number nine could be an attribute of a group of substances. Indeed, in requiring that numbers be attributes of groups, the abstractionist account exacerbates the first problem. This account fares only a bit better on the second problem. As long as the mathematician is really dealing with physical substances, the attributes that he ascribes to mathematicals should clearly be attributes of the substances themselves. The mathematician might speak of the line as straight or curved, he might, that is, suppose that straight and curved are attributes of the line; but in the most proper ontological sense the straight and the curved must somehow belong to the things from which lines have been abstracted. Likewise, odd and even must somehow be traced to the things from which number has been abstracted. But the first problem emerges again here: how could "even" be an attribute of a plurality of substances? If we could just solve the first problem, the recognition that mathematicals are abstracted from substances and that their attributes are thus some-how attributes of substances might lead us to a solution of the second problem.

An alternative to the abstractionist account of the origin of num-bers has been advanced by Jacob Klein and has recently been endorsed by others.[14] According to Klein, intrinsic to the Greek notion of "number" (*arithmos*) is the process of numbering or counting: num-ber is always the number *of something*. In contrast to Plato, Aristotle thinks that it is sensibles that we count.[15] Klein's key text for Aristotle's discussion of counting is *Metaphysics* X.1. There Aristotle claims that one is the measure of a genus, most properly the genus of quantity from which it has been extended to other genera, "for the measure is that by which quantity is known; quantity *qua* quantity is known by one or by number, and each number is known by one" (1052b18–22). According to Klein, the first move is to regard each substance or each instance of another genus as a single individual, to remove in thought all that is not numeric. Then, number is derived by counting several of these individual units.

It seems to me that the main difference between this view and that of the abstactionists is that here abstraction is always confined to a single individual. Once we regard the individual as a unit, we can use it to measure other instances of the genus. This approach represents a major difference because it arrives at number without assuming that number is an attribute belonging to a group.

But just what sort of an entity is number? According to Klein: "A number is not *one* thing but a 'heap' (*sōros*) of things or monads."[16] This is a peculiar claim, for Aristotle reserves the term "heap" for what has little or no ontological status, for matter or what does not exist. In *Metaphysics* VII.16, he denies that earth, fire, air, and so forth are substances on the ground that each is but a mere "heap" until it is made into something one (1040b8–10). Seeking the cause of being in *Metaphysics* VII.17, Aristotle inquires into the cause of unity: why is something like a syllable and not like a heap (1041b11–12; cf. 1041b25–27).[17] It seems that to be something is *not* to be a heap. Perhaps, though, this conclusion is too general; the reasoning shows only that no substance is a heap. Could a number be a heap? There are several passages where Aristotle accuses his predecessors of being unable to account for why number is one (see I.9.992a1–2; VIII.3.1044a3–5; XII.10.1075b34–36; XI.2.1060b10–12); failing this, their numbers are heaps of units (VIII.3.1044a4–5; XIII.8.1084b21–22). The clear implication is that Aristotle believes he has a way to account for the unity of a number and so to avoid making them heaps.

Somehow Klein does not see that Aristotle takes being a heap and being one to be contraries. For he maintains both that Aristotle's numbers are heaps and that Aristotle also offers a cogent account of why each is one.[18] He thinks that the reason that each number is one is that it is measured by a unit; thus, in each case the principle of unity is the measure of the count. I shall return to this contention shortly.

The question that should be addressed first is whether Klein's view of number resolves either of the problems. Could a number that is a heap measured by a single nature be an attribute of some substance? It is surely not a quantity of the individual that serves as a measure, nor is it apparent how it could be an attribute of any other individual. Even if it were somehow an attribute, how could the heap-number have its own attributes? Not only does Klein fail to provide us with an account of how such a number could have attributes, his number's lack of ontological determination—its being a heap—seems incompatible with its having any per se attributes. In short, Klein's account does not solve the two problems.

The notion that numbers can be defined through counting is, though, too promising to give up so soon. Let us grant that Klein is mistaken to think that numbers defined by counting are heaps. Could they be understood in some other way? What sort of entities could they be? It might be suggested that numbers somehow belong to those people performing the act of counting. This would make number second intentional, and we would have to explain how it is that numbers and other mathematicals can be attributes of substances. An alternative is to say that the numbers or counts are attributes of genera; perhaps this is what Aristotle means when he says that numbers are measures of genera. Let us suppose that I intend to count the horses in a barn. I choose one, abstract all other sensible characteristics and focus on its indivisibility. Then, by means of this unit I can count the other horses.[19] Say there are five horses. This number five does not belong to any individual horse. Does it belong to the genus that was counted? No, for it does not characterize the genus of horse: it characterizes the horses in the barn. But "horses in the barn" is not a genus; horse is the genus here. Could we say, instead, that there being "five in the barn" is an attribute of the genus horse? This is, I think, a genuine generic attribute; but it is also an attribute that belongs to particular instances of the genus, for each horse in the barn belongs to a group of five that are in the barn. It seems to me perfectly legitimate and entirely unproblematic to say that numbers belong to a genus and thus to instances of the genus, if what is meant is that the attribute of being part of a group with x members belongs to each of the x things in the group: five belongs to a group of horses in the sense that each horse has the character of belonging to a group of five horses. But this point of view makes number a relative, for the attribute five signifies the *relation* of the one horse to the others in the group. There is some basis in the *Categories* for numeric relations (6.5b14–6a11; 7.6a39–7b1), but what about the primary sense of number, the number that falls within the genus of quantity? How could numbers that exist as the counts of a plurality be quantitative *attributes* of any individual counted, of the group that is counted, or of the genus counted? However we understand it, Klein's characterization of number by means of counting does not help to answer the first problem. Nor does it explain the second problem, the attributes of number. Perhaps we could say that these attributes are "third intentional," but this does not help to explain why mathematicals admit of attributes, and it seems thoroughly incompatible with Aristotelian mathematicals' being properties of substances.

Klein's discussion of number serves to highlight still another problem that needs to be faced: in virtue of what is a number one? As I noted earlier, Klein thinks that the source of unity is the unit that is counted, the measure of the count. This has a certain intuitive appeal, for surely the key element in any count is the nature whose instances are counted or—as we might say—that description which enables us to pick out instances, and surely any group can be counted provided it can be suitably described. Granted, the nature that is counted, the measure, does supply a sort of unity to the count. Unfortunately, though, it cannot be the unity possessed by a number; for nothing in the particular nature counted or in the particular description in accordance with which we pick out instances determines how many instances we will count, and the collection of instances has no substantial nature. There could be any number of instances of the measure; we could say that the *horses* are five—if they are five—or whatever number they happen to be. There would be a sort of unity here in that the horses are what is numbered, but there is no particular reason why there should be five horses or fifty horses, as far as the nature of horse goes. Most importantly, the nature that is numbered does not supply unity to the plurality of units because the nature does not unify its instances: they remain a plurality of horses or whatever else. The group of five horses—or of any other number of horses—do not constitute a single nature. How could their number be a single being? A single description might enable us to pick out instances; it does not make the count of those instances one nature. Measures or descriptions may explain how we go about counting and how we decide what things to count; they do not explain the ontological status of number.

The counting and the abstractionist accounts of number are sometimes both ascribed to Aristotle, on the presumption that different books of the *Metaphysics* could well have been written at different times and thus could reflect distinct paths taken toward a solution of a problem.[20] It is not clear that XIII.3 and X.1 are incompatible because XIII.3 does not speak of abstracting number from a plurality and because X.1 still presupposes the abstraction of a unit presumably by the process described in XIII.3. But there is no need for me to delve any further into this two positions view, espoused by Julia Annas, because it is already clear that neither position by itself will resolve the problems.

Thus far, I have pointed to two problems in understanding Aristotle's ontology of number and I have considered the two prevailing accounts of Aristotelian mathematics and a third view that attempts to combine them. None of these accounts resolves the problems. When we reflect on how simple and obvious the problems are, it seems highly unlikely that any of them could be right. We are hampered by not having an Aristotelian work devoted to mathematics. But if we find an account of number that is consistent with the texts we have and resolves the problems, we ought rather to accept it as likely to be Aristotle's. It is well to remember too that there is no question that we can arrive at numbers by means of some sort of abstraction and that counting involves measuring a genus. (The texts upon which the two accounts rely are clear.) At issue is whether counting or abstracting *as described by the commentators* is compatible with the ontological status of number.

There is one text that concerns number that is not usually discussed in this context, Aristotle's treatment of the infinite in *Physics* III.4–8. I propose that this treatment provides an essential clue towards understanding Aristotle's philosophy of number. In this portion of the *Physics* Aristotle is interested in deciding whether the infinite exists and if so how. His overall motivation is to refute the Pythagoreans who posit the infinite as a first principle and thereby to lay the groundwork for a refutation of Zeno's denial that there is motion, but this need not concern us here. As I suggested earlier, the mathematical infinite needs to be examined by anyone intent on maintaining that the universe is finite and that mathematicals are attributes of things. Of course, Aristotle must deny that there is an infinite in length—there can be no infinitely long lines in a finite universe. But a line can be divided infinitely, and this fact supports the existence of two types of infinite: the infinite in division (infinitesimal magnitude) and the infinite by addition (the infinite in number). Why the infinite in number? Because we can count the divisions (III.7.207b10–15).[21] Aristotle's mathematical realism dictates that there could not be numbers unless there were things to be counted (cf. *Met.* XIV.5.1092b19–20).[22] It is the points on a line that we can count, and since the line is always capable of being divided further, we can always count further.[23] This capacity for further division and thus for further counting is intrinsic to the Aristotelian notions of the infinitely small in length and the infinitely large in number. Aristotle's infinite is sometimes termed a "potential infinite" and contrasted with the "actual infinite" proposed by the Pythagoreans and by their modern counterparts, like Cantor. For present purposes, there is no need to examine the adequacy of Aristotle's account of the infinite.

My intention is to apply this description of infinite number to finite number. If it is possible to speak of numbering as infinite because a line segment can always be divided further and numbers abstracted from points of the division, then why not say that a finite number is derived from a finite number of divisions of a line? Thus, the things that are counted are the divisions of a line or points on a line. This is not, of course, to suggest that number is identical with these points on a line; what I am proposing is simply that number is abstracted from the points or the divisions of a line. This is entirely consistent with those texts where Aristotle speaks of the unit as what is indivisible in all ways, in contrast with solids, planes, lines, and points, which are more divisible (V.6.1016b23–31). He calls units "points without position" (XIV.8.1084b26–27; *An. Po.* I.27.87a35–37; 32.88a33–34). Units and, thus, numbers seem to be the last of a series of abstractions (cf. XI.12.1069a12–13; *Physics* V.3.227a27–32).[24]

On this account, though, number is not abstracted from a group of things, as in the abstractionist account. This is its major advantage, for we can see at a glance that the problems that undermine the two alternative accounts pose no difficulty for this one. Since numbers are attributes, and attributes belong to individual substances, numbers should be attributes of individual substances. It is now obvious how this is possible: we can ascribe six to Socrates because we can find six divisions in a line that is part of his shape or, to put is more perspicuously, Socrates is six because he has six parts; for example, head, arms, legs, and trunk. This number can be ascribed to Socrates because we can count his parts. Further, because this number belongs to Socrates, any attributes, that it may have, could—with suitable reference to the number—be ascribed to Socrates. We cannot say that Socrates is even—though we might wish to say that he odd—but we can say that he has an even number of parts. By recognizing that number is included in their definitions, and that the attributes of number are particular kinds of number, we can see that the attributes of numbers amount to attributes of the substances to which the numbers belong.[25]

The reason that all the attributes of mathematicals can be ascribed to the substance in which the mathematicals inhere is that the attributes of mathematicals invariably belong to the second type of per se attributes described in the *Posterior Analytics*, the attributes whose definition includes their subject (I.4.73a37–b3). Thus, to define odd or even we need to mention number. Each is a particular sort of number. But if number is itself an attribute of a substance, then any per se character that belongs to number would be just a further specification of that attribute that belongs to the substance, and so itself an attribute of the substance. If odd = number + some specification x, and number = sensible substance + some other specification y, then odd = sensible substance + $(x + y)$. On this analysis, what seems to be an attribute of an attribute turns out to be an attribute of a substance. From this more proper metaphysical perspective, number is not a substance that receives attributes but a sort of genus that includes numbers of various sorts—odd numbers, even numbers, etc.—all of which belong to substances, as does their genus.[26] In short, mathematical properties are not, strictly speaking, properties of quantities; they belong to *things* (*pragmata*) insofar as those things are lines, planes, or numbers (XIII.3.1078a5–9; a24–26; cf. 1077b17–20).

From this metaphysical perspective, mathematics is concerned with what we could think of as clusters of properties of things. The mathematician shows that in virtue of one of those properties, others in the cluster must belong to the substance. Through a convenient shorthand, mathematics can treat that property in virtue of which others in the cluster belong to the thing as a nature in which the others inhere.

I warned earlier that the solution to the two problems would be simple. My claim is merely that number is not primarily some plurality of substances, as everyone else supposes, but simply a plurality of parts of one substance. What the mathematician treats as attributes of this plurality of parts are properly attributes of the substance. With these simple moves both problems are easily solved.

Nevertheless, some uneasiness may be felt about this picture on at least two counts. First, there is the seeming arbitrariness of the divisions. Are we to count Socrates as six, as twenty-two (the number of fingers, toes, head, and trunk), or perhaps as the number of movable parts Socrates has? Since Socrates is a solid that contains infinitely divisible line segments, we could assign any number we wanted to Socrates. Moreover—this is the second problem—Socrates has these parts only potentially. In order to make these parts actual, we would have to make the actual divisions; we would need to chop Socrates up. It seems as though the parts must actually exist to ascribe number to Socrates, but the existence of actual parts—the actual division of Socrates—would make it impossible to ascribe number to Socrates. Once we actually divide Socrates, he ceases to be: there would remain no substance to which we could ascribe the number.

Both of these problems are easy to resolve. The actuality of the parts of Socrates cannot lie in Socrates, for were his parts actual, he would not be. Rather, the actuality of his parts lies in us and our process of abstraction. As I said earlier, by "abstraction" Aristotle does not mean the assembly of a plurality of entities and the distillation of some common character. What he usually means is the omission or *subtraction* of some characters. He describes our leaving aside our color, heaviness, and so forth and focusing attention on the mathematical character that remains, apparently the shape of a solid (XI.3.1061a28–35). This first step of abstraction is easy. We perform an additional abstraction when we separate the plane figures that constitute the surface of this solid and concentrate on only one of them. Here we are taking something that exists in the solid only potentially and actualizing it somehow through thought. Aristotle denies that the solid is made up of planes (*De Caelo* III.1.299a2–11), just as he denies that the line is made up of points (*Physics* IV.8.215b19; 11.220a18–21; VI.1.231a21–232a22; *G.C.* I.2.317a1–12). The points are in the line potentially; they become actual when the line in divided (*Met.* VII.13.1039a4–7). The division that takes place through abstraction is a division that is effected by thought. There is one place—unfortunately, only one place—that I know of where Aristotle explicitly corroborates this notion: it is his otherwise puzzling description of constructed lines in proofs (IX.9.1051.21–33). His examples are the proofs that the angles of a triangle equal two right angles and that the triangle inscribed in a semicircle must be a right triangle, both proofs that require the construction of an additional line.[27] Aristotle maintains that the line is there potentially (1051a29–30). This potential is actualized by our actually drawing the line; not, of course, actually drawing it in the sand or on the paper—these are not the proper subject matter of the proof—but actually drawing it in thought:

> Thus, it is clear that potential things are discovered by being brought into actuality. The cause of this is the fact that thinking is an actuality. And so it is by actuality that the potential becomes actual; and on account of this, people know by making [mathematical constructions], for actuality in respect of number is posterior in generation to potentiality. (1051a29–33)

At least some mathematical objects come to be actual by human agency.[28]

Consider Aristotle's claim that a line is infinitely divisible. This is obviously not an empirically supported contention: if we try to divide a line physically, we find fairly quickly that there are a finite number of divisions we can see, no matter how fine our pen point is.[29] The assertion of infinite divisibility could only rest on the conceptual grasp of the nature of a line. Past a certain point, divisibility of the line would only be possible in thought. Accordingly, when we abstract points on a line, there is no need to *physically* divide the line segment or the substance in which it resides. The actualization is effected by thought: the process of abstraction amounts to a conceptual actualization. Thus, by means of a process of abstraction we could arrive at numbers that belong to individuals; by virtue of abstraction these numbers would have actual existence even though the individuals to which they belong do not have actual parts. Aristotelian abstraction involves a kind of mental construction.[30] In one passage he links the existence of numbers to the activity of the soul: "If it were impossible that there be a [soul] counting, then it is impossible that there be something counted; so that it is clear that neither would there be number. For number is what was counted or what is countable" (*Physics* IV.14.223a22–25). It would scarcely be consistent for Aristotle to suppose that numbers exist only in the soul; they require the soul because they are actualized through abstraction performed by the intellect.

Once we see how abstraction works, the answer to the first problem I raised earlier, the problem of the arbitrariness of the numbers assigned to individuals, is easy to resolve: the numbers are arbitrary, but this is no problem. The process of abstracting that Aristotle describes does not properly belong to the discipline of mathematics; it is what the metaphysician or mathematician must do—consciously or unconsciously—in order to secure the existence of the subject matter.[31] That is to say, the mathematician does not *qua* mathematician deal with Socrates; he deals with the number or numbers that have somehow been abstracted from Socrates. For the discipline it matters little where these numbers came from; what matters is that they somehow be available.[32] Indeed, Aristotle, like Plato, distinguishes between the numbers as they exist in sensibles and the mathematical numbers.[33] That virtually any number could exist in nearly any individual substance is just another reason to insist on this distinction.

Indeed, the possibility of continued division enables us to account for the possibility of arithmetic operations and to understand a criticism that Aristotle directs against Plato. One of his many objections to the Platonic doctrine of the inassociable units—the doctrine that there is a form of twoness with two units and a form of threeness with three units and that the units of these and other such forms cannot be combined—is that it precludes mathematical operations on units. Even in the *Phaedo* Plato puzzles over these operations (96e–97b). He asks: How could some one and another one be brought together to make two? Are they not already two? Surely their position cannot make them two. How is it possible for Aristotle, a realist who insists that each number is an attribute of an individual, to admit mathematical operations? If six belongs to Socrates and three to some other substance, how could the two numbers be added or subtracted? If I have understood him correctly, Aristotle has an answer to such problems. We add three to six by further dividing some substance, through a process of abstraction. We subtract three from six by removing the divisions in thought. Mathematical operations do not involve a plurality *of substances* but a plurality of parts. This plurality inheres in some individual. In this way, what the mathematician does can be given a metaphysical legitimacy.[34]

The foregoing account of abstraction has a very important consequence that I want to note before proceeding further. One of the most persistent objections to Aristotle's philosophy of mathematics is that the objects of mathematics cannot be in sensibles as Aristotle thought because we perceive only imperfect shapes, figures, and so forth.[35] The real triangle, it is often said, could not be any triangle that we see because no surface that we sense is perfectly straight, no figure perfectly triangular. This is a Platonic point, and it is so obvious that Aristotle could not have missed it. If he is willing to endorse the existence of mathematicals in sensibles, he must think he has an answer: it is easy to reconstruct one from the account of abstraction that I have given. Again, let us start with Socrates and abstract away all sensible characteristics: what remains is an odd shape. By dividing this shape—again, the process must be mental—we could arrive at any solid figure we wish. The point is that once we recognize the character of a solid, we can see that it contains within itself an indefinite number of geometric figures at least potentially, just as—to use Aristotle's example—Hermes is in the stone potentially because the sculptor can make the stone into a statue of Hermes. Mathematicals are, Aristotle claims, "divisions of bodies" (III.5.1002a18–19): no surface is in a body more than any other (1002a20–24).[36] Mathematicians are not generally concerned with the solids that are abstracted immediately from sensible things but with the products of additional abstraction. These figures are in sensibles, even though we need to work to grasp them there. They are in sensibles not actually, but potentially or, as Aristotle puts it, materially (XIII.3.1078a29–31).[37]

Though it may not be apparent at first glance, my contention that Aristotle's mathematicals exist as potential parts of bodies is a way of preserving his realism in the face of his denial that mathematicals exist separately. Potential existence in bodies is real existence, and it is closely connected with the character of quantities. Consider a plane figure that would be studied in geometry. It cannot exist as an actuality in space apart from a body because all spatial actualities have three dimensions. The only spatial existence it could have would be as some sort of part of a body. This is true whether the figure is the surface of a body or the limit which divides the body into solid parts. Now any part exists potentially until it has been separated from the other parts (VII.13.1039a4–7). But the figure, whether surface or division of a solid, *cannot* be separated in space from the other parts. Hence, the figure could only exist in bodies potentially. The same could be said of all the other mathematicals, even mathematical solids, for solids cannot exist separately from some substance to which they belong. The mathematician treats as separate what is not separate: he treats as actual what exists only potentially. This much of my interpretation ought to be widely accepted.

The more controversial part is my idea that, despite the actualizing role of thinking, mathematicals really exist in sensibles and not just in mind. Since I require mind in order to bring them to actuality, it might seem that they really exist as mental entities. Aristotle would then seem to be some sort of constructivist. Though my interpretation highlights the constructive dimension of Aristotelian mathematics, I do not think that he is a constructivist in the modern sense. The key difference is his insistence that mathematicals have a spatial existence. Again, the way to understand what he says is to consider the character of quantities. Quantities can always be divided into other quantities (V.13.1020a10–11; 25.1023b12–15). In making and grasping these divisions, we are not constructing something new but coming to grips with forms that are (somehow) in the thing, exactly what we do when we grasp the form of any sensible thing. The lesser quantities are contained in the greater. (Academic doctrines of inassociable numbers deny this, and that is part of Aristotle's objection to them.) The case of volumes is the most obvious: a cubic centimeter is contained in the liter as a constituent. Likewise, when we recognize the triangle that is part of a square, we grasp something that is a constituent of the square. In general, the mental construction of a geometric object involves finding certain spatial parts of substances.

Similarly, the numbers that we can abstract from a substance are really there in the substance, at least potentially (cf. 1002a24–25). The substance is one; it is divided—at least in thought—so as to admit of numeric predicates. A number derived by abstracting all of the substance's other sensible characters possesses a unity by virtue of belonging to the same substance.

Aside from resolving the two difficulties mentioned earlier, this account of the abstraction of number has a major advantage for us: it is immune to a powerful criticism that Frege leveled against abstraction. Frege's argument goes like this: the whole notion of abstracting everything from a substance until it is a unit and then counting up other similar units is nonsense because once we remove all sensible characteristics from substances, they become indistinguishable and there is no possibility of having a plurality of them.[38] The solution, it seems to me, is to start with a single substance, divide it into parts, and then abstract out all but the sensible characteristics. The result is a plurality of units, and one unit is exactly like the others. But the units together belong to the substance from which they have been abstracted. Insofar as we grasp these units as parts of some single substance, it is possible to speak of a plurality of units. In other words, the units are identical by virtue of abstraction, but distinct insofar as they are parts of a whole. Thus, the Aristotelian process of abstraction never requires that we first generate identical units and then compare them; we generate the identical units from nonidentical parts. Only in virtue of the substance in which they inhere can we recognize these units as constituting a single number.[39]

Interestingly, the very reasoning that answers Frege is what I think Aristotle intends to use against Plato. I mentioned earlier that in several places Aristotle complains that Plato could not explain why the form-numbers are one. Typically, he does not tell us how he would solve this problem. It seems to me that Aristotle thinks the reason why Plato could not solve this problem is that he lacked precisely what Aristotle insists upon throughout, a substrate in which the units inhere. The Platonic form of twoness consists somehow of two units; the Aristotelian two consists of units that inhere in a substance. It is this substance from which the units have been abstracted but in which the units exist that gives unity to the many units. I propose that the principle of unity of numbers lies in the substrate to which the units belong, the substance from which they are abstracted.[40]

But if number belongs primarily to an individual substance, as I am proposing, then how are we to understand counting many substances? It is here that I think we need to turn to *Metaphysics* X.1. First, I remind you of a rather puzzling text in the *Physics* where Aristotle claims that the ten sheep and ten dogs are distinct tens (IV.14.224a2 ff.). No one seems to know quite what to do with this claim, but it plays beautifully into my account and helps to explain X.1 (see also XIV.1.1087b33–1088a14). There Aristotle defines one as "the first measure of a genus, especially of quantity from which it has been extended to the other [genera] (1052b16–20)." The one that is in the genus of quantity is just the one that belongs to each individual substance. It measures numbers, but it has also been extended to other genera. How? The extension is based upon an analogy: just as the unit measures numbers, individuals in other genera are used to count instances of the other genera (1052b20-34). Thus, a single horse is used to measure the genus of horse, for we count instances of this genus as so many horses. This number of horses stands to one horse as a particular number stands to one. Apparently, the number that measures the horses differs from number per se, the number that belongs to the genus of quantity. We can see right away why the ten of the dogs is not the same as the ten of the sheep: each is a count that is based upon a distinct measure. However, the two are analogous— because they are both analogous to the ten that belongs to the genus of quantity and is measured by the unit. That this latter ten should have its own nature apart from the sheep or any other particular being is a consequence of Aristotle's distinguishing a distinct categorial genus of quantity. The ten that exists in the genus of sheep is merely analogous to the ten that exists in the genus of quantity; and this latter is—if what I have said so far is correct—the number that belongs to an individual substance. If all this is right, then counting and many of our other uses of numbers are strictly derivative; they are based upon analogies drawn with the genus of number, that is, analogies with parts of individuals. The treatment of one in X.1 cannot define the number one, as Klein and others maintain; for it locates ones in other genera by reference to one in the genus of number. The discussion assumes that we *already* know what one in number is. The plain sense of Aristotle's discussion is that it is through an analogy with numeric one that we are able to find a unit with which we can count instances of other genera (1052b18–20, 1052b35–1053a2).

Side by side with cases where an instance of a genus is the unit by which other instances are counted, Aristotle mentions cases where the measures are more intensive: white is the measure of color because all colors (except black) are somehow composed of it; the quarter tone is the measure of tones because it is the smallest discernible difference and all tones consist of quarter tones. I was puzzled by these latter examples, apparently cases where very different sorts of measures are at work, until I saw their close connection with the genus of number. One is the measure of numbers because each number is composed of ones, of units. Apparently, the analogy by which one and number are extended to other genera is broader than it first appears. Not only is each instance of a genus countable as a one, but each can, at least sometimes, be measured by some primary instance in its genus. Thus, the instances of a particular genus stand to some primary instance of the genus as numbers stand to one: these instances can be measured internally by some primary instance of the genus (see X.2.1053b28–1054a9). Just how to understand this difficult doctrine is a question that, fortunately, need not concern us here. The main point to notice is that the measuring of a genus includes the measuring of individuals within the genus. The quantities measured in this way belong to individual instances of the genus. Thus, number somehow belongs to *each* instance of a genus—exactly what we would expect from Aristotle's stipulation that quantities be attributes of individuals.

It is important to realize that only quantities can be properly counted; we are always counting the units in a number. But through an analogy, we can use the numbers to count instances in a genus: we need to recognize that instances of a genus stand to some particular instance just as numbers stand to the unit. When Aristotle claims that it is from numbers that one has been extended to other genera, what I think he means is that we count instances of other genera by making an analogy between them and number. The instances of the genus are "that which is counted"; the number is "that by which we count" *(Physics* IV.11.219b6–9).

This explains how counting instances of other genera is possible, but it does not explain the ontological status of the particular count. Just what sort of being is the ten of the dogs? Where among Aristotle's categories does it fall? The only answer that I can see to this question is that the ten belongs to the categorial genus of relation. Just as being double some *x* or half of some *y* belongs to an individual substance as a relation—at least on Aristotle's ontology, so too belonging to a group with ten instances is a relation that happens to belong to each of the dogs. Ontologically, the ten of the dogs is quite different from the ten parts of a particular dog: the latter is a quantity, the former is a relation that is analogous to a quantity (X.1.1052b20–23).

But what evidence is there that Aristotle advances a doctrine of relational numbers? In his discussion of relations in V.15, Aristotle describes a class of relations in respect of number (1020b32–1021a14). All these relations are defined in terms of one, the "principle and measure of number" (1021a12–14). Though he mentions relations like double and half, it seems that any number stands in relation to one. Later, in X.6, Aristotle distinguishes two different ways that one and many are opposed as relatives:

> The one and the many in number are opposed as measure to measured, and these are opposed as relatives, relatives that are not per se. Elsewhere we have distinguished two ways that relatives are said: (1) as contraries, and (2) as knowledge is relative to the knowable, by something else's being said relative to it. (1056b32–1057a1)

The one stands opposed to the many in number as measure to what is measurable, and these are opposed as relatives, as non–per se relatives. . . . In one way, as has been said, these [many and one] are divisible and indivisible, while in another way they are relative as knowledge is to knowable, if plurality is number and one is a measure. (1057a14–17)

In the last clause, the one measures indefinite plurality; but determinate pluralities, that is, particular numbers, are apparently relatives in the other sense, the sense in which contraries are relatives. They are opposed as white things are opposed to something white and ones to one (1056b17–25). This reference to white and whites shows that Aristotle's concern here is not simply with relations that may be thought of as within the genus of quantity, but with numerical relations in other genera. Just as the white things are related to their measure, so too pluralities in other genera are defined through their relation to a measuring instance. In short, there should be no doubt that Aristotle regards some numbers as relatives. On the other hand, in another place, V.13, he treats numbers under the heading of "quantity," and there he proceeds differently. Though he claims that numbers are countable, he defines them as "what is potentially divisible into non-continuous parts" (V.13.1020a7–11; see also *Categories* 6.4b20–22; b25–26; 5a24–26). Both sorts of numbers are characterized by divisibility, but relational numbers are divisible in respect of some measure, whereas quantitative numbers are divisible per se (1020a14–17). While the former are ordinals, quantitative numbers are cardinals. It is entirely apt to speak of the quantitative numbers as standing in relations, and even as measurable by one (e.g. X.1.1052b20–23; 6.1057a3–4), but I suggest that these relations do not define quantitative numbers because they apply also to instances of other genera. In sum, there is no doubt that one is a measure, and that many things can be counted, but such counting cannot define the numbers that are objects of mathematics; at best, counting defines relational numbers.

All this shows that my interpretation is consistent with Aristotle's various claims about number. It is also consistent with some of the things Greek mathematicians said about numbers. It is well known that Greek mathematicians conceive of number in spatial terms. They speak of a number as square or oblong (e.g., *Theaetetus* 147e–148a). If my account of Aristotle is correct, then he shows us the conceptual basis for such talk: numbers are abstracted from individuals and thus, ultimately, from figures. I have spoken of the abstraction of numbers as proceeding from points or lines, but I do not see anything in Aristotle that confines him to abstraction from these, and it is easy to see that we could perform the abstraction of numbers from any solid. Aristotle's account is consistent with Greek mathematics in a way that Plato's is not.

Lack of Aristotelian texts precludes a conclusive determination of his mathematical ontology. But the interpretation that I propose here enables us to draw together some rather diverse and difficult remarks of Aristotle on numbers—remarks that I would be hard pressed to make sense of without it. At the same time, this account constitutes a philosophy of mathematics that is more substantial than anything else that has been ascribed to Aristotle and, I think, worth taking seriously.

In philosophy of mathematics Aristotle provides a common sense mixture of moderate realism and constructivism. He is a realist because he maintains that mathematical objects exist objectively as entities. But they exist in sensible substances: they exist mixed with other things. It is up to us to abstract them, and this process of abstraction has a kind of quasi-constructive character. It is we who divide the line into points and thus abstract numbers. The numbers are, though, really in things, at least potentially. It is all so simple that the only surprise is how so many careful thinkers could have missed it. But perhaps this is not so surprising after all. We are used to thinking of philosophy of mathematics as realistic (Gödel), formalistic (Hilbert), logistic (Russell), or intuitionistic (Brouwer). Aristotle fits squarely under none of these heads. At least part of the reason is that, unlike contemporary philosophers of mathematics, he is willing to divorce our coming to know mathematical objects and mathematical truths from the way that mathematicals exist in things.[41] Because for contemporary mathematicians truth is constituted by proof,[42] this distinction has become hard or impossible to draw. Still, it is well to remember that there is no intrinsic necessity to identify mathematical ontology and epistemology and that the burden of proof ought to lie with those modern philosophers who make the identification.

I began by noting that Aristotle is not usually thought to be much of a mathematician, and by pointing to his mathematical ontology as a probable reason for this. I have not given you any reasons for thinking that Aristotle was really a better mathematician than he is given credit for. For all we know he was held back by lack of talent, as most of us are. All that we can say is that if what I have proposed here is correct, then Aristotle was not held back from achievement in mathematics by his mathematical ontology.

Chapter 8

ARISTOTLE'S
ACCIDENTAL CAUSES

Aristotle's expression "accidental cause" (*aition kata* [or *ōs*] *sum-bebēkos*) (*Phys.* II.5.196b23–29; 6.198a5–9; *Met.* V.2.1013b34–1014a6; VI.2.1027a8; see also: V.30.1025a24–29; XI.8.1065a6–8) sounds like a contradiction. We usually think of an event as accidental just because it lacks a cause. In general, we suppose that events that were caused *had* to have occurred. A cause is a sufficient condition; it necessitates what it causes.[1] To be sure, we often speak of things and events as causes when they would not by themselves bring about an effect; we say, for example, that the matches were the cause of a house's burning, not mentioning the flammability of its materials, the presence of oxygen in the atmosphere, and so forth. We are also apt to refer to habits and predilections as causes of behavior, even though they do not always bring about their effects. But such "causes" do not shake our faith in the possibility of specifying sufficient causes for each event, for they fail to bring about their effects because they are merely partial causes. Were all the causal components present, the effect would inevitably, we continue to suppose, come about. To specify a complete cause we need only add the requisite conditions to the matches and the triggering circumstances to the habits, and these are possible to indicate, at least in principle if not always in fact. Such a complete cause would *always produce its effect.*

Though this classical picture has been challenged by a number of recent writers, the objections typically turn on the difficulty of finding and stating causal components. Armstrong, for example, contrasts "oaken laws" that do not necessitate an effect with necessitating "iron laws." But the difference is not one of principle; rather, events described by an "oaken law" have additional, possibly infinite, conditions not stated in the law.[2] Davidson argues that a cause can be designated even if it cannot be completely specified; the difficulty we have in specifying a cause concerns its description rather than the causal event.[3] Causal events do, he thinks, necessitate their effects; and events are governed by causal laws, even if our descriptions often fail to capture these laws. Thus, even though both Armstrong and Davidson question whether complete causes can be specified, neither denies that there are causal laws or that causes necessitate effects.

There are, however, some philosophers who do deny that causes must necessitate their effects. Richard Sorabji, for example, considers an unpredictable nucleus decaying and its product striking a detector, and he claims that the detector's response would be caused but not necessitated.[4] His point is apparently that we are willing to *call* certain things or events "causes" even though they do not necessitate effects. If we do speak this way, it may stem from imprecision: the nucleus is not always a cause, rather it is only a cause *when* it decays in a particular way and then it necessitates its effect. In any case, it is ironic that examples advanced by scientists to show the consequences of quantum mechanics unintuitive and troubling should be repeated by philosophers as examples of ordinary usage. The reason such examples are troubling is that the possibility of accidents has not been shown: how is it that in a world where each event seems to have a sufficient cause, there could be chance and lack of determinacy? Sorabji's example simply assumes that chance exists.

In short, though the term "cause" may have a wide usage, we continue to understand a cause to necessitate: always, provided it is complete, it acts to bring about its effect, and like causes produce like effects. The idea that a complete cause might be present and an effect not occur—that, for example, the matches, the wood, the right atmospheric conditions, etc. could all be present but the house still not burn—strikes us as impossible, indeed, as fantastic. Could this be what Aristotle means by an accidental cause? If so, it is extremely troubling.

Think of the standard Aristotelian examples of accidental events: someone on a trip to the marketplace might encounter a creditor, or he might not; though an acorn usually develops into an oak tree, it might not. Such examples are apt to seem akin to matches and predilections; surely, we suppose, it is possible to specify precisely circumstances in which one would always encounter a creditor or in which the acorn would always develop. But what would that mean? Suppose that under certain circumstances we would always encounter a creditor; when do those circumstances arise? We should be able to account for them with similar causes, and so forth. If we *could* spell out the circumstances under which the putatively accidental event would always occur, and, then, the circumstances under which those circumstances always occurred, and so forth, we could formulate a law that accounted for what was taken to be accidental. The accidental character of the event would vanish; what seemed to be merely accidental would turn out, on closer consideration, to be the product of causal laws. Or would it? Perhaps the retort will be made, "the event is still accidental because those causal circumstances may not occur." And when will they occur? "When certain other circumstances occur." And those circumstances will, in turn, be caused by others: we are back to a causal chain. But still the *connections* of circumstances can be spelled out in laws; they are not accidental. Hence, the causal circumstances that might not occur are not any of the intermediate circumstances; these causal circumstances could only be the initial conditions. Thus, following the reasoning of the retort, we see that it could only be a set of accidental initial conditions that qualify an event as accidental. But all initial conditions are accidental; a law predicts only what will happen in some hypothetical set of circumstances. No law posits a set of circumstances as existing. So if the accidental character of an event rests on accidental initial circumstances: *all* events will be accidental. Even if all this were so, *causes* would still not be accidental. A set of circumstances X would always cause circumstance Y; what would be accidental is whether X obtains. X itself would not be an accidental cause.

This reasoning shows that to maintain that some events are truly accidentally caused Aristotle would need to be committed to denying that it is always possible to provide a causal law. Further, the inability to supply a causal law could not always be due to our lack of knowledge of all pertinent circumstances and triggers or to other deficiencies on our part; it would need to be a matter of nature. A genuine accidental cause would require that exactly the same set of circumstances might in one case cause an event and in another not. But, surely, nature is not like that.

There is a parallel, if less immediately apparent problem with Aristotle's notion of accidental being (*to on kata sumbebēkos*). Either a thing exists or it does not exist. What could it mean to say that it exists accidentally, that it is an accidental being? Is it semi-real? A musical builder is out of the ordinary and this is a sign, Aristotle thinks, that it is an accidental being. But does the musical builder have less existence than the builder or is he any less a being? The standard Aristotelian answer is that the builder has a nature, whereas the musical builder does not. But just why not? Saying that accidents have no nature does not provide us with any insight into what accidents are unless we understand why they have no nature, but this is, of course, just as mysterious as the question of how there can be accidents.

In short, the existence of accidents and accidental causes is problematic. Moreover, these characteristically Aristotelian doctrines seem out of place even in his own philosophy. Typically, Aristotle accounts for phenomena by referring to some nature; references to natures are the modus vivendi of Aristotelian science. Why is it that there are some events and causes (accidents and accidental composites) that are not and cannot be subject to science? The aim of this chapter is to answer these questions.

I

The Aristotelian corpus contains three discussions of accidents. In *Metaphysics* V.30 Aristotle describes accidents (*ta sumbebēka*) as follows:

Something is said to be an accident if it belongs to a thing and is truly said of that thing, but not out of necessity nor for the most part; for example, if someone digging a hole for a plant found a treasure. This—finding the treasure—is an accident for the person digging the hole. . . . And someone who is musical might also be white. . . . (1025a14–20)

From this passage it is clear that Aristotle regards a coincidence like finding a treasure as the same sort of entity as being white or being musical. Finding a treasure is an attribute that could "belong" to the digger, just as being white or musical is an attribute that might "belong" to some person. The text goes on to assert that the cause of an accident is indefinite and indeterminate:

So that since there is something belonging to something else, and sometimes what belongs is of such a sort and at some place and at some time, but not because it is this or now or there, it will be accidental. Nothing, then, is a definite cause of the accident, except chance (*to tuchon*); and this is indeterminate. (1025a21–25)

As an example of an indefinite cause, Aristotle mentions someone's going to Aegina not because he decided to go there but because a storm blew him off course. "The accident has occurred or exists not *qua* itself, but *qua* other, for the storm was the cause of his coming not to the place he intended to go" (1025a28–30).

It is usually thought that Aristotle is wrong to give the same account for accidental attributes and accidental events.[5] The notion that events belong to substances is, to say the least, a strange one. Yet, in an ontology of substances and their attributes, how else could Aristotle understand an event? Just what type of entity could an event be?

What is perhaps more puzzling is the notion of an indeterminate cause. Aristotle's example of an indeterminate cause is the storm that blows someone off course. But surely the storm is determinate. It has a character or nature, just as any other entity. I propose that it is just in the context of this problem that we can understand Aristotle's insistence that the accident exists not *qua* itself but *qua* other. The storm is not an accident insofar as it is a storm. It is an accident insofar as the ship is concerned. It is an accident because it does not belong to the ship per se;[6] that is to say, the storm could not be demonstrated from the essence of the ship (cf. 1025a30–32). Something is accidental only in respect of something else, in respect of something of which it or the relation between it and the subject is the attribute.

In sum, two important points emerge from V.30: (1) accidental events are attributes of substances, and (2) they are accidents not in themselves but in respect of some other thing.

A second discussion of accidents occurs a bit later in the *Metaphysics*, at VI.2–3. Here Aristotle aims to show what accidental being is and that there can be no knowledge (science) of accidents (1026b3–5; 1027a26–28). One of his arguments turns on the infinity of accidents: The builder could not intentionally make all the accidents of the house he builds because these accidents are infinite (1026b4–10). It follows that the builder did not have knowledge of the accidents. The implicit assumption is that there cannot be knowledge of what is infinite. Also, it is assumed again that accidents belong to some nature. The person who knows the nature of the house, the builder, should be the one who knows its attributes; but because these attributes are infinite, the builder could not know the accidents, nor could anyone else.

Another argument for the unknowability of the accidents begins from the characterization of accidents as what are neither always nor for the most part. Since knowledge is of the universal (that is, it is of what is always the case), it is impossible to know what is accidental (1026b19–22).

These arguments presuppose the existence of accidents. Later on in the chapter, Aristotle advances what has been taken to be an argument for the existence of accidents: "So that, since not all things are or come to be from necessity or always, but most are for the most part, it is necessary that accidental being exist" (1027a8–11). In other words, the reason that there are accidents is, apparently, that there are things that are not always but only for the most part. The cases when these latter do not obtain are the accidents.[7] As an argument for the existence of accidents, this one begs the important question of why there are things that are only for the most part.

There are good reasons to doubt that this is Aristotle's argument. First, it is sandwiched by two other similar texts (1026b26–30; 1027a16–17), and in between them are examples of accidents. Second, the argument is introduced with "so that" (*hōste*), indicating that not the conclusion but the entire argument follows from those examples. It seems that Aristotle offers us a series of examples of things that are for the most part: If the weather is cold during the "dog days" of summer, this is accidental because the weather is always or usually stifling (1026b33–35). A man is pale accidentally, but not accidentally an animal because the former is not and the latter is always or for the most part (b35–37). The builder that heals is an accident (b37–27a2), as is the pastry maker who produces health (a3–5). In each case, a regular occurrence fails to occur or is altered. The existence of accidents follows from the occasional irregularity of particular types of events. It is not that the existence of what is for the most part tells us that there must always be accidents, but that the existence of accidents tells us that certain sorts of events are not necessary but for the most part. The argument is not conceptual and *a priori*, as usually supposed, but empirical and inductive.

Just because it is empirical, the argument seems inadequate. How do we know that there is not some more fundamental principle that determines when the dog days are cold or when a baker is also a healer? At the end of VI.2 Aristotle mentions the case of a remedy for fever that works every day except when there is a new moon: such a regularity would render it nonaccidental (1027a21–26). W. D. Ross sees in this passage evidence that Aristotle thinks that "nothing is objectively accidental," that "if we knew more about [events that present themselves as accidental] we should know that they obey laws of their own."[8] This cannot be Aristotle's view because it would mean that there is no truly accidental being. That Ross could make this claim testifies to the apparent inadequacy of Aristotle's argument proving the existence of accidents as well as to the difficulty we have in understanding the possibility of accidents.

The difficulties in formulating an adequate existence proof of accidents are deeply rooted in the Aristotelian conceptual scheme. In order to offer one Aristotle would need, according to the *Posterior Analytics* (II.2.90a5–11),[9] to show that their nature or essence exists. But an accident has no essence; that is why it is unknowable. Our quandary is that we are seeking the essential accidental, but an accident is nonessential. Indeed, if there is an essence of the accidental it is just to lack an essence. At first hearing this may well seem to be mere word play. Surely, we suppose, "accident" can have an essence even if no particular accident has an essence. But Aristotle does not think that words or phrases by themselves have essences; it is things that can have essences. Consequently, an essence of accidents would need to be a character that all accidental beings share—but, again, what they all have in common is not a character but the absence of a character. Given this characterization of accidents, it would seem that the way to prove their existence is to show that some things that have natures need not always occur. This is, I think, that aim of the examples that Aristotle advances here, cool weather in the dog days and the builder-doctor. Again, such examples do not still doubts about the existence of broader causes.

Metaphysics VI.3 looks to be a promising source of a proof that accidents exists, for it is often taken to contain an argument against determinism. In fact, though, Aristotle mentions as the absurd conclusion of a reductio argument that "all will be of necessity" (1027a31; b8–9). If this is just taken to be absurd, then Aristotle cannot be arguing against determinism. He is just assuming that determinism is wrong. Since determinism is wrong, a claim implying it must also be wrong; and so it is that Aristotle asserts that there are principles and causes that are and are not without being in the process of coming to be and being destroyed. Without such causes, all would be determined.

What is the reason that causes that come to be causes (over time) lead to determinism, and how is determinism avoided if there are causes that do not become causes through some process? Much has been made in the literature of the difficulty of VI.3.[10] I suggest that the source of the problems has been a widespread misinterpretation of one crucial line in the argument. Let me begin with the part of Aristotle's argument that is straightforward and well understood. Suppose that each cause comes to be a cause; that is, that each cause acts in time. Then, given the present conditions, we could work back to determine the past; and given a set of past conditions, we could determine the present. All would be necessary. But this is absurd. Thus, it seems that not all causes act in time. That is, not all causes act in time *if* this stipulation would somehow remove the threat of determinism. The difficult problem is how nontemporal causes could help us avoid determinism. Aristotle's example is the case of the person who eats spicy food, gets thirsty, goes to a well, and at the well encounters ruffians who kill him. Eating spicy food has, it would seem, caused his death. But this causal chain was not accidental, Aristotle suggests, but necessary (1027b4–9). And this is supposed to be absurd:

> All that will be must, of necessity, be; for example, that the living thing must die. . . . But whether [the living thing die] by disease or by violence is not yet [determined], but [it will be] if something [else] would come to be. Accordingly, it is clear that [the principles] are led as far as some principle [(or) led back to

some beginning], but this not into another. *This* is the principle of the fortuitous, and it has no other cause of its coming to be. (1027b8–14)

To what does "this" refer? What is the principle of the fortuitous? According to Pseudo-Alexander and, so far as I can tell, every other commentator who came after him, "this" refers to eating the spicy food.[11] The idea is that (as Ross puts it) once he eats the spicy food, "his fate is sealed . . . but before he eats it there is no condition from which it necessarily follows that he will eat it."[12] That is, the accident is taken to be what happens *before* a causal sequence is initiated. But, first, this is wrong because even after he ate the spicy food it is still not necessary that he meet a violent death: suppose he goes to another well or decides to endure his thirst? Second, it makes the whole chapter incoherent because the causes that do not come to be causes play no role in avoiding determinism. By reinterpreting the "this" we can skirt both problems. When Aristotle says that the principles "are led as far as some principle," he might mean that they "are led *back* to some beginning"—this is the way it is generally understood—or he could mean that they are led *in the other direction*, forward, to some terminus. This is the way I take the passage. The principle of the accident is not what happens *before* he eats the spicy food. It is an event that follows this: "But whether [the living thing die] by disease or by violence is not yet [determined], but [it will be] if something [else] would come to be." That is to say, the cause of the violent death is not only in the spicy food, but also in something else, the ruffians he encounters at the well. These ruffians *are* a cause of his death without *becoming* a cause of the death—neither he nor the ruffians contemplated or planned the encounter; it was not in the process of coming to be; it happened instantaneously at the moment when they met. Without such instantaneous encounters with other things, all would be necessitated.

This latter is precisely the point of Aristotle's claims that the principles are led as far as some principle "but this not into another" and that "it has no other cause of its coming to be." The "something else" that causes the man's death is the presence of the ruffians. There are, of course, causes for the ruffians being at the well and causes for these people being ruffians, but these causes operate over time, that is, they come to be causes; and they are not, Aristotle is saying, properly causes of the man's death. Rather the cause of death is simply the

encounter with the ruffians. This cause, unlike the others, is instantaneous: it is (*genetai*—1027b11) a cause without having come to be a
cause (cf. 1027a29–30). In other words, Aristotle is not denying that
the ruffians are caused or that the meeting at the well is caused: he is
denying that anything else that causes the ruffians causes the meeting. No cause of the ruffians' coming to be is a cause of the man's
death, for such causes produce regular and, thus, predictable, effects
over time. Were the death at the well the product of such causes, such
tragedies would always occur and all would be determined.

Let me recapitulate Aristotle's argument. First, he argues that if
all causes are in time, then all is necessary. Then, he shows how recognizing some causes that do not come to be causes enables us to
avoid this inference. That someone eating spicy food would need to
take a trip to a well could be predicted; that he would encounter ruffians who would kill him, could not because this encounter does not
come to be a cause but is a cause all at once.

In short, with one relatively simple change in the traditional
interpretation, VI.3 becomes cogent. There are two points to note: (1)
the accidental cause was in some other thing, and (2) the accidental
cause makes a significant difference to the event. Unlike the case of
the builder-doctor where the doctor's activities are not influenced by
his also being a builder, the accident described in VI.3 affects the outcome of the event.

The third discussion of accidents that I mentioned at the beginning appears in *Physics* II.4–7, Aristotle's treatment of fortune (*hē
tuchē*) and chance (*to automaton*). Aristotle's aim here is to steer a middle course between those philosophers who leave no room for accidents (II.4.195b36–196a24) and those who allow accidental causes too
much importance, philosophers who account for the universe by
chance (196a24–b7). In other words, Aristotle is not simply trying to
vindicate chance against necessity but also to vindicate natural causes
against chance. Once again, the force of his argument rests in large
part upon well-chosen examples: "it is not any chance thing that
comes from a given seed but an olive from one kind and a man from
another" (4.196a31–33); "the housebuilding ability is the cause of the
house per se, the white or the musical accidentally" (196b26–27;
197a14–15); and the man who, aiming to collect money, goes some-
place for some other reason, but while there is able to collect the
money (196b33–197a2).

To the discussions of accidents in the other passages, the *Physics*
adds a characterization in terms of final cause:

So that it is clear that of those things which come to be for the sake of something, whenever they do not come to be for the sake of what results and the cause is external, we say they are from chance. Things are from fortune if they are from chance and they come to be from the choices of beings capable of choice. (6.197b18–22)

The assumption is that nature *is* for the sake of something, as is craft. When the agency intrinsic to either does not attain that at which each aims, but does attain something else, we have chance or fortune. As Aristotle puts it elsewhere, chance is the privation of nature, fortune the privation of art *(Met.* XII.3.1070a6–9). Notice again that the cause of the chance event is external. Aristotle's troubling claim of purpose in nature is mitigated somewhat by his identification of formal, final, and efficient causes in natures (7.198a24–27), for the end sought by each nature is nothing other than the preservation of its own nature. Nevertheless, a teleology poses potential obstacles for an account of accidents; I shall return to them later.

The central argument in this section of the *Physics* shows that fortune and chance depend upon natures and mind:

Since [1] chance and fortune are causes of that of which mind or nature might have come to be the cause but which were caused from something accidentally, and since [2] nothing accidental is prior to what is per se, [3] it is clear that no accidental cause is prior to a per se cause. Thus, [4] chance and fortune are posterior to mind and nature. (6.198a5–10)

The crucial assumption is the second; it is also the most problematic. But we have already seen this idea at work in VI.2. An accidental event occurs when an event that is "for the most part" does not. It is just when the course dictated by nature does not obtain that there is an accident; when, for example, the dog days are cool. The accidental is the privation of nature or art; its cause is the absence of the cause at work in nature or in artistic production. In *Metaphysics* V.30 Aristotle assumes that a nature is a substrate in which an accidental attribute inheres. Here in *Physics* II we see that nature and art are efficient or formal causes. Chance and fortune can produce what nature and art do (198a23), even though they lack an essence. A pilot can guide the ship to harbor through art; fortuitous winds can achieve the same end by producing the same movements as the pilot would. By generating the movements that art would make, fortune produces what art could produce. The sequence of movements is a form or follows from a form, and this, I take it, is what is prior to fortune.

This last idea helps to explain why Aristotle asserts, immediately after the quoted passage, that even if chance is a cause of the universe, mind and nature are prior causes (198a10–13). Even if a number of particles could have somehow come together to form the universe, the sequence of events leading to the universe would be or follow from a form. Since (according to assumption [2] above) nature or art is prior to chance and fortune, there would need to be a natural or artistic process of universe formation that would precede any chance formation. This argument is plausible but not decisive because it lacks compelling assurance that the universe is not an exception to the assumed priority of nature. An earlier argument is more explicitly an appeal to plausibility: if the generation of animals and plants is "by nature," then processes that are even more regular and orderly—and what is more regular than the motions of the heavens?—should *a fortiori* be from nature or mind rather than chance (4.196a28–31; *P.A.* I.1.641b20–23). Neither argument is conclusive.

This brief discussion of Aristotle's three treatments of accidents is, therefore, disappointing. None contains a conclusive proof for the existence of accidents. Aristotle does not advance arguments that assuage our concern that there are general causes of all things, nor does he show adequately that all things could not have come about through chance.

II

Though Aristotle's treatments of accidents do not in themselves resolve the problem of concern here, several important points emerge from them that can form the basis for a reconstruction of his doctrine and for a consideration of interpretations of it advanced in the literature. First, his discussions make clear that there are two types of accidents. One type, the musical carpenter type, is not particularly troubling. The carpenter builds the house because he is a carpenter. His also being a musician does not prevent him exercising his knowledge of housebuilding, nor does it contribute to this knowledge. The conjunction of musical and carpenter in one person is benign in the sense that nothing results that cannot be explained by one or the other of these characters individually. But there is also second type of accident, the discovery of the buried treasure or the death at the well. Such accidental events cannot be explained by an individual character: it is not simply the man's eating spicy food that causes his death but the presence of ruffians at the well. This second group of accidents are anything but benign; they are causes of events.

Aristotle treats both types of accidents in the same way. Both are attributes of some nature. The musical carpenter consists of a nature with two unrelated attributes. The accidental event is also an attribute of some nature; thus, the discovery of the treasure belongs to the digger. Besides belonging to some substrate nature, an accident also presupposes nature in another way: it *could* have come about "by nature," as for instance if someone with the art of metal detection, rather than the digger, would find the treasure. Nevertheless, insofar as it is a genuine attribute of a nature, the accident is a real being.

These observations call into question some interpretations of accidents advanced in the literature. First, there is the widespread notion that Aristotle's accidents are events not yet explained. This is ultimately W. D. Ross's view.[13] He thinks that an event appears accidental because we do not know what its cause is; further study would show us that it has a cause. This approach trivializes the difference between Aristotle and modern science, as well as the difference between Aristotle and his philosophical contemporaries (cf. *Physics* II.4.195b36–196a24). Aristotle thinks that an accident is an irreducible type of being.

Ross's heirs are those who, perhaps following Davidson, declare that particular accidental events do have particular causes, but that their causal connections do not exemplify typical (or universal) patterns.[14] This has an advantage over Ross in that the accident is irreducible, but the view is at bottom the same: accidents have causes much as does everything else. The cause is taken to be accidental either by its rarity or, perhaps equivalently, by virtue of the way we know it. In either case, once it is said that all events, whether accidental or not, are caused, we seem—in the absence of some escape route—to be committed to determinism.

The opposite tendency in the literature is to maintain that accidents are uncaused. Sorabji ascribes this position to Aristotle because he reads *Metaphysics* VI.3 to maintain that some causes are not themselves caused.[15] Accidents are, in effect, the uncaused starting points of causal chains. (I have already argued for a different reading of VI.3.) What is uncaused, on Sorabji's account, is not a man's going to the well or the ruffians' going there, but the simultaneous occurrence of these two events, and it is uncaused because there is no connected explanation of them.[16] Sorabji thinks that Aristotle infers from the event's being uncaused that it must also be unnecessitated—in which case the existence of accidental events would refute determinism. But this inference is wrong, Sorabji maintains, because necessitating conditions, unlike explanations, do not require some connection: a coincidental event is necessitated provided only that there are sufficient conditions for each constituent.[17] Since, as we have seen, VI.3 does not argue against determinism but assumes that it is wrong, we can set aside Sorabji's criticism. The larger issue here is why Sorabji concludes, or thinks that Aristotle concludes, that there is no connected explanation. Though no connection is obvious, it would seem that if we traced the causes far enough back, if we could take a sufficiently comprehensive overview, or if we had more knowledge of the causes, we would indeed find a connection. Thus, a determinist would insist that, contrary to appearances, the man's going to the well and the ruf-. fians' also being there are ultimately connected and, thus, caused. The notion that there must be a cause for every event is a familiar one. What needs to be explained is what the world could be like in order that there be events without causes. Sorabji ignores the problem. Perhaps claims by contemporary physics that atomic decay is unpredictable and that subatomic events are probability distributions inure us to the difficulty of conceiving an uncaused event. Still, it does need to be explained just how accidents could be possible.

To summarize the positions advanced in the literature, either Aristotle thinks that accidents exist only because with our limited knowledge we are unable to explain all the causes or unable to arrive at a universal formula relating cause to effect, or he thinks that there are some events that are truly uncaused. Either way, Aristotle seems to be participating in one of the great debates in modern philosophy. It is just this seeming relevance of Aristotle to the problems of another era that ought to set us on our guard. Aristotle did not accept the dichotomy between the caused and the accidental that modern philosophers would come to see as obvious, for he speaks of accidents as caused. Aristotle's notion of an "accidental cause" has no place in the modern scheme; it neither causally necessitates nor fails to be a cause.[18] From this analysis we see that Aristotle's position on accidents is more radically different from our own than the literature would allow. Understanding that position is more difficult, but perhaps more rewarding.

III

In each of the three passages where Aristotle treats accidents, he contrasts them to natures, and he insists that natures are prior to accidents. Hence, to understand Aristotelian accidents, we need to understand Aristotelian natures. Moreover, since accidental causes, chance and fortune, are genuine causes in Aristotelian physics, the proper place to start to understand them is the key notion in Aristotelian physics, nature.

It is well known that Aristotle defines a nature (*phusis*) as an "internal principle of motion and rest" (*Physics* II.1.192b13–14; *Met.* V.4.1014b18–20). The things that have a nature are "animals, their parts, plants, and the simple bodies, such as earth, fire, air, and water" (*Phys.* II.1.192b9–11). Thus, dogs have a nature, as do the olive tree and human beings. Each nature is an essence that can be expressed by a definition. It is the task of an Aristotelian scientist to discover and demonstrate attributes that belong to instances of a nature in virtue of this essence; these are the nature's per se attributes. One of many Aristotelian examples of a per se attribute is respiration, "the alternate discharge and reentrance of heat and the inflow of air," (*P.A.* I.1.642a35–36, Oxford trans.). This is necessary for animals like us if they are to live. A scientific account of respiration should show why it belongs to animals in respect of their nature.

Interestingly, the example of respiration shows that an essential attribute of one nature can involve some other nature, such as that of air. That air should enter our lungs is an essential attribute of our nature. But the converse is not the case: that air should be breathed is not among the essential attributes of air. Nothing in the air's nature causes it to be present to animals; it is possible that an event such as an explosion would deprive animals of air. The point is that we have here two distinct entities, human beings and air, each with its own essential attributes. That these two beings interact is necessary for the survival of one of them, but not necessary for the other. Nothing in the nature of either accounts completely for the interaction. To put the problem more broadly, because the mode of explanation in Aristotelian science is to trace an attribute to a substance, it cannot fully account for the interactions of substances.[19] Human actions and characteristics are understood in terms of human nature; the motions and characteristics of air are understood through its nature. Whatever interactions there are between these two substances can only be understood as attributes of each of the substances

It is just Aristotle's inability to account fully for the interactions of substances that leaves open the possibility of accidents. That we breathe is an essential character of our nature, but in respect of its own nature the air has its own set of motions. We cannot account for the motions of the air by referring to our nature, nor can we account for our attributes by referring to the nature of air. Because the interaction of these two substances is a function of *both* natures, and because knowledge (for Aristotle) involves a single nature, the interaction escapes knowledge. Whether air is present to animals or whether it is absent, as for example in a death by drowning, can only be matter of chance. There is no one nature that could account for it.

The development of an acorn into an oak is one of most hackneyed examples of what Aristotelian physics takes to be a natural process. What is left out of the standard accounts is that most acorns never complete the process. Their internal principle of motion is blocked in the actualization of its potential by the absence of water or other necessities (cf. *Phys.* VIII.4.255b13–31), or, often, by the acorn's being eaten by squirrels. For the developing oak, the squirrel is simply an accident; the squirrel's eating the acorn cannot be accounted for from the nature of the oak. On the other hand, the squirrel itself is, in eating the acorn, acting according to its nature. The example shows vividly how an accident, the destruction of the acorn, results from the interaction of two beings each acting according to its own nature. This accident is not uncaused, nor is it an aberration from the orderly processes of nature. On the contrary, it is the result of those orderly processes. But because the principles of order reside in individual natures, the existence of an actual interaction of two natures can only be accidental.

With this analysis we can see the significance of Aristotle's claim in *Metaphysics* VI.3 that the cause of an accident is something else. Eating spicy food may cause a trip to the well, but the eater's death was caused by the ruffians he met at the well; it was caused by other natures that were not previously connected to him (cf. 1027b11–12). There is no way to account for the encounter from the nature of the person who ate the spicy food, from his decision to eat the food, or from his character as a spicy-food eater. Were it otherwise, the eating of spicy food would regularly result in death at the well and eating spicy food would be done for this purpose. Ross is right to say that we see here the intersection of different causal sequences. What he does not recognize is that the causal sequences spring from distinct natures and the connection between the sequences is inherently unexplainable.

In moving from physical natures to the spicy food example, I have implicitly extended the notion of nature to actions. But this is a thoroughly Aristotelian move: he is often concerned about the further attributes that follow from the presence of some particular attribute. The trip to the well follows from someone's eating spicy food, parallel to the way that breathing follows from our nature.

In short, it is just Aristotle's account of the physical world in terms of natures and their attributes that leaves open the possibility for accidents. Each thing acts according to its nature. In doing so, it can bump into something else acting according to its nature, and this interaction can alter the activities of either or both.

This alteration is contrary to nature in the sense that it does not spring from nature, and it can be so profound that one or more of the things that are interacting can lose its nature. Thus, the acorn can be eaten by the squirrel and lose its nature as an acorn. The possibility that accidents engender substantial change gives them significance in Aristotle's conceptual scheme. Other ancient philosophers who distinguish between different types of natures also have the possibility of accidents. Thus, the interaction between different Democritean atoms is accidental. But Democritean atoms never lose their natures. They are already the most fundamental of beings. Consequently, though in a way everything in a Democritean world is accidental, accidents make no difference to what is. On the other hand, because Aristotle identifies natures with something other than matter, his accidental interactions have the possibility of destroying natures into their matters. Thus, even though the Aristotelian account of substance is not required in order for there to be accidents, it is bound up with the particular account that Aristotle offers.

This broad account of the possibility of accidents needs to be refined. First, let us notice that what may seem to us as a single event, the encounter at the well or the squirrel's eating the acorn must be, for Aristotle, at least two events. There is an encounter that is an attribute of the eater—this is an accident that is caused by others, the ruffians—and there is an encounter that is an attribute of each ruffi-an—this too is an accident that is caused by another person, but here the other is the eater. Analyzing the event into at least two attributes is not intuitive, but it solves an otherwise sticky problem. Let's go back to the squirrel-acorn example. The eating of the acorn turns out to be two events. Eating the acorn is an attribute of the squirrel, whereas being eaten by a squirrel is an attribute of the acorn. The for-mer is apparently an essential attribute; the latter is accidental. Now suppose for the moment that Aristotle went with intuition and claimed that the squirrel's eating the acorn was one event. He would need to say that whether or not that event is accidental depends on our perspective or the way that we describe the event. This claim—which is, in fact, endorsed by some scholars—really undermines the doctrine of accidental being, for it implies that a being is not intrinsi-cally accidental. On the other hand, in understanding what seems to be a single event as attributes of two different substances, Aristotle is able to distinguish intrinsically accidental beings, such as the attribute of the acorn, from essential beings, such as the attribute of the squir-rel. Accidental beings and accidental causes are not simply a matter of our perspective but stem from the activities of natural beings.

Second, it is apparent from this analysis that individuals are accidental. It would seem to be the nature of the squirrel to eat acorns, but that this particular squirrel eats this particular acorn is due to chance. The only way it could be otherwise would be if we could trace the particular acorn to the nature of the squirrel. But a particular squirrel's finding a particular acorn does not follow from the nature of the squirrel—whether that nature is a nature that all squirrels share or a nature that belongs to a single squirrel. Aristotle's science is not sufficiently refined to explain which individuals are encountered. There is, thus, a sense in which the eating of the acorn is accidental for both squirrel and acorn: the meeting of these two individuals could not be predicted from either nature. It is just in this way that the acci-dental event resembles accidental attributes such as the paleness of Socrates: both individuality and accidental attribute spring not from form (or nature) but from matter, the individuating principle of the composite (cf. *Met.* X.9.1058a29–b25). Thus, eating acorns is a per se attribute of a squirrel, but eating this particular acorn, though it is an instance of this attribute, is an accidental attribute that may belong to some squirrel at a particular time. This is not to say that the eating of an acorn is both accidental and essential, depending on some subjective perspective; it is always both. In just the same way the growth and development of a child is both by nature and accidental: the sequence of stages and their approximate length is by nature, whether one stage is slightly shorter or longer is accidental because it is due to something besides the nature, such as matter or external circumstances.

Third, we see from all this why the notion that an accident is somehow uncaused is misleading. There is no reason to think that there is a suspension of causal mechanisms. On the contrary, accidents arise from a *plurality* of causes. Nevertheless, it is tempting to say that such an accident is uncaused because there is no one cause that can account for the accident, that is, because there is no overarching cause that coordinates the operation of the plurality of causes. The causes of the encounter at the well are the victim's eating spicy food and the presence of the ruffians, but the simultaneous operation of these causes is, apparently, uncaused. However, as we have just seen, this accidental encounter is not one event but a group of attributes that belong to those present at the encounter. Each of these attributes has a cause, a substance different from the one to which it belongs. What we are missing is a cause that causes the different substances to cause the accident. Without such a cause, there is no way to determine when or even if this accidental attribute will belong to a substance. But this is true of all interactions of substances. Aristotle's causes are substances, particular entities. The only way to explain the interaction of two substances would be through some *other substance.* But then we would have the problem of explaining the interaction of these *three* substances. Clearly, introducing a fourth substance for this purpose would lead us again into the same problem, and so on indefinitely. There seems to be no alternative other than to accept that interactions of multiple substances can have no cause other than themselves. In a metaphysics of substance and attribute any interaction between a plurality of substances must have a plurality of causes. Multiple causes and, thus, accidents are intrinsic to the Aristotelian conceptual scheme.

In short, accidents arise because there are a plurality of different substances. In acting in accordance with its own nature, each substance interacts with other substances, and the interaction is, to some extent, accidental because it is caused by the other substance.

We can see from the foregoing examples that there are various ways in which there are a plurality of causes. The pluralities are:

species-species plurality (such as the squirrel-acorn interaction), individual-individual (the particular squirrel and the particular acorn, or even two squirrels), and individual-species (Socrates—both his form and his matter—and the species human being). (It is because of the last of these pluralities that pale can be an accidental attribute of Socrates.) Though Aristotle does recognize principles prior to these pluralities, he has no principle that accounts for their interaction. Thus, his accidents are irreducible.

Aristotle's inability to account for interactions of substances and the consequent irreducibility of accidents is troubling on several counts. First, some interactions between species are regular, and Aristotle assumes that what is regular is essential: "all that is by nature comes to be either always or for the most part, but none of what is from fortune or chance" (*Physics* II.8.198b34–36). Hence, regular interactions between different types of substances should not be accidental. Second, since nature acts for the sake of an end (199b7–8), what occurs always or for the most part should be for the sake of some end. Though Aristotle declares that the rain does not fall for the sake of the crops but of necessity (198b18–19), the usual occurrence of rainfall during the season when it benefits the crops suggests that rain does fall for the sake of the crops. In this case, the interaction between the two substances would not be accidental. Third, Aristotle sometimes arranges species hierarchically as if they formed a structure: in the *Metaphysics* he speaks of all species as constituting a whole ordered by first principles, the unmoved movers, in the way that an army is ordered by a general (XII.10.1075a11–15); in the *Politics* he speaks of a hierarchy of species that exist for the sake of man (I.8.1256b7–26).[20] The existence of such suprageneric ontological structures would seem to imply, again, that species-species interactions are nonaccidental.

Aristotle's response to all three difficulties would be the same. He would rely on a point made earlier: just as respiration, an interaction of an animal and air, is an essential attribute of the animal, so too all the above interactions are essential attributes. He does not express this general point, but we can see that he holds this view by looking closely at his treatments of species interactions and hierarchies. Thus, in *Physics* II.8 Aristotle insists that the regular occurrence of rain and heat in particular seasons indicates that they are due to a nature and for the sake of an end (198b36–199a8). Yet he does not say they are for the sake of the corn; and when he explains the summer heat and winter rain in the *Meteorologica* (I.9), he makes no mention of the corn.

Their end is their own nature or that of the region of the heavens in which they occur. Similarly, Aristotle's examples of things for the sake of ends are attributes of a nature; such as, the leaves of a plant and the web of a spider (199a23–30). In all these cases, the end is the nature or part of the nature in which the attribute inheres—not another nature. That the rain must fall for the corn to grow is a necessary attribute of the corn. It is not an attribute of the rain. Because the rain and the crops are not governed by the same nature, the crops could be lost due to the rains' not falling or falling at the wrong time. And the rains might not come in winter or—what is apparently part of the same phenomenon—the dog days might not be hot because of some other factors (*Met.* VI.2.1026b33–1027a2). Thus, accidents are compatible with Aristotle's teleology (cf. *Physics* II.8.199a33–b7).

Aristotle's assertion of a teleology in nature conjures visions of a benevolent force guiding and shaping the interactions of substances. But this picture is not only unaristotelian and unwarranted, it is hard to reconcile with accidental failures: is the guiding force insufficiently powerful? are the accidents for the sake of some other end, such as moral enlightenment? Such problems vanish and Aristotle's teleology becomes benign once we see that interactions for the sake of some nature are *attributes of that nature*. Each thing acts in accordance with its own nature, and in doing so is necessarily bound up with other natures. The interactions of Aristotle's natures resemble Chinese handcuffs: each nature is bound to others not by some external force but through its own natural activities.

The point is that interactions between substances cannot themselves be substances. If they were, then the constituents of those interactions would lose *their* substantial character. If an interaction cannot be a substance, then it can only be an attribute of some substance. Analogously, Aristotle's hierarchical arrangement of substances cannot itself be a substance—were it so, its constituents could not be substances. It too can only be an attribute. The hierarchy of the *Politics* is clearly an attribute of man. Perhaps there would be different hierarchies were the attributes of other substances at issue.

In sum, neither the regularity of species-species interactions, the teleology of nature, nor the hierarchical relations of substances can seriously challenge my account of accidents. All represent Aristotle's attempts to deal with what must be pressing problems for a philosophy that relies on particular substances to provide the principles of explanation. It should be apparent that despite claims of teleology and hierarchical structures, Aristotle is unable to account fully for the interactions of substances.

To put this problem in relief, let us mention in passing two ways that other philosophers account for interactions. Thomas Aquinas denies the existence of accidents by tracing the interactions of substances to God.[21] He admits that there are no *natural* causes of interactions, but he posits divine causality to fill this hole. Since the divine cause is supremely good, it follows that interactions are arranged to promote goodness: every seeming accident is for the best. Spinoza, on the other hand, avoids the problem by arguing that there can only be one substance.[22] Then there can be no possibility of accidental interactions, for there *is* no other substance to cause an effect that cannot be accounted for from the nature of the affected substance. Since there is only one substance, every event can only be accounted for from its nature. Thus, nothing is accidental.

The contrast between Aristotle, Aquinas, and Spinoza on substance and accidents serves to highlight the really profound metaphysical problem inherent in Aristotle's treatment: what is the metaphysical status of interactions of substances? If each substance is intelligible in its own right, then there could be no way to grasp the interactions of a plurality of substances. On the other hand, in order to account for the interaction we would need to give up the independent intelligibility of what interacts (by, for example, making them parts of some larger whole or introducing some transcendent cause). Neither alternative is without its difficulties. Nor is it satisfactory to blithely ignore the problem by insisting that the universe is governed by laws of nature: in what do those laws inhere? If we answer this question by saying that the laws inhere in nature or the world, then we are implicitly making the world one thing—that is, we are adopting the Spinozistic approach. This is, I think, what most modern thinkers have unwittingly done; the Spinozistic picture underlies scientific claims of force fields that extend throughout space. In consequence, individuals come to be thought of as mere aberrations in the field, and this, in turn, along with other consequences, is incompatible with the existence of ethics.

IV

Some of Aristotle's paradigmatic examples of accidents reappear in the *Nicomachean Ethics*: "The involuntary comes to be either through force or ignorance. Force is that whose principle is outside, the principles being of such a sort that the one acting or suffering contributes nothing in it; for example, if the wind carries him away somewhere or if men overpower him" (III.1.1109b35–1110a4). The ship that was blown off course and the spicy-food eater who was overpowered at the well were acted upon involuntarily. Because these actions are involuntary, they fall outside of the scope of ethics. No one can be praised or blamed for involuntary actions, for their "principle is outside" (also: 1110b1–3; b15–17). This is just the way that Aristotle characterizes accidents (*Met*. VI.3.1027b10–11), as we saw. The very same accidents that are not in accordance with nature appear, at first glance, antithetical to ethics as well.

But besides these totally involuntary actions, Aristotle recognizes a class of mixed actions. In the former the subject makes no contribution to the action, in the latter she can make some partial contribution. The passenger on that ship blown off course in the storm may need to decide whether or not to throw the cargo overboard (1110a8–11). Since for this decision she can be praised or blamed, it is closer to a voluntary decision than to an involuntary one. Perhaps Aristotle has in mind the ruffians at the well when he suggests that one should be praised for refusing to do certain ignoble actions even at the threat of death (1110a26–b1). In any case, by only slightly varying the same examples, Aristotle illustrates accidents, involuntary actions, and voluntary actions. For our purposes what is especially interesting is that accidents have not only the potential to prevent ethical acts, but some of them also constitute the *occasions for* ethical actions. The storm and the encounter at the well provide opportunities for noble action, opportunities that would not be present in a world where all went according to plan or where all went according to law.

Accidents thus provide part of an Aristotelian answer to the contemporary problem of free will. This is not a problem that Aristotle actually confronts, and we can see why. As it is usually formulated, the problem of free will is as follows: since, as science tells us, every event in the world is governed by laws, even my will must be subject to laws and so determined; but since I am aware of the ability to make choices and since ethics depends upon the possibility of free choice, my will must be free. Thus formulated, the problem of free will is precisely parallel to the problem of accidental causes. Just as laws of nature seem to preclude the possibility of accidents, so too they seem to exclude free will. I suggest that Aristotle skirts both problems in the same way. Both spring from a dichotomy between the caused (or necessary) and the uncaused. Aristotle's treatment of accidents shows us that this is a false dichotomy, for events can be caused but not yet necessary. This *tertium quid* depends on the existence of a plurality of natures, each of which operates causally. One nature experiences an accidental event when some other nature impacts upon it. The event was caused by the second nature, but it is not necessary because it follows from neither nature. Almost exactly the same circumstances obtain in moral action. We have a plurality of individual agents, and each acts in accordance with its own choices. The actions of one agent will have consequences for other agents. Thus, one agent will experience an event that does not follow from its nature or its choices. This event could afford the agent no possibility for further choice, as, for example, the storm that forces the ship to sail to Aegina. But, often, accidental events provide new circumstances for making choices, such as, whether to throw the cargo overboard. So long as the principle of choice is in the individual agent, and so long as it is exercised, her action is free despite the external circumstances that occasion it, and to say that the action is free is not to deny that it is caused. To put the point another way, external circumstances need not deprive an agent of the possibility of choice; most often they provide opportunities for new choices for the agent, choices that that agent comes to by assessing both the circumstances and his own nature. Because choices depend upon a conjunction of multiple causes and upon the agent's assessment of these causes, they are unpredictable.

The reason that Aristotle has no problems with the existence of either accidents or free will is that he does not have the type of laws that are at work in modern philosophy. Modern laws are supposed to apply universally to all things. Insofar as all events are law-governed, everything seems to be determined. Aristotle has no such universal laws. His causal principles are particular natures. Events occur because of these natures, but there are no principles that fix the interaction of natures. Philosophers like Kant who insist on the dichotomy between the law-governed and the free, argue for the existence of freedom by marking out a realm that is, somehow, not subject to physical causality. Aristotle has no need of such a device because physical causality is not governed by universal law. Such a physical world does not prevent ethical action; it occasions it. The activity of choice is simply part of the exercise of reason, something that we do by nature but also because of circumstances' being what they are.

This relatively simple solution to the problem of free will is not likely to gain many adherents, for it requires that we renounce scientific laws as they have come to be used in modern science. The value of this solution lies rather in its making clear the metaphysical assumptions that generate the problem of free will and, likewise, the Aristotelian metaphysical assumptions that make it a non-problem for him. We can see that, from his metaphysical perspective, ethical interactions closely resemble physical interactions. In each case, different things, each acting in accordance with their own nature, impact upon each other, creating something that is not caused by one nature alone. This interaction could be purely physical, such as the ship being buffeted by the storm, or the product of human choice, such as the encounter at the well. In either case, the accident provides, at least sometimes, an occasion for action by the nature that experiences it.

Whether the action is from nature or from choice, it is, Aristotle maintains, equally teleological: both sorts of action aim to preserve the agent. The difference between physics and ethics lies in the nature from which action springs and which it aims to preserve. Physically, I am defined by my capacity for reason, but insofar as this capacity is realized in a developed faculty for some rational or moral endeavor, I possess a "second nature." Since this second nature has come about through the exercise of the faculties, with each further use of the faculties, I continue to have a formative effect upon it. Thus it is that moral choices reimpact upon the agent. All this adds a level of complexity to human interactions that is not present in physical interactions. No wonder Aristotle decries the possibility of attaining in ethics and politics the same sort of precision to be found in physics (N.E. I.3.1094b10–27).

Some of the choices that we make for ourselves, such as the choice to pursue knowledge or to develop a talent for music, seem to be purely self-related and so independent of chance. However, even such choices require a set of other choices about external things, such as books, musical instruments, and teachers. And since these external things, no matter how integral to my functioning, are governed by their own natures, even my most self–related decisions depend upon the existence and availability of other things, that is, they depend upon chance and fortune. It follows immediately that chance and fortune must play some role in happiness.

The role of external goods in human life and happiness has exercised recent commentators.[23] I treated this problem in an earlier chapter,[24] and there is no need to return to it here. My point is just that the discussion in the preceding paragraphs shows the problem to be a consequence of Aristotelian metaphysics. Other entities are necessary for proper human functioning but they have natures of their own. Hence, the possession of those other entities cannot be accounted for by human ethical nature alone. In contrast, the usual view is that Aristotle accords external goods a role in human happiness because he accepts common opinion. There is no question that Aristotle uses conflicting common opinions to pose problems or that his solutions preserve important common opinions (*N.E.* I.8.1098b–12; b23–29). However, even if there were no common opinions about external goods, he would need to include them in his account of happiness; and his treatment of them is a consequence of his notion that natures are the principles and causes of everything else and that, consequently, no additional principles can account for interactions among natures. That Aristotle assimilates the problem of external goods to the problem of accidents is clear from a passage in the *Politics*.

> He is happy and blessed through none of the external goods, but through himself alone and being of such a nature, since good fortune must differ from happiness in these respects. For chance and fortune are the cause of goods external to the soul; but nothing from fortune or through fortune is the cause of justice or moderation. (VII.1.1323b24–29)

Since external goods are caused by fortune, the reason for them lies in the account of fortune in the *Physics*. In short, Aristotle's position on external goods follows from metaphysical considerations. That this solution accords with common opinion is a strong point in its favor, but to try to understand it solely through common opinion is to miss what supports it.

Trying to understand the doctrine of external goods in terms of common opinion has other detrimental consequences as well. External goods are "for the sake of the soul"; they are by nature (VII.1.1323b18–21). To live in a good state, to have good friends, and to have sufficient food are not accidents, but essential attributes of human beings. What needs to be explained is not why we have them but why they are lacking. In other words, it is not—as common opinion would have it—the presence of external goods that is accidental but their absence. In this respect, external goods are exactly parallel to physical accidents. That a tree needs water is part of its nature; the drought that deprives it of water is contrary to nature, accidental. No matter how favorable the circumstances in which the tree grows, its path of development and its quality as a tree have been set by nature. Analogously, the external goods can cause harm if we are accidentally deprived of them, but their capacity to benefit us is only limited because our happiness depends fundamentally upon our nature (1323a36–b18). Commentators who have tried to understand external goods through common opinion have overemphasized their importance for happiness, perhaps because the desire for them is so widespread. Due attention to Aristotle's discussion of accidents and natures is the proper antidote.

V

We have seen that the existence of accidents both physical and ethical, arises from a certain type of metaphysics. It is a metaphysics that locates principles in individual natures and identifies individuals with their activities. Because the activities of one individual can interfere with and impede those of another, an accident is possible. Because Aristotle defines a thing by its activities, something impeded by an accident risks losing its nature. In this way, accidents can have a profound impact on the world.

Finally, we can return to the problem broached at the beginning of the chapter. How is it possible for there to be accidental causes? Does Aristotle really maintain that the same circumstances might in one case generate an effect and in another not? How could it not be possible to find a law correlating cause and effect? The answers to these questions should now be apparent. The simple answer to the puzzle of how one set of events might at one time generate an effect and at another time not is that there is never two instances of precisely the same set of events. In every case the accidents are indefinitely many, and these accidents could be responsible for, could generate, or impede an effect. We would like to spell out all the relevant circumstances and relate them together in some formula: whenever I eat spicy food and go to the well and there are ruffians there, etc. But Aristotle's notion is that this is impossible precisely because there are an indefinite number of circumstances that might intervene. Think of the causes of the house burning: we first mention of the match, then, with a bit of prodding the air, the flammability of the material, proximity, etc. Aristotle would deny that we can spell out the "etc." There are any number of ways the necessary ingredients for a fire can be hindered: a sudden cramp might prevent my arm from lighting the match, yesterday's rain prevents the house from catching fire, and so on. Our first impulse is to add these to the list of specifications stated in the law. But if there are an infinite number of specifications, the case of two events exactly alike, one of which causes the effect while the other does not, could never arise. The two events could be alike in essence and they could share many attributes, but they could not have exactly the same infinite set of attributes—for one thing they would exist in different places or at different times.[25] We could think hypothetically of two things exactly alike, but any two real things would have an indefinite number of accidental attributes and so an indefinite number of ways in which they could generate or fail to generate their effect.

Why could there be an infinite number of accidental attributes and why does it make such a difference? The reason is that there are an indefinite number of natures and those natures interact with each other. Essential attributes come from a thing's own nature, accidental attributes come to a thing from other things or from other parts of itself (such as its matter). Because there are an indefinite number of other natures and other instances of natures, there are an indefinite number of accidental attributes. Given the Aristotelian metaphysics there could not be laws that excluded accidents. Modern physics has had to alter metaphysics drastically to be able to speak of laws. It contains its own problems, but they are metaphysical problems and the notion that somehow modern science has escaped metaphysics is only a myth. Understanding the metaphysics that makes accidents necessary also enables us to understand the metaphysics that renders them impossible. Most importantly, both alternatives help us to come to grips with the problem of interaction. My account of Aristotle's accidents has not aimed to make his metaphysics attractive, but to elucidate a metaphysical problem that gives rise to it.

Part III

REASON

The last two papers in the metaphysics section show the limitations of the applicability of actuality. Some of what we ordinarily think of as entities, such as types of interactions and numbers of items in groups, cannot be full actualities. They lack proper forms. Now, the extent to which things can be said to have forms is also the extent to which they are intelligible: actuality is not merely a principle of things in the world, but a principle of intelligibility. Hence, entities that lack forms are unintelligible. To recognize that certain things lack forms and intelligibility is to recognize that the world is not fully intelligible.

There are two radical challenges to this position. The first denies all intelligibility to the world; the second insists on the complete intelligibility of the world. The former was the path of Nietzsche; the latter that of Hegel. This final part explores these two alternatives.

The Nietzschean denial of intelligibility is best understood by considering art. This is the sphere where he applied his position and where his views, or views like his, have had the greatest impact. I contend that experimentalism in contemporary art manifests a Nietzschean view of art, but that this is an untenable view. If the denial of rationality fails even in the sphere of art, then *a fortiori* it should be rejected in other spheres as well.

To motivate the Hegelian notion of complete rationality, the final chapter considers a problem in Aristotelian metaphysics, whether the differentia belongs to the genus it differentiates. This is part of the more general problem of how to make a distinction without using terms or entities that themselves fall under the distinction. Because there are arguments both for and against the inclusion of the differentia, the problem seems intractable. However, Hegel shows the problem can be solved if the differentia of the genus is just the genus itself. This requires that the genus be a type of process which it itself can undergo. Though it is a significant modification of the Aristotelian scheme, the self-differentiating genus still exemplifies the activity that is its own end, the actuality that Aristotle identifies as form. The difference is that this activity belongs solely to reason. Some such extension of Aristotle's self-reflexive scheme is necessary if all is to be intelligible.

Chapter 9

IS CREATIVITY GOOD?

Nietzsche's *Thus Spoke Zarathustra* defies rational analysis. It is not merely that Nietzsche justifies his position by caustic polemics nor that the exact details of this position are often difficult to determine. A more important deterrent to coming to grips with Nietzsche is his forthright denial that his position is rational. The existence of an objective rational order is one of the illusions of Platonism, in Nietzsche's eyes a fundamental mistake of western culture. How then can we assess Nietzsche? In this chapter I shall counterpose Nietzsche's views to the influence they or similar views have had. I shall argue that the two are at odds and that the discrepancy ought to cause us to reflect seriously on the validity of Nietzsche's position.

I

The first step is to advance an interpretation of *Zarathustra*. The central message in this work is, I contend, the importance of creativity. Much of Nietzsche's criticism of others boils down to their failure

185

to be creative. Creativity is always the creation of new values, and it always involves the overthrow of old values. Not only great art but also the laws laid down by the great law-givers are examples of creating values. But creativity is more than the triumph of an individual over other individuals; it is inevitably a self-struggle and self-overcoming. Much of *Zarathustra* examines the psychological struggle of the creator; and, as an account of the agony and isolation inherent in creation, the work is probably on good ground.

The creative act is always intrinsically good. Its value does not depend on either what it produces or what it overthrows. Creativity is good for its own sake. Accordingly, creative acts are neither motivated by reason nor evaluated by rational standards. It follows that creativity is not a rational process in any sense. According to Nietzsche it stems from the will and is a manifestation of the will to power. Reason is merely a tool of the will, an instrument through which the will may realize its objective of setting a law for itself. Further, there is no objective standard by which to judge a creative act. One law or one work of art is not objectively superior to another. Ultimately creativity is arbitrary: newness is valuable for its own sake. And the creative process is neither logical deduction nor rational analysis; it is play.[1]

There are, though, creations that Nietzsche does value more than others. They are the creations that "affirm life." Nietzsche sometimes uses "affirmation of life" as a kind of standard by which to compare creative acts. All creativity is worthwhile, but creativity that is life-affirming is most valuable. It is this standard that accounts for Nietzsche's occasionally ambiguous attitude to Christianity. On one hand, he recognizes Christianity as the product of a creative act, and he has some genuine respect for its saints (e.g. *Zara.* I.2). On the other, Christianity denies life and thus fails to be truly creative. Sometimes it appears that to affirm life is to affirm physical desire over asceticism, but Nietzsche regards physical desire as merely a manifestation of a will to power—and probably a perverse one at that. It is not merely that Christianity advocates asceticism, but rather that Christianity views the world as already created by God. "God is dead," Nietzsche claims, and at least one of the meanings of this enigmatic slogan is that it is up to man to create himself. "Affirmation of life" looks like it might be helpful in characterizing which creative acts are intrinsically worthwhile, but when Nietzsche cashes it out, to affirm life amounts to being creative, and the reason that Christianity does not affirm life is that it does not promote creativity. If what seemed to be a standard by which to evaluate the creativity of a work boils down only to creativity, then there is no standard by which to judge whether a work is creative except its newness. The value that Nietzsche himself creates is creativity, and Christianity is at once an example of this value and an example of the denial of this value.

Zarathustra is the story of the creation of creativity as a new value. The key to the story is, I think, the discussion of the three transformations that appears at the beginning of the first part: the camel, the lion, and the child.[2] These three transformations are the three steps on the path to being a creator. Each step represents an act that is part of the process of creativity. The three steps also correspond to the first three parts of Zarathustra. (The fourth part was conceived and written later and deals with the disciples of Zarathustra rather than the self-struggle of the creator that is the theme of the first three parts.) The first transformation is called the camel: the potential creator takes a burden on his back and grows strong in the process. The burden that Zarathustra takes on his back in the first part is the recognition of the subjective character of values. This comes out most clearly in the section titled "A Thousand and One Aims." There Nietzsche explains how each lawgiver gives a value to his people and how the value is opposite to the character of the people. Here, as throughout the first part, all the values are on a par. None is intrinsically better or worse, and Zarathustra shows respect even for priests because they too are creators of value. In the second part, though, the part that Nietzsche calls the lion, Zarathustra does reject the values of others. Following the characterization of the lion in the first chapter of the first part, the second part shows Zarathustra destroying old values. It is here that he rejects Christianity and Platonism on the ground that they amount to a denial of life. As I explained earlier, they are creative, at least initially, but they stifle further creativity. In the second part values are embodied in individuals, and they are termed "virtues." This new perspective allows Nietzsche to play off the values people profess with the will that really motivates them (see the section titled "The Virtuous Ones"). The third part shows Zarathustra becoming a child: he stops "nay-saying" to the old values and introduces new values for himself. The title of the crucial section refers to the "new tablets." Here Nietzsche makes explicit the new value that Zarathustra has been pursuing all along, creativity.

Creativity is the ultimate value because it is what underlies all the other values. What all values share in common and what makes them values is just that they have been posited as values. Indeed, since Nietzsche rejects objective reality and objective standards of judgment and evaluation, the only character that could mark a value as such is just the fact of its being accepted as a value: a value is a value because someone has created it as a value. And the act of creation of a value is nothing more than the removal of the old value and its replacement with something new. All past creators valued creativity, for it was implicit in their creation of their own values. Nevertheless, by focusing on particular creations, they missed the significance of creativity itself. Nietzsche's idea is that the creative act is itself independently valuable quite apart from anything it may produce. The new value that Nietzsche creates is creativity.

Creativity is, however, an extremely problematic value. Any single act of creation is inevitably the creation of something in particular; it is the creation of a particular value. However, this new creation tends to stifle further creativity. For further creativity to occur, this new value must be overthrown, and something still newer put in its place; and then the process repeated. Creativity could only be realized as a value if what was once new is constantly overthrown and replaced with something else. The difficulty of realizing this value is apparent in the fourth section of *Zarathustra* and also in the much discussed doctrine of "eternal return." As I see it, the idea of eternal return has no connection with anything mystical. Instead, Nietzsche refers to the perpetual need for the creator to face the same obstacles to creation—the creator is always confronted with the same self to overcome. To embrace creativity wholeheartedly as a value, someone would have to create constantly and thus to be constantly overcoming himself. (Nietzsche uses the word *ewig* like the Greek word *aei*; a translation better than "eternal return" might be "constant return.") The real creator can never rest content with a past creation. He needs constantly to throw down his own past and do something new. True creativity is a constant struggle.

This description ought to make creativity seem like a goal nearly impossible to attain, as indeed it is—not simply because of our human limitations, but because the creator is constantly destroying himself. Nevertheless, this is the picture that Nietzsche paints of Zarathustra.

II

How can we assess these ideas? One way to evaluate the thought of a philosopher is to consider the consequences of putting it into practice. In Nietzsche's case, this approach is encouraged by the influence Nietzsche's ideas and ideas like his have had in the recent history of art. References to Nietzsche abound in artists of the stature of Mahler and Thomas Mann, and in a host of lesser ones as well. Nietzsche's work had a direct and profound influence on important artistic innovators, but there is no need to assess the precise extent of his historical influence here. For the sake of evaluating Nietzsche's ideas in practice, we need only see that the artistic climate of the recent past reflects what art would be like if it had been influenced by Nietzsche.

Somehow, we have come to value creativity. The fact is that we commonly praise artists and art works by calling them creative. To someone with a classical education—someone such as Nietzsche— praise of creativity is striking. For the Greeks innovation is not a virtue. When Aristotle introduces his unmoved movers in *Metaphysics* XII, he carefully points out that they do not really differ from what the ancients meant when they spoke of the gods. Plato often ascribes his new ideas to the Egyptians or to mythical figures from the past. Both presume that the veil of antiquity renders an idea more credible. Similarly, through the Middle Ages, philosophers buried their own ideas in commentaries on other thinkers. Only in the modern period are philosophers so bold as to declare their work original. The reason is not simply immodesty. Rather, only in the modern period do progress, improvement, and creativity come to be desirable.

This endorsement of creativity as a value does not, by itself, reflect a Nietzschean perspective. The ideal of scientific progress dates from the seventeenth century, at least. The Romantics virtually deified creativity. Thus, the classical perspective had been abandoned long before Nietzsche. Yet his endorsement of creativity as a value still represents a new departure, and it is the Nietzschean ideal that has come to seem synonymous with creativity today. The idea of scientific progress—at least, as it was understood until recently—is the idea of a gradual, cumulative development of knowledge. The type of change which Nietzsche advocates is neither gradual nor cumulative. There is no preparation for the *Übermensch*; he emerges out of nowhere. He does not represent a development of what is implicit in the past; the *Übermensch* is a radically new beginning.

Nor is Nietzsche's creativity at all like the creativity so valued by Romantics. For them poetic creativity is a cognition of the highest reality.[3] In contrast, Nietzsche denies that there is any reality apart from creation. The existence of an objective reality presumed by the Romantics is just what Nietzsche is so anxious to deny. Unlike the Romantics, Nietzsche praised newness for its own sake.

The Romantics are, though, similar to Nietzsche in that they share the common heritage of Kant's "Copernican Revolution." Kant attempted to explain reality and experience as constructs of our faculties, and the faculty of imagination plays an important role in this construction. The Romantics extended Kant: if the imagination is responsible for the construction of the objects of experience, then the pure use of it will yield some special insight into these objects. Consequently, the use of the imagination to create a poem can lead us to a cognitive insight into truth. The creativity praised by the Romantics has to do with the veridical use of our faculties.

Nietzsche too regards experience as constructed by our faculties, but he differs from the Romantics in denying that there is a canonical use of the faculties. Reference to his own categorical imperative (*Genealogy of Morals*, Preface § 3) indicates that Nietzsche regards reason as peculiar to the individual rather than a faculty that legislates categorically for all. He agrees with Kant that we lay down laws for ourselves, but there is no reason to think that either everyone does this or that the laws will be the same in each case. Further, there is no standard by which we could distinguish the better from the worse. No particular laws are intrinsically good except perhaps for the law to be creative. Nothing intrinsically good or real exists apart from creation. Thus, all creation is valuable for its own sake. Whatever is new is good. Unlike Kant, Nietzsche regards reason as a tool of the will rather than its end.

Once we understand Nietzsche's view of creativity, we can easily see just how pervasive it has become. Its influence is particularly important in the fine arts. As I said, there is no need to consider the historical question of the extent to which Nietzsche was actually responsible for artistic developments. My point is that the conception and execution of art in this century reflects what Nietzsche would regard as desirable tendencies. A central characteristic of twentieth century art is the profusion of artistic genres. This creation of new genres and the stylistic transformations that constantly occur within genres go under the general name of "experimentalism." Unlike scientific experimentation which aims to test a hypothesis and thereby to advance knowledge, artistic experimentation seems to have no goal besides the production of something new and different. Although justifications were generally advanced for the various "avant garde" artistic movements of the present century, it is difficult to escape the conclusion that their newness is, in large measure, the source of their attraction.

For example, assessing the cubist movement, a recent writer denies that it can be defined in terms of style, subject matter, techniques, or aesthetic theory; but, he insists, an essential element in it is its dismissal of old conventions and the endorsement of the new.[4] A like emphasis on newness for its own sake is manifest in serial music, abstract expressionism, and current choreography to mention merely a few areas. While Duchamp's submission of a urinal for an art exhibit was an attempt to mock traditional views of art, his view of the arbitrariness of the standards by which art is evaluated has become the accepted standard: art is what we decide to take as art. On this basis his urinal qualifies as art, not because of any intrinsic beauty it may have, but because it was a new idea to call a urinal art. There is no standard by which to judge a work of art except its newness, and we often hear art praised for the novelty of its effect. In short, newness is an important quality in contemporary art, both as an element in art and as a standard for judgment.

A second characteristic of contemporary art is its manifest antirationalism. For one, the emphasis on design and formal elements that predominates in painting is intended to appeal to the viewer's nonrational faculties. Much current art contains no rationally cognizable content. In addition, the antirationalism of much current art is apparent in its thematic content. Much sculpture and music has centered on sexual themes. Perhaps more characteristic are the colored rectangles that Hans Hofmann painted in the fifties. These paintings were not only intended to appeal to our primal color instincts, simple colors constituted their entire content. Similarly, current music, both popular and serious, often attempts to express the disharmony and disorder of the world and to elicit nonrational emotions. As we might expect of any sweeping statement about twentieth century art, there are many exceptions and qualifications. Still, it remains that antirationalism is an important characteristic of much contemporary art.

Whatever the historical sources of this antirationalism are, it accurately reflects Nietzsche's subordination or denial of the rational. He maintains that the source of creativity is the irrational will. Reason is at best a reflection of the will and its tool. If the source and end of art lie in the will, then art has no need of rational content. What we see in much art are Nietzsche's views concretely applied. Of course, it would be an exaggeration to lay all artistic antirationalism at Nietzsche's feet. The association of art and creativity and the denial of any rational ground for the evaluation of art can be seen in thinkers as diverse as Heidegger and the logical positivists. Many artists must be credited with making these values manifest by creating new art forms; some, such as Wagner, even preceding Nietzsche. Again, I think that Nietzsche was directly responsible for a good deal of artistic antirationalism: no thinker or artist explicitly propounds creativity as a value in the way that he does. But my goal here is not to show Nietzsche's historical influence. My point is that the experimentalism and antirationalism that we find in art are concrete counterparts of a Nietzschean view of creativity as a value. It is difficult to understand them in any other way. The particular art works produced by artists, our evaluation of those works by assessing their creativity, and our consciousness of value in art all reflect, to a large extent, the thought of Nietzsche.

III

To some extent the artistic movements to which I have been alluding are passé. Experimentalism has gone by the boards, and artists are returning to more traditional modes of expression. Composers are writing in keys; painters are depicting recognizable figures. We are now in a position to assess the artistic experimentalism of the recent past and also, if what I have said is correct, to assess Nietzsche as well.

Surveying the history of art in this past century, we can easily see that, by and large, experimentalism has failed. To be sure, individual artists have done much fine work, but much that has been touted as art falls far short of the mark. Despite an historically large number of practicing artists this century has produced little that rivals the work of past masters. How could any artist thoroughly master a style if every few years he or she needed to alter it in order to remain creative? The return to more conventional styles in recent art signals an abandonment of experimentalism as an ideal.

For our purposes the interesting point is not the failure itself but the reason for it and what this reason, in turn, tells us about Nietzsche. If my analysis is correct, recent views of art reflect Nietzschean ideas. However, the notion that art reflects philosophy is inconsistent with and antithetical to the Nietzschean philosophy. Nietzsche thinks that the source of creativity lies in a will to power. Paradoxically, his own philosophy, or one like it, seems to have had just the impact that he denies philosophy can have. A Nietzschean philosophy has impelled artistic experimentalism and the dynamic development of new styles so important in this century. Yet it is a tenet of that philosophy that this development has some nonrational source. If Nietzsche were correct, then his philosophy should never have had the influence that it apparently did have. Ironically, in denying the importance of reason and thought for art, Nietzsche has exercised a tremendous influence over art—influence that no philosopher should have had if Nietzsche were right in denying the importance of reason in art. While Nietzsche says that reason and philosophy do not generate art, *his* philosophy has, in fact, generated art.

This accusation of contradiction could be disputed on two counts. First, I have spoken of art as reflecting a Nietzschean philosophy, but I have not shown any historical link between Nietzsche and artistic experimentation. Even if there is a contradiction here it need not be a criticism of Nietzsche. Second, even if artistic experimentation does reflect Nietzsche's philosophy, it does not follow that Nietzsche or any other philosopher was the cause of the experimentation, for Nietzsche could simply have been accurately describing the way that artists operate. Perhaps artists have simply followed views that they had arrived at on nonphilosophical grounds.

Neither of these objections holds. The historical link is unnecessary for my analysis. All that I need for my point is the agreement that if Nietzsche had influenced artists, they would have experimented with artistic styles in the way that twentieth-century artists actually did experiment with them. My claim is that recent art illustrates the contradiction in Nietzsche's philosophy because something like it *would* result from putting Nietzsche's philosophy into practice.

Purists will cringe at the suggestion that art ever reflects philosophy. If either exerts an influence on the other, they will say, it is the artists who influence the philosophers. Along this line, it would be

Nietzsche who derived his inspiration from art: he was merely describing what artists do or were doing at the time. After all, he had before him the recent innovations of Wagner as well as the innovations of Beethoven. Was he not merely pointing out the path of all great musicians and artists? To suggest this line of thought is to fail to see Nietzsche's own innovation. His observation that the great artists have bent the "rules" to serve their own ends is accurate and perceptive. But we are not simply talking about change here. Nietzsche's philosophy sanctions constant change, that is, experimentalism. This is an ideal that he could not have derived from the solely from the activities of artists because there are no examples of great artists who exhibit this ideal: there neither were nor are any *Übermenschen*. Nietzsche sees himself as the herald of something unprecedented. As I have said, it makes no difference whether he had the impact he sought. Nor is it necessary for me to trace current trends in art to other philosophers. Artists themselves have conceived of their goal as creativity. Those who have written about their work—as surprisingly many have done—have made claims similar to Nietzsche's. We find artists themselves trying to explain and to justify the nonrational basis of their work. We face in these writings self-contradictory attempts to offer reasons for the denial of reason.

This same contradiction is even more forcefully apparent in individual works of art. As I have mentioned, much of the art of this century is openly irrational both in content and appeal. Yet artists justify such works with elaborate theories, and the work can be appreciated only by an audience that is acquainted with those theories. A case in point is Hans Hofmann's colored blocks. These paintings are exhibited along with Hofmann's description of his theory of primal color perceptions. Without some knowledge of what he was trying to do here, someone viewing these paintings would be at a total loss. Similarly, Arthur Danto once imagined an artist illustrating Newton's first and third laws with two identical paintings, each consisting of a line drawn horizontally a third up from the bottom of the canvas.[5] While the paintings were identical, the artist understood each of them differently. For Hofmann's work and for Danto's imaginary artist, artistic appreciation depends on grasping something that is independent of the painting. While the art work itself is irrational, it depends on an artistic theory for its success and intelligibility. The denial of reason is illusory: works of art can omit reason only because their creators presuppose a particular type of rational understanding in their audience. The result, of course, is not works that appeal to primitive color instincts or to anything else that is primitive, but extremely esoteric works that can be appreciated only by those who either understand the artist's theories or who are so familiar with similar theories that they can grasp the theory from a few examples. The hope that paintings such as Hofmann's colored blocks can help us to return to a primitive way of viewing the world before we were corrupted by modern society is ill-founded. There is no evidence to suppose that human beings ever perceived the world in this way. What we find in these theories and the works influenced by them is a sophisticated intellectual analysis masquerading as primitive instinct. In short, the claim of contemporary art to spring from a source other than reason is a sham. Current art draws heavily on the results of reason. Artists omit reason because their thinking leads them to the conclusion that reason is unimportant. Their art works are inconsistent in both denying and presupposing reason.

The problem with the artistic experimentation of the present century is that it has proceeded under false pretenses. Creative work has often been motivated by rational considerations but those rational considerations have led to the conclusion that reason ought not to be present in a work of art. The result has been work that is esoteric, but also work that has not been truly creative. Much of what passes for innovation is merely a slight variation on old ideas. Many artists have claimed that art should appeal to something primitive. Whether this primitive reality is color, as Hofmann thinks, or lines or shapes or something else, the idea remains the same. It is merely another manifestation of the Nietzschean idea that reason is subsidiary and that reality lies somewhere else.

While I have said a good deal about art in this chapter, my primary aim is assess Nietzsche's view of creativity. Is creativity a value that ought to be sought in all circumstances? Is it always good? It is trite to say that what is new and different is not necessarily better. Moreover, Nietzsche's response to this is that nothing is better than anything else because there is no standard of judgment. Nevertheless, what emerges from my look at Nietzsche's views in practice is that much which purports to be new is not truly new at all. The only way to judge newness accurately is to grasp the ideas involved. But these ideas are hidden or excluded from contemporary art. The result is that contemporary art de-emphasizes exactly what it needs to reach its goal, reason. Only on the basis of carefully thought out views of art can a particular art work be genuinely innovative. The key to creativity is reason.

After this analysis, the same type of problem is apparent in Nietzsche's own work. On the one hand, Nietzsche belittles reason and advances the will to power as the source of creativity. Yet Nietzsche's own work is carefully and rigorously thought through. Despite the appearance of irrationality, in *Zarathustra* especially, Nietzsche has rational arguments for the subsidiary role of reason. Further, what makes creativity a truly plausible value is Nietzsche's criticisms of other values, his insight that this value is implicit in all other values, and the argument that we cannot specify anything else that makes a value creative except its newness. Despite what Nietzsche suggests, the idea that creativity is the ultimate value is a rational insight. Yet the effect of this reasoning is to deny the power and efficacy of reason. Nietzsche's work is much like the art that he helped to spawn: it denies its own rational basis and in so doing becomes esoteric

What makes Nietzsche's work creative is his ideas; and, to the extent that current art is creative, it is due to its ideas. Where Nietzsche goes wrong is in neglecting the importance of thinking in creativity. The reasons that his ideas seem to be so untenable in practice is that those who have embraced them have flitted from style to style and that, in denying the importance of thinking, they remove thought from the sphere of creativity. In espousing constant creativity, they restrict creativity. Moreover, reason is the only faculty that can approach the constant creativity that is Nietzsche's ultimate goal. Creativity without reason is an illusion. To conclude, creativity is good only when it springs from reason.

Chapter 10

HEGEL AND THE PROBLEM OF THE DIFFERENTIA

It is a minor scandal that, with the extensive treatment the works of Aristotle have received, particularly of late, virtually nothing has been said of a blatant and devastating difficulty with his account of the categories. The problem is the status of the differentia. It is a problem that I think Hegel recognized and resolved or at least thought he resolved, and in this chapter I will explore what I take to be his solution and some of its ramifications.

I

First I need to explain the problem. It is this: It is only possible to divide all things into categories if we can expound the characteristics of the categories, if, that is, the categories can be characterized and distinguished from each other. What is supposed to do this is the differentia or, in English, the difference. An entity is defined by giving its genus and its differentia, but because Aristotle maintains that each differentia falls under only a single genus (and under the genera that include this genus), a definition really requires only the differentia.[1] The question immediately arises as to whether this differentia belongs to the genus it differentiates. The answer Aristotle ordinarily gives is no, and the reason is easy to see. If the differentia did belong to the genus, then it would not explain why the genus differed from other genera nor would it characterize the instances of the genus. If X, Y, and Z are the instances of genus A, then X does not distinguish X, Y, and Z from instances of other genera, nor does it characterize Y and Z. So the differentia must not belong to the genus it differentiates. Indeed, the differentia must belong to some entirely distinct category.[2] But we then face the disastrous prospect that that entity by which A differs from other genera and by which A is what it is, that entity which is what A is most of all, is not A. Since, for example, the differentia of human being, a particular type of rationality, seems to be a quality, the nature of a particular substance, namely, us, is not to be a substance, but to be a quality, rationality.

Aristotle must have been aware of the problem because in a peculiar passage in the *Categories* he denies that the differentia of a particular substance is "in" the substance, as its attributes are; it is rather "said of" the substance, a characterization implying that the differentia belongs to the category of substance (5.3a21–28). Nearly all current scholars dismiss this claim of Aristotle as some sort of slip, for it would undermine the neat distinction of categorial genera.[3] Unfortunately, these scholars do not explain how to avoid the problem: they do not even see the problem. Perhaps, part of this blindness arises from the unfortunate tendency to read the *Categories* either as a work about language or about the application of language to things. The presumption is that problems at the linguistic level are somehow subjective and not ontologically troublesome, but Aristotle's categories are classes of things based upon the natures of those things. Surely the nature that marks off the category ought to belong to the category, and so Aristotle implies that the differentia does belong to the category. The alternative to Aristotle's solution is worse. If a differentia did not belong to the category it differentiates, the nature of each category would lie in some other category.

In placing differentiae within the categories they differentiate, Aristotle broadens the notion of a category to include not only the entities that are properly instances of the categories but also the essential characteristics these have.[4] These two, instances and characteristics, somehow belong to the same category, but they have a different status. We are supposed to be able to recognize qualities in the genus of substance. But if they are in the genus of substance how could they be qualities? How could we know them as both? Despite the advantages this solution has over the alternative, it is scarcely more intelligible. The problem undermines the existence of independent categories.

As I said, current philosophers have not been concerned with this problem, and my account of it is apt to strike some as artificial. I suggest that the reason for this is that most current philosophers have embraced what I shall call one-level distinctions. When Gilbert Ryle distinguishes "knowing how" from "knowing that" he offers his readers a set of examples.[5] Somehow we are supposed to see what he means from these examples or, rather, to see how to use the distinction. I suppose that those who distinguish categories in this way do not regard the distinction as anything that could be—or should be— intelligible: these are just ways we speak, and it is impossible to find more than family resemblances among distinct instances of knowing that, etc. But I think there is really an element of self-deception here. In recognizing how to make the distinction we do grasp characteristic features. The problem is that these features have a different ontological status from the entities being distinguished. What do family members have in common?, Wittgenstein once asked.[6] Not the nose, the lips, or hair color—not anything that we could see. As long as we insist that the common feature be perceptible, we need to reject universals and intelligible categories. But we understand the family by its common heritage. This is nothing we can see or point to, but it is the way that we grasp what they have in common. Heritage is an implicit second level that allows us to characterize the first level: it is what all the instances of the family share. Without this second level it would be impossible to speak of the difficulties of finding characteristics possessed in common by what is marked out by the first level, the family in this case. The reason this case seemed paradoxical to Wittgenstein is that the principle of intelligibility, the second level, does not resemble the items on the first level.

These reflections allow us to see the problem of the differentia as a general problem with all distinctions. To distinguish A from B we need another distinction C and D: A differs from B because A is C and B is D. But C and D must be what A and B are, yet they must also differ from them; they are on another level. Moreover, since the issue is the intelligibility of A and B, it is natural to posit C and D as ideas or other intelligible entities, but this leads to the problem that what characterizes A is something of an entirely distinct ontological order, an idea.

The differentia is the principle of intelligibility of a category. The Aristotelian approach to the categories locates this principle of intelligibility in things. That is, C and D belong to the same ontological order as A and B. The differentiae of the categories are instances of the categories. As I said, the consequences are devastating, but there is a certain consistency and appeal here because Aristotle tries to include among the categories everything that is. In contrast, if what I said about Ryle and Wittgenstein is correct, their C and D are thoughts that are somehow excluded from the things we can usefully talk about. As a result, the thoughts are themselves unintelligible.

Exactly the opposite of this latter approach is the Kantian treatment of the categories. Kant characterizes his categories through judgments. They represent the various ways we can combine subject and predicate. Here all the reflections concern the intelligible content. The intuited matter, A and B in the previous scheme, even though it comes to be subsumed under an intelligible category, remains unintelligible.

Kant's criticism of Aristotle is that his derivation of the categories is unsystematic, a deficiency Kant aimed to remedy by deriving the categories from the logical functions of judgment. If we ask Kant, What really characterizes each category?, it seems to me that his answer is not ultimately better than that of many current philosophers. He takes his start from the "technical distinctions recognized by logicians" B 96),[7] and his categories are read off of these judgments. Aside from examples, the only remarks that Kant has by way of characterization concern the derivation of the three entries that fall under each of the four main headings. But insofar as these can be derived from each other, or from some other scheme, the three are not independent categories at all. There are, then, really four Kantian categories, and they are not justified by anything else. These categories *have* no differentiae; but they *are* the differentiae of intuited things.

The Kantian categories apply to intuition; they are that by which we think intuition. Because these categories belong to thought, Kant faced the enormous problem of justifying their application to something that is unthought. This problem is tackled in the "Transcendental Deduction" of the first *Critique*, and Kant's conclusion, that we need thought in order to have an intuition, seems to undermine the problem rather than resolve it. But I will not examine Kant's reasoning here. Instead, I want to return to my original question, what is it that characterizes or differentiates entities within a single category? For Kant the entities are intuitions and the differentiae are concepts or what he terms "categories." The concepts or differentiae are supposed to be just what the intuitions are, but they cannot be because they belong to a distinct faculty.[8] The attempt to differentiate intuitions by means of concepts must fail because intuitions and concepts remain ontologically distinct. Even if we know A as a C, we recognize that A is not C and that C fails to characterize it. In speaking of A, we are conceptualizing it and thus treating it as something that is thought. Paradoxically, Kant maintains that we need to think through the nature of A to recognize it as something that cannot be thought. Something is terribly wrong with categories that both are what they apply to and cannot be what they apply to.

II

All this serves to motivate and to justify the Hegelian categories, for these categories avoid the problem. As we saw, the problem of the differentia is the problem of making categorial distinctions intelligible. So long as the principle of intelligibility lies either within the things or in some distinct realm, such as thought, the problem will persist. Hegel's move is to locate both the categories and their differentiae within thought. We can see that this is a kind of response to Kant, for it eliminates the difficulty posed by intuitive content that is thought and yet remains unthought. At the same time, Hegel's move seems tautological: surely the only way for us to consider categories is through thought; so any category or distinction that we recognize must ultimately be a category of thought. Recognizing that all our experience must somehow be thought provides Hegel with an answer to the most persistent of objections to his *Logic*, the notion that in recognizing the rationality of all things, Hegel has left out something of paramount significance, the objectivity of things. Any attempts that we could make to speak of things must treat these things as the objects of our thoughts. Even in insisting that they *cannot* be known we betray our knowledge of them and we recognize their intelligibility.

Hegel's conception of the categories is the mirror image of Aristotle's. While Aristotle's categories are things that are distinguished by things, Hegel's are thoughts distinguished by thoughts. That is to say, both recognize the differentia as ontologically of the same order as what it differentiates. Can the Hegelian categories avoid the problem of the differentia?

There are two features of the Hegelian categories that allow them to avoid the problem; both spring from the character of thought and could not apply to categories of things. The first is self-reference. The requirement of self-reference is implicit in the recognition that the differentia must belong to the same order as what it differentiates. Clearly, no self-reference is possible as long as what falls under the categories belongs to one realm and what makes them intelligible belongs to another. Nor is there any self-reference possible on the Aristotelian scheme because, whether or not the differentia belongs to the same genus as what it differentiates, it must be a different sort of thing. The Aristotelian differentia is either an instance of another category or it belongs to the same category but is distinguished from what it differentiates as its quality. In contrast, if the objects in a category are thoughts and if their differentia is also a thought, then it is possible for the differentia to have exactly the character that the objects have.

Exactly how they could be the same will be clearer once we recognize the second feature of the Hegelian categories, dynamism. Hegel speaks of the categories unfolding and of one category passing over into another. Most readers tend to discount these claims. Hegel is usually viewed as simply describing a group of categories, rejecting them for various reasons and himself passing on to others. How could process lie within the categories?

My contention is that the dynamism of the categories and their self-reference are consequences of Hegel's solution to the problem of the differentia. Let us begin with an arbitrary category, A. To make A intelligible we need to say what it is: we need to give its differentia. This requirement raises the same question we considered before, does the differentia belong to A? Again, insofar as the differentia is just what A is, it must belong to A; but because no mere instance of A could serve to differentiate A from anything else, the differentia cannot belong to A. It seems as if we face the same dilemma as before, but Hegel provides a way to skirt the problem. The only thing that could, without contradiction, characterize A and differentiate it from the others is A itself. What Hegel does is to show that the category does differentiate itself. That is to say, rather than characterize A by C and face the difficulties of sorting out the relation of A and C, Hegel characterizes A by A. At first glance this is apt to seem vacuous: surely, A is A. This is a tautology that seems to tell us nothing. But this appearance is mistaken. The Hegelian categories, like the categories of Kant, are thought relations. To apply one to itself is no simple endeavor. It involves showing that the particular category is itself an object of the thought relation that it expresses. As I understand the *Logic*, the argumentation aims to show for each category that some sort of self-relation holds.

These self-relations are essential because they differentiate the categories. They make the categories intelligible, or as Hegel often puts it, they express the "truth" of the category. But Hegel's self-relations avoid the difficulties that beset the Aristotelian categories only by introducing a further level of complexity. In differentiating his categories, in finding their truth, Hegel destroys them and they pass over into other categories. Again, the reason is easy to see if we bear in mind our earlier reflections on the problem of the differentia. Aristotle's problem is that the differentia of a category should belong to both the category it differentiates and another category. Hegel avoids having a differentia that belongs to some other category by self-differentiation, a move that is possible only because he makes both the category and its differentia thought relations. But then, showing that the category is indeed differentiated, showing that it is characterized by itself, amounts to introducing further thought relations into the content of the category. So differentiation amounts to transformation. And the cycle repeats itself.

It seems, then, that Hegel is keenly concerned with the problem of the differentia and that he advances what amounts to a solution. Since the differentia is the principle of intelligibility of the categories, by speaking of categories of thought, Hegel places both category and differentia on the same ontological plane. As a result, the differentia can belong to the category. While this seems to avoid the difficulty, the differentiation of the category adds new content to it and so transforms it into another category. If all this is right, the problem of the differentia acts as a kind of engine to produce the dynamic that we see in the *Logic*.

III

All this is quite abstract, somewhat empty, and drastically in need of qualification. There is not time here to work out the details—I would need to discuss the entire *Logic* to make a really convincing case. Let me merely draw your attention to some passages where Hegel differentiates his categories: Being is and, thus, is nothing (*Logik* I, 68; 82); "Their vanishing [that of being and nothing in becoming], therefore, is the vanishing of becoming or the vanishing of the vanishing itself. . . . Becoming as this transition [i.e., as this becoming] is *determinate being*" (*Logik* I, 93–94; 106);[9] "determinate being is *a determinate being, a something*" (*Logik* I, 103; 115); "being-for-self is first, immediately, *a* being-for-self—the One" (*Logik* I, 144, 151; 157, 163); "real discrete quantity is thus *a* quantity, or quantum" (*Logik* I, 192; 201); "quantum as thus *self-related* . . . is *quantitative ratio*" (*Logik* I, 236; 240); "*in this very externality quantum is self-related*, is *being* as quality . . . this is the truth of quantum, to be Measure" (*Logik* I, 320; 323–24); "Absolute indifference [Indifferenz] . . . [is] determined as *indifferent* [gleichgultig]. . . . But . . . it is the very nature of the differences of this unity to sublate themselves, with the result that . . . its indifference [proves] to be just as much indifferent *to itself*, to its own indifference, as it is indifferent to otherness. . . . Being, in its determining, has thus determined itself to essence" (*Logik* I, 381–83; 383–85). All these categories belong to the sphere of being. As we can see from these passages, in this sphere any self-relation immediately sublates a category into another. That is to say, the process of expounding a differentia, the process of setting forth what a category is and what distinguishes it from another category, adds new content to the category and so transforms it into something else. For these categories, the process of differentiating is a failure because what should be the essence of the category turns out to be another category. Yet it is this very failure that serves to characterize the categories of being: the categories of being are categories whose essence lies in another.

To put this same analysis in somewhat different terms, my claim that Hegel avoids the problem of the differentia by the self-differentiation of the categories seems to be false not because there is no self-predication—that there is should now be obvious—but because this type of predication does not succeed in remaining within the category it differentiates. But Hegel recognizes the transformations engendered by self-differentiation as part of the nature of the categories of being. Consequently, though self-differentiation transforms a category into a new category, this new category is the "truth" of the original category and thus, somehow, the same. Once we see that the category necessarily transforms itself, then we recognize the very transformation as its nature; consequently, self–differentiation, understood now as a dynamic process, does not alter the category.

This recognition of transformation as part of the nature of a category reflects a movement to a new sphere, essence. The categories of essence are distinguished by the relations they have to the contrary in terms of which they are defined: thus, for example, identity is defined through difference (*Logik* II, 265; 417) and positive through negative.[10] In this sphere, the differentia is included in the category it differentiates as its essence. However, this essence contains a reference to its contrary and thus also fails to express the nature of *just* the category.

This reference to a contrary is eliminated in the sphere of notion, for the categories of notion posit themselves together with their relations to themselves. Describing the development of universal notion into particularity, Hegel makes a claim that characterizes self-differentiation in the sphere of notion while indicating the significance of this process in the determination of other categories:

> It [the true, infinite universal] *determines* itself freely; the process by which it makes itself finite is not a transition, for this occurs only in the sphere of being; *it is creative power* as the absolute negativity which relates itself to its own self. As such, it differentiates itself internally, and this is a determining, because the differentiation is one with the universality. Accordingly, the universal is a process in which it posits the differentiae themselves as universal and self-related. They thereby become *fixed*, isolated differentiae. The isolated *subsistence* of the finite . . . is, in its truth universality, the form with which the infinite Notion clothes its differentiae—a form that is, in fact, one of its own differentiae. (*Logik* III, 36–37; 605)[11]

In other words, the universal notion differentiates itself without passing into or presupposing another category. Its differentia is just that self-relation that is its own nature. Though the universal notion is differentiated by itself, insofar as it is a differentia, a determination of the universal, it contains an additional dimension and is, thus, another category, particularity. Ultimately, it is only the absolute whose differentia is just what it is; only the absolute is in and for itself.

Thus, the character of self-relation is transformed as the *Logic* progresses. Even in the sphere of being, the various modes of self-relation are diverse. Nevertheless, the "truth" of a category in any sphere still adds content that is not contained in the category and so transforms the category into a different one. Hegel arrives at the "truth" of these categories by making them intelligible, that is, by finding their differentiae. The diversity of the modes of self-reference may seem to call into question my treatment of the problem of the differentia, but it really supports my analysis—or it would if I could work out the details here—because it shows how an analogous operation is used to generate new categories and, thus, that the entire development is rational.

I have expounded the problem of the differentia as if it were a completely general problem that could somehow apply in all categories, and in a sense it is. In another sense, though, the relations developed within each category are unique and arise from the character of the category itself. In each category of being, Hegel argues for self–relation to effect differentiation, but each argument differs and the mode of self-relation differs for each. In essence and notion, self-relation also effects differentiation, but what counts as self-relation is vastly different. This difference is a sign of progress: to the extent that self–relation is contained within the category, the category comes closer to the absolute. Once the differentia of the category is just the category itself this ultimate has been reached.

Part of the difficulty in tracing the problem of the differentia through the *Logic* is that the terms of the problem are transformed; they depend on the category being considered. What I have called Hegel's treatment can at best be the hollow shell of his position, for it lacks the recognition of the necessary diversity and richness of the development. It is misleading to speak of Hegel's response to the problem as if the problem of the differentia were one problem rather than a problem to be faced anew in each category.

It is easy to confuse my account of the problem with exactly the positions Hegel rejects. From Aristotle through contemporary philosophers, the discipline of logic has been conceived as a method that is applicable to a wide variety of diverse contents. Logic has been taken to be a canon of reasoning. All valid arguments can, it is supposed, be expressed in logic. In contrast, the Hegelian logic is content dependent. Its arguments properly apply only to its own categories, and Hegel denies that any universal canon could ever be extracted. For just this reason it is a mistake to accept any account of the problem of the differentia that purports to apply to all the categories. Such an account must separate the logic of the differentia from the diverse contents of categories. On the other hand, the virtue of the universal account that I have given is that it shows how Hegel uses the *rejection* of the distinction between logic and the content of logic, that is, the distinction between what the category is and the way it is differentiated or characterized, to solve the problem of the differentia. So, even though my account is universal and thus inherently inadequate, it, or something like it, must be correct.

The problem of the differentia and what I take to be Hegel's response to it point up the difficulty inherent in any categorial thinking. We can—and do—apply the categories, but when we try to think them individually, as they are in themselves, we are led to other categories. We find ourselves in the position of Plato in his *Parmenides*, a dialogue much admired by Hegel: everything is related to everything else. What Hegel does is work through these relations organically and systematically. What is simply a problem for other thinkers is, for him, a dynamic tool.

Chapter 1

1. It is often supposed that Plato does define the forms in his middle dialogues. Does he, then, set aside the view expressed in the *Phaedo*? This is not the place to address this question thoroughly, but let me suggest that though Plato does provide formulae of the virtues, some constituent of each formula remains undefined. Hence, the formulae are not properly definitions. Moreover, Plato arrives at these formulae after making hypotheses. Hence, they fall short of the unhypothetical principles sought in the early dialogues.

2. Examining the presuppositions inherent in Socratic dialectic, R. E. Allen ("Plato's Earlier Theory of Forms," in *The Philosophy of Socrates: A Collection of Critical Essays*, edited by G. Vlastos [Garden City, N.Y.: Doubleday, 1971], pp. 333–34) argues that in most important respects, the forms of the early and middle dialogues are identical. This position is developed in more detail in his *The Euthyphro and Plato's Earlier Theory of Forms* (London: Humanities Press, 1970).

3. E.g., Vlastos, "Introduction: The Paradox of Socrates," in *The Philosophy of Socrates*, edited by G. Vlastos, pp. 1–21.

4. This is a central theme in Vlastos' work. His most recent book, *Socrates, Ironist and Moral Philosopher* (Ithaca, N.Y.: Cornell University Press, 1991), reached me too late to incorporate into this essay.

5. Stories of Vlastos' helpfulness to younger scholars are legion. To them, I can add that Vlastos generously read and commented upon an earlier

version of this chapter. His pointed criticisms have helped me formulate my argument more cogently.

6. Richard Robinson (*Plato's Earlier Dialectic*, 2nd ed. [Oxford: Clarendon Press, 1953], p. 2) identifies five ways Plato is commonly misinterpreted, one of which he terms "misinterpretation by inference":

> "Plato says p, and p implies q; therefore Plato meant q." The conclusion does not follow; for Plato may have thought the p did not imply q; or, more probably, the suggestion that "p implies q" may never have occurred to him at all; or, most probably of all, even the proposition q itself may never have occurred to him. . . . Even those consequences which now seem to us to follow most obviously and directly from a given proposition were often not realized by the acutest of earlier thinkers, as the history of thought shows again and again.

This would be more plausible had Plato written treatises. As it is the problems are: (1) it is never Plato who says p but some character in a dialogue; and (2) Plato does not draw conclusions from the dialogues, and this is probably intentional. That Robinson's book emphasizes dialectic and Socratic methodology is not accidental—these are most identifiable as Socratic assumptions.

7. The legitimacy of the distinction between the philosophical and the literary aspects of the dialogues has recently been called into question by, among others, Michael Stokes (*Plato's Socratic Conversations: Drama and Dialectic in Three Dialogues* [Baltimore: Johns Hopkins University Press, 1986], see esp. pp. 1–36). Stokes argues against the assumption that a question that Socrates asks need reflect his own opinion. Though I agree with the thrust of Stokes' position, it is also important to see that the questions Socrates raises do indicate the lines of an argument. The approach I explain and illustrate later in my text has, I think, the same goal as Stokes's approach.

8. The definition proposed in the *Charmides* looks to be something different from an example, but Socrates refutes it in the same way that he refutes examples, by showing that there are cases where it would not be moderate.

9. The *Charmides* might seem to be an exception to this analysis because it offers what appear to be six definitions and because the identification of moderation with knowledge raises the question of how this knowledge could have any object. In fact, the six definitions fall neatly in the three groups, a pair to each group. The last and most extensively treated pair consider whether the knowledge that should be moderation knows everything or nothing.

10. At *Laches* 191d–e, Socrates advances a series of examples, and claims that "there are people who are brave in all these ways." However, it is clear that he advances these examples on Laches' behalf. The punctuation of Burnet's text suggests that Laches' quick response to Socrates' remark comes before the remark is complete: we would expect Socrates to continue with a characteristic "or is this not so?" were he not interrupted. The passage is part of an argument for the existence of a single standard by which to judge the instances of courage, an argument that requires initial agreement from the interlocutor that there are indeed many instances of courage. Only the standard is perfect courage. So the context speaks against 191d–e's expressing Socrates' view. Even if all this is wrong, it would still not be clear that Socrates asserts the existence of examples of courage in *Laches* 191d–e; for in saying that "there are people who are brave in all these ways," he probably means to emphasize not the various individuals but various types of bravery. That is to say, the argument divides courage into its species in order to argue that there must be one character that serves as a standard. Thus, *Laches* 191d–e is not a counterexample to my claim that the examples are advanced by interlocutors other than Socrates.

11. Socrates ascribes moderation to Charmides (175d–e), but Charmides himself denies this (176b). The reader, of course, knows that, as one of the thirty tyrants, Charmides is not moderate and could not have been moderate at the time the dialogue was set. Charmides' willingness to use force to coerce Socrates into speaking about moderation shows ironically how far he is from being moderate.

12. Drawing on the assumption that capacity is fine, the *Hippias Major* contains an argument showing, what is acknowledged as impossible, that the fine is not good (295c–297c). Though capacity here is not limited to knowledge, the idea that someone who possesses it will be both fine and good parallels the unity of virtue arguments.

13. On this passage, see note 15.

The *Hippias Minor* concludes with an argument showing that the virtuous person is the one who is unjust, clearly an absurd conclusion. In this case the conclusion neither implies nor presupposes the unity of virtue, but this argument plays the role in this dialogue that unity of virtue arguments play in other dialogues.

14. Terry Penner's "The Unity of Virtue" (*Philosophical Review* 82 [1973]: 60–66) is an exception. See also Vlastos' appendix to his "Unity of Virtue" paper: "The Argument in *La.* 197E ff." in his *Platonic Studies* (Princeton: Princeton University Press, 1973), pp. 266–69.

15. Vlastos maintains that the aim of *Euthyphro* 11e–15b is to get Euthyphro to consider what part of justice piety is, and that this project makes no sense if justice and piety are the same ("The Unity of the Virtues in the *Protagoras*," *Review of Metaphysics* 25 [1972]: 421). That Socrates does get Euthyphro to consider what part of justice piety is is clear, but this path fails. The immediate aim of the argument is to show that the differentia that Euthyphro proposes to distinguish piety from the rest of justice will not work. There is no evidence in the dialogue that Socrates' aim is to find the correct differentia. If his aim is rather to show that there is no differentia, not only would the argument still make sense, but it would also be consistent with the *Protagoras*. Whatever the aim, it is not realized: Euthyphro declines to continue the investigation (15c–d).

Behind the supposition that Socrates rejects the unity conclusions of dialogues other than the *Protagoras* is the tendency to derive his own views from questions he asks others. On this type of error see Stokes, *Socratic Conversations*, p. 4.

16. G. Vlastos, "The Unity of the Virtues," pp. 415–58. Vlastos terms claims such as "justice is pious" "Pauline predications" when what is asserted is piety of those who have justice (p. 446).

17. Penner, "The Unity of Virtue," pp. 39–41. Penner claims that Socrates is not interested in the "philosopher's question," the conceptual analysis of courage, etc., but the "general's question," the question of what (state of mind) makes a person courageous. He thinks that the text strongly supports a non-referential sense, but that interpreters reject it because the intensions of virtue terms are obviously distinct.

18. Vlastos, "Unity of the Virtues," pp. 418–24.

19. See Penner, "Unity of Virtue," pp. 36–37.

20. Dorothea Frede ("The Impossibility of Perfection: Socrates' Criticism of Simonides' Poem in the *Protagoras*," *Review of Metaphysics* 39 [1986]: 729–53, esp. 748) proposes that a portion of the section interpreting the Simonides poem, from 343c–347e, was written and inserted in its present place around the time the *Symposium* was written and that this text manifests the latter dialogue's understanding of the relation of being and becoming. At the end of her paper, Frede remarks that students of the dialogues often discover "that even an early dialogue cannot be quite as early as others have thought" (p. 752). Though the similarities she finds to *Symposium* 343c–347e are intriguing, they do not prove that this section of the *Protagoras* must be a later addition. Though both dialogues suggest that knowledge itself belongs

to the flux, this notion is put to different (ironical) uses in each. More importantly, the "Platonic" doctrines that Frede finds in this portion of the *Protagoras* (p. 746) not only appear elsewhere in the dialogue; they are integral to this dialogue and to others, as I have been arguing here. Indeed, the problem Frede confronts in her paper is exactly the problem I am considering: how to understand the apparently Platonic elements in the *Protagoras*. She does not consider the possibility that the distinction between the Socrates of the early dialogues and Plato is overdrawn.

21. It is also worth noting that Aristotle frequently characterizes Platonic forms by their unity; e.g., *Met.* I.7.988b4–6. The suggestion that Aristotle got something right in discussing Plato may strike some as heretical.

22. Norman Gulley (*The Philosophy of Socrates* [London: Macmillan, 1968]) is but one representative of this view. Terence Irwin (*Plato's Moral Theory: The Early and Middle Dialogues* [Oxford: Clarendon Press, 1974], pp. 40-41) maintains that Socrates' renunciation is genuine; Socrates renounces knowledge but supposes that he has true belief. The issue is incisively discussed by Gregory Vlastos in "Socrates' Disavowal of Knowledge," *The Philosophical Quarterly* 138 (1985): 1–31. According to Vlastos, Socrates genuinely renounces certainty, but actually supposes he has some knowledge, elenctically justifiable knowledge (pp. 12, 18). The former is "divine knowledge," the latter what the *Apology* calls "human knowledge" (p. 29). I shall comment on this article shortly. My question—raised by none of the commentators—is whether the apparent contradiction in Socrates' claims to knowledge and denials of knowledge is due to the peculiar nature of the objects of knowledge.

23. See the preceding note.

24. Vlastos ("Socrates' Disavowal," p. 28) suggests that Socrates' reaction is religious rather than analytic.

25. I have dwelt on Vlastos' dualistic view of knowledge because of its similarity to the view I endorse and because it might at first glance seem able to help Socrates skirt the seeming contradiction of the super-argument. Vlastos could, I think, make virtually the same moves as I have in part I in response to the super-argument: the knowledge mentioned in (2) and (3) above is "divine knowledge," what Vlastos regards as certainty; if certainty is a requirement for virtue, then it would apparently have no human embodiments—so (1) must be rejected. But Vlastos maintains that virtue *does* have human embodiments; he clearly regards Socrates himself as such an embodiment of virtue. Were he somehow to reject (1), his position would amount to mine.

Chapter 2

1. A. E. Taylor (*Plato: The Man and his Work* [New York: Dial Press, 1936], p. 64) maintains that the *Lysis* is the "unnamed source from which Aristotle derives most of the questions discussed in a more systematic way in the lectures which make up the eighth and ninth books of the *Nicomachean Ethics*." Taylor later remarks that "all the conflicting points of view of [the *Lysis*] are taken up, and each is found to have its relative justification" (p. 74). Unfortunately, he does not elaborate on these interesting remarks.

Robert G. Hoerber ("Plato's *Lysis*," *Phronesis* 4 [1959]: 26) maintains that Aristotle's criteria are "closely parallel" to the triad to be found in the *Lysis*. I shall have more to say about Hoerber's position in a later note.

2. David Sedley, "Is the *Lysis* a Dialogue of Definition?" *Phronesis* 34 (1988): 107–8. I find Sedley's suggestion for repunctuating the text plausible, but the new punctuation is consistent with other interpretations, as argued in my text. Sedley accepts Richard Robinson's view that "the explicit question of the *Lysis* is not 'what friendship is' but what its condition is" (*Plato's Earlier Dialectic*, 2nd ed. [Oxford: Clarendon Press, 1953], p. 49). I do not understand what is being asked in the question, "What is the condition of friendship?"

3. Being the friend of someone indifferent is not excluded by this argument. Thus, thorough reciprocity is not assumed here. It seems that what Socrates objects to is calling a friend someone whose friendship *could* not be reciprocated. As yet, only the possibility of reciprocity is assumed.

4. T. J. Saunders, *Plato: Early Socratic Dialogues* (Harmonsworth, England: Penguin, 1987).

5. Vlastos also remarks on this point in "The Individual as an Object of Love in Plato," *Platonic Studies* (Princeton: Princeton University Press, 1973), p. 8 with p. 5. Vlastos does not notice the reciprocity criterion at work in the *Lysis*.

6. Cooper thinks that this is the essence of friendship: "the central idea contained in *philia* is that of doing well by someone for his own sake, out of concern for him." ("Aristotle on the Forms of Friendship," *Review of Metaphysics* 30 [1977]: 621). Well-wishing captures what Cooper takes to be the altruistic dimensions of Aristotle's friendship. His grounds for emphasizing well-wishing are a passage from the *Rhetoric* (1380b36–1381a2) and Aristotle's claim in the *Nicomachean Ethics* that "friendship is good will when reciprocated" (1155b31–34—Cooper's trans.) which he understands—rightly, I think—to characterize all three types of friendship (pp. 623–26). Since the *Rhetoric* describes what is ordinarily said and believed about friendship, it is not a good source for Aristotle's considered view. In the passage from the *Ethics*,

Aristotle is emphasizing that well–wishing must be reciprocated in order for there to be friendship. He wants to exclude friendship with inanimate objects, such as wine, whose good fortune we do not wish (1155b27–31) and friendship with people who do not wish us well in return (1155b31–34). (In this respect, well–wishing *does* function in the way that reciprocity functions in the *Lysis*.) Friendship requires that well–wishing be reciprocated, but the passage does not say that well–wishing suffices for friendship. Indeed, Aristotle immediately expresses dissatisfaction with the claim that friendship is reciprocated well–wishing (1155b34), and after apparently correcting the problem by insisting that the parties be aware of the good will they have for each other, he concludes only that such reciprocated well–wishing is necessary for friendship (1156a3–5). Nothing in Aristotle's subsequent treatment suggests that reciprocated well–wishing defines friendship; indeed, as I explain in my text, Aristotle characterizes well–wishing as an attitude or emotion necessarily distinct from friendship, an activity. Initially, Cooper speaks of well–wishing and well–doing in the same breath, but the texts he cites speak only of well–wishing, and by the end of his article Cooper himself has fallen into speaking of well–wishing as an attitude (p. 644).

The well–wishing Aristotle describes here resembles the nameless virtue that he locates between obsequiousness and grouchiness, the virtue he declares to be "closest to friendship" but to be lacking in affection (IV.6.1126b11–23). (At II.7.1108a26–30 he actually refers to this virtue as friendship.) Those with this virtue will choose to share pleasures with others as is appropriate to their worth, but neither too much nor too little (1126b36–1127a5). The friendship under consideration in books VIII and IX is a much stronger relation that involves living and working together. The nameless virtue may be necessary for friendship, but it is certainly not sufficient.

That well–wishing is common to all three forms of friendship indicates not its significance but its relative insignificance, for the forms of friendship are defined in respect of their primary instance, not through a common character. Aristotle's idea of well–wishing is exemplified in newspaper stories of the "hometown boy makes good" sort. Though we are typically unacquainted with the subject, we take a certain satisfaction in his success and wish that it continue. He, in turn, may have the same attitude towards us. Again, such mutual well–wishing is still a long way from friendship.

7. The phrase "such as pleasure" suggests that there are other cases when friendships endure because "the same comes from each other. " In fact, Aristotle's context here is a discussion of friendships for the good; he is claiming that they also endure for the same reason as friendships for pleasure, "the same comes from each other." Later, I shall argue that it is this mutual exchange of "the same" that makes friendships for the good pleasurable. It follows that friendships for pleasure are not the only friendships that involve

shared pleasures; friendships for the good do as well. But we need not conclude that there are reciprocal relations besides sharing pleasures.

8. Aristotle's claim that the lover and beloved do not share precisely
the same pleasure seems to be at odds with his earlier use of falling in love as
an example of friendship for pleasure (1156a34–b2). The distinction he may
have in mind is that between two people who share affection and the more
standard situation of older lover–younger beloved.

9. For a similar claim, see Socrates' analysis of Simonides' poem at
Protagoras 343e–345c.

10. Vlastos's argument in "Is the *Lysis* a Vehicle of Platonic Doctrine?"
(Appendix I of "The Individual as an Object of Love in Plato," in *Platonic
Studies*, pp. 35–37) that the *Lysis'* discussion of "first friend" need not be a
transcendent Platonic form is well taken. There is no compelling reason to
suppose that the dialogue *assumes* the existence of such forms, nor, as Vlastos
also argues, of participation. But the issue should not be what the dialogue
assumes about the first friend, but what it shows. If, as I shall argue, transcendence is a consequence of the dialogue, I can accept Vlastos's argument while
rejecting his main point, that the *Lysis* does not reflect a commitment to Platonic, transcendent form.

11. R. G. Hoerber ("Plato's *Lysis*") maintains both that the *Lysis* contains a deeper and more positive philosophical content than its inconclusive
conclusion might suggest (pp. 16–17) and that the many triads in the dialogue
are the key to understanding this content (pp. 17–25). Hoerber takes this
deeper content to involve the three types of friendship that Aristotle also distinguishes. The triadic relation that I advance as the definition of friendship is
not only consistent with most of Hoerber's analysis, the latter provides strong
support for my conclusion. The reason that I think Hoerber misses this is that
he clings to a notion, expounded by Cicero, that "utility is not the essence of
true friendship" (p. 23), which he takes to mean that utility has no place within a true friendship. The only support Hoerber offers for this claim is the refutation of the account of friends as unlikes. As I have shown in the text, this
refutation need not be understood in this way.

Laszlo Versenyi ("Plato's *Lysis*," *Phronesis* 20 [1975]: 186–87) agrees with
Hoerber that the *Lysis* contains a positive account of friendship. However, he
emphasizes friendship's *utility* (pp. 197–98) rather than the criterion of
reciprocity. The utility he has in mind is educational, and he maintains that
this could be mutual, as displayed in the *Lysis*. This is right as far as it goes.
The problem is that Versenyi leaves out the good as the third pole of the relationship. He argues that the good, the first friend, is likely something like
eudaimonia (p. 194). I shall argue against this Aristotelian view shortly. What
Versenyi does not see is that the utility of the two interlocutors to each other

is quite different from the utility envisioned earlier in the dialogue, where it is a relation of a better to a worse.

12. A nice dramatic wrinkle is the position of Socrates: he is at times one of the interlocutors, and at other times himself, as it were, a surrogate for the good.

13. Versenyi ("Plato's *Lysis*," pp. 192–95) argues that the first friend need not be one entity but is relative to individual needs, and he identifies it with *eudaimonia*. Versenyi acknowledges that these conclusions are inconsistent with 220e–221c, a passage that he dismisses as "inconclusive and inept" (p. 196). The doctrine of that passage is that someone would desire the good even without what was earlier assumed necessary, the presence of the bad. Since, as I have noted, this doctrine is virtually equivalent with the standard Socratic-Platonic dictum that all people desire the good, it is wrong for Versenyi simply to dismiss it. The interpretation of the dialogue that Versenyi advances resembles Aristotle's view of friendship for the good; the problem is that the *Lysis* does not support it.

14. John M. Cooper ("Friendship and the Good in Aristotle," *Philosophical Review* 86 [1977]: 295, 296) denies that the other self claim contributes to answering the question of what motivates someone to seek friends. Instead, he maintains that the value of friends lies in the psychological benefit of helping us to sustain interest in our work by providing (1) "confirmation of the worth of one's endeavors and pursuits" and (2) expanded experience, pride, and satisfaction in the fruits of a shared endeavor (pp. 306–7). First, there is no textual support for this view. Second, it is unlikely that Aristotle would rely on *psychological* benefit given that friendship contributes to happiness and happiness is an activity, not a feeling. Third, what Cooper describes would not be limited to the virtuous—it would apply equally well to players on a baseball team and to Nazi concentration camp guards. Fourth, and most important, the feeling of mutual confirmation of one's value that Cooper thinks friends provide is simply not valuable—it produces complacency. It is also unnecessary, for Aristotle thinks that the goals of a virtuous person are objectively valuable, and that the individual needs to know this, at least to some extent, to be virtuous. Real friends challenge us to know it better. See, for example, the rivalry between Lysis and Menexenus that Plato describes (e.g., 211a–c). More on this point later.

15 Cooper's notion that the friends provide us with a feeling of the worth of our endeavors ("Friendship and the Good in Aristotle," pp. 306–7)—discussed in the previous note—is antithetical to what I have identified as the position of the *Lysis*. I think that Aristotle also regards genuine friendship more as a challenge and a spur than a confirmation.

16. On the second dimension, see Eugene Garver, "Aristotle's Genealogy of Morals," *Philosophy and Phenomenological Research* 44 (1984): 471–92.

17. David O'Connor ("Two Ideals of Friendship," *History of Philosophy Quarterly* 7 [1990]: 109–22) terms such a relation "friendship as partnership" and contrasts it with the more common and contemporary "friendship as intimacy" model. O'Connor does not emphasize the triadic character of friendship, but his excellent discussion is otherwise compatible with my account.

Chapter 3

1. G. E. L. Owen's influential "*Tithenai ta Phainomena*" (in *Aristote et les Problèmes de Méthode,* edited by S. Mansion [Louvain: Publications Universitaires de Louvain, 1961], pp. 83–103) sets out this view of Aristotelian method. Difficulties arise from inconsistencies in the *phainomena*, and Owen argues that this term encompasses both observed facts and what people say about them. Hence, the task of the philosopher is to reconcile conflicts between observations, between opinions, and between opinions and observations. Martha Nussbaum (*The Fragility of Goodness* [Cambridge: Cambridge University Press, 1986], pp. 240–63) argues for a still more radical view. She denies the existence of a "Baconian realm of fact" that exists apart from what is said. Consequently, she sees inconsistencies in *phainomena* as simply conflicting claims made about the world (pp. 243–45). With this move, Nussbaum can only appeal to consistency criteria to reconcile conflicts in phainomena, and ethics becomes entirely the practices of a community.

2. T. H. Irwin ("The Metaphysical and Psychological Basis of Aristotle's Ethics," in *Essays on Aristotle's Ethics*, edited by A. O. Rorty [Berkeley: University of California Press, 1980], pp. 50–51) argues that the view that Aristotle derives his ethics from common opinion is "at best a half-truth." The other half of the truth is that Aristotle's ethics depends upon his psychology and, thus, upon his metaphysics. Since the latter cannot be the whole story, Irwin needs to rely on common opinion. Notice that Irwin would base ethics upon *other* Aristotelian sciences. This would violate Aristotle's assumption that ethics is an autonomous science.

Richard Sorabji ("Aristotle on the Role of Intellect in Virtue," in Rorty's *Essays on Aristotle's Ethics*, pp. 201–19) argues that the intellect has more of a role in virtue than is usually accorded it, but he concentrates on practical wisdom, and has little to say about Aristotle's account of the moral virtues.

3. John McDowell, "Virtue and Reason," *Monist* 42 (1979): 336–42.

4. A host of objections have been raised against the function argument. A persistent one is that reason is not the only distinctively human trait.

Bernard Williams (*Morality* [New York: Harper & Row, 1972], p. 64) suggests as alternatives: making fire, having sexual intercourse without regard to season, despoiling the environment and upsetting the balance of nature, and killing things for fun. Robert Nozick (*Philosophical Explanations* [Cambridge: Mass.: Belknap Press, 1981], p. 516) proposes telling jokes. It seems to me that an Aristotelian response to such objections would consist of showing that these and all other uniquely human traits—assuming they are all uniquely human—derive from reason. Nozick's objection that the uniqueness of a property is not morally significant (pp. 516–17) is beside the point. It is only a character that belongs to us uniquely that could serve to characterize our nature and to mark us off from other things. (Surely, characteristics common to many species cannot be the sole cause of characteristics that belong to us uniquely.) Only from such a character could our unique moral characteristics, the moral virtues, be demonstrated. Though I shall not show how other unique human characteristics follow from this principle, my account of how the cardinal moral virtues derive from reason indicates the way such derivations might look. The present chapter is an example of what Christine M. Korsgaard ("Aristotle on Function and Virtue," *History of Philosophy Quarterly* 3 [1986]: 259) terms the "indirect method" of defending the function argument: I show how it fits into the argument of other portions of the *Nicomachean Ethics*. For a brief summary of objections to the function argument, see Korsgaard, pp. 259, 278n.

5. See J. L. Ackrill, "Aristotle on *Eudaimonia*," reprinted in Rorty's *Essays*, pp. 26–29, and David Keyt, "Intellectualism in Aristotle," in *Essays in Ancient Greek Philosophy*, II, edited by J. P. Anton, and A. Preus (Albany: SUNY Press, 1983), pp. 364–68. Both argue for the inclusive interpretation. The exclusive view—that the human good involves *only* the best virtue, intellectual virtue—has been endorsed by W. F. R. Hardie ("The Final Good in Aristotle's *Ethics*," *Philosophy* 40 [1965]: 280); and A. Kenny (*The Aristotelian Ethics* [Oxford: Clarendon Press, 1978], pp. 203–6). Also, J. M. Cooper (*Reason and Human Good in Aristotle* [Cambridge, Mass.: Harvard University Press, 1975], pp. 99–100) presents arguments for the exclusivist view. The interpretation that I will advance here obviates this issue; if it is right, neither side is correct.

6. Ackrill ("Aristotle on *Eudaimonia*") slips back and forth between the notions that happiness includes everything desirable (pp. 25–26, 31–32) and that happiness includes practical and theoretical rational activity (p. 27). The former includes acts of moral virtue; the latter would probably not.

7. Cooper (*Reason and Human Good*, pp. 147–48) argues that the first and tenth books defend a conception of happiness different from that which is implicit in the middle books.

8. Ackrill ("Aristotle on *Eudaimonia*," pp. 30–31) considers and rejects the view that actions are virtuous insofar as they promote *theoria*. He also finds that Aristotle gives no satisfactory answer to the question of what makes virtuous actions virtuous nor to the question of the relation of *theoria* and action. I suggest that Ackrill's depressing conclusion arises from mistakes about the character of actuality; the inconsistencies are his own. See my preceding remarks on the inclusive interpretation.

In a particularly interesting article, Christine Korsgaard considers what contribution to rational activity is made by the moral virtues and the appetitive portion of the soul ("Aristotle on Function and Virtue, " pp. 260 and 262). Though this is just the converse of the issue I deal with here, Korsgaard actually explains (pp. 276–77) how reason could determine what counts as moral virtue: "What the morally virtuous person . . . judges to be good, is the kind of activity that keeps reason in control of the soul" (p. 276). However, she does not explain how reason determines the specifics of moral virtue; she thinks that "no more than this [schematic account of the role of reason] can be theoretically conveyed" (pp. 276–77). Though I think Korsgaard is right both about the role of reason and its limitation, I shall argue here that reason gives us more than a merely schematic account.

9. Charles M. Young's "Aristotle on Temperance" (*Philosophical Review* 97 [1988]: 531) argues that the distinction between common and peculiar appetites is a distinction between different grounds for having appetites; for example, "I want to eat the Athenian pastry before me both because I am hungry and because I like to eat Athenian pastry." Only the former, the common appetite, is physical (p. 532). I have drawn on this distinction in my discussion of explanation (3). Though Young does not discuss this latter, he too emphasizes the rational component of moderation (pp. 541–42).

10 Cooper (*Reason and Human Good*, p. l08–9) argues that if moderation did serve reason, Aristotle would not recognize pleasures of the body as valuable and would urge asceticism. But Aristotle does not regard asceticism or insensibility as a viable human option (1119a5-7). I shall say more later and in the next chapter about why particular acts of moderation are intrinsically valuable.

11. Ackrill ("Aristotle on *Eudaimonia*," p. 32) claims that an endorsement of intellectual virtue would imply that "one should do anything however seemingly monstrous if doing it has the slightest tendency to promote *theoria* ."

12. Clearly, there are also circumstances where the rational and right thing to do would be to refuse to fight in battle; for example, in a repressive state or when there is little or no chance of success. The courageous person *risks* his life in battle; that does not mean that he must die in battle.

13. Though Plato thinks that virtue should be completely intelligible, there is some question whether such knowledge can be attained in human life or even applied to human life. In practical matters Plato is in much the same position as Aristotle: he denies that laws can adequately cover all cases, as he notes in several places (e.g. *Statesman* 294b–c; cf. *Timaeus* 29b–d). But he ascribes this failing to the irrationality of the sensible world, and it does not cause him to question the rationality of virtue. Because the virtues are rational, the way to come to possess them is to come to know them. But knowing them would not necessarily make one better in acting in this world—among the shadows of the cave (cf. *Republic* 516e–517c).

14. See Cooper, *Reason and Human Good*, pp. 163 and 107–8.

15. R. A. Gauthier and J. Y. Jolif (*L'Éthique à Nicomaque*, 2nd ed., vol. 2, part 1 [Louvain: Publications Universitaires de Louvain, 1970], p. 7) regard it as one of the fundamental incoherencies of Aristotle's moral philosophy that morality is both absolutely valuable and a means to something else. Aristotle, however, does not have in mind a means-end distinction; rather, he distinguishes what is useful and valuable from what is only valuable.

Similarly, Plato distinguishes things valued both for their own sake and for their consequences from the things valued only for their own sakes and from things valued only for their consequences (*Republic* 357b–358a). He places justice in the first class.

16. At IX.8.1169a3–6 Aristotle appears to equate "living in accordance with reason" and "desiring the noble." The latter is manifested in acts of moral virtue. See also 1169a17–18.

17. John McDowell, "Virtue and Reason," pp. 33–42. McDowell's argument is implicit. My objection here is not to McDowell's emphasis on "salient facts," but to his denial of any objective basis for their being salient. McDowell's claim that Aristotle's "thesis of uncodifiability" entails that a "conception of how to live" is "not intelligible independently of just such appreciation of particular situations as is involved in the present 'perception' of a salience" (p. 345) is, if I understand it correctly, incompatible with Aristotle's claim that we deliberate not about the end, but about what relates to the end (III.3.1112b11–12); for McDowell's "conception of how to live" seems to be just the real or apparent good (cf. 4.1113a22–24), and this Aristotle insists we desire but do not deliberate about, not because it is particular or "uncodifiable," as McDowell would have it, but because we are all in basic agreement about the end. It is the particulars that relate to this end that Aristotle thinks we *do* deliberate about.

18. This seems to be Cooper's question; see *Reason and Human Good*, pp. 166, 167, and 178. Cooper thinks that a thorough intellectualist would be

entirely lacking in emotion, a notion that I think motivates the following remarks:

> However often he may perform the just or the temperate or the liberal deed, anyone who organizes his life from the intellectualist outlook cannot care about such actions in the way a truly just or temperate or liberal man does. He will not possess the social virtues, or any other virtues, because he will lack the kind of commitment to this kind of activity that is an essential characteristic of the virtuous person (p. 164).

For reasons which I make clear here, I reject this sharp dichotomy between the life of moral virtue and the life of intellectual virtue. So far as I can see, a person who is morally virtuous has no commitment to emotions; he has a commitment to their *proper* exercise.

19. Without entering into the various controversies about the interpretation of the *Philebus*, I suggest that my account of Aristotle's moral virtue bears affinities with Plato's description of the mixture of reason and pleasure in that dialogue (22a–e, 64c–65e). To see the affinity, substitute emotion for pleasure. Cooper's suggestion that a genuine intellectualist would entirely lack emotion recalls what that dialogue terms the "life of intellect" (21d–e).

Chapter 4

1. Stephen A. White ("Is Aristotelian Happiness a Good Life or the Best Life?" *Oxford Studies in Ancient Philosophy* 8 [1990]: 106–7) states the problem concisely. White's answer to the title question is "a good life," and he speaks of the "sustained satisfaction found in the pursuit of certain goals" that such a life would provide. He also thinks that such a life "preserves the maximalist's [the one who advances the alternative answer] demand for a composite good" (p. 135). I do not see that either sustained satisfaction or a composite good has a hand in Aristotle's reasoning, but White's interesting paper was part of what stimulated the present chapter.

2. Ackrill, "Aristotle on *Eudaimonia*," pp. 18–28.

3. W. F. R. Hardie, *Aristotle's Ethical Theory*, 2nd ed. (Oxford: Clarendon Press, 1980), pp. 22–26.

4. See White, "Aristotelian Happiness," p. 14–15.

Ackrill, "Aristotle on *Eudaimonia*," is inconsistent. Though he usually argues that happiness includes everything desirable (pp. 25–26, 31–32), he also interprets activity of the rational element in the function argument to be practical and theoretical reason (p. 27). Since practical reason cannot be equated with moral virtue, the latter interpretation would omit something essential from happiness.

5. For additional criticisms of Hardie's position see Ackrill, "Aristotle on *Eudaimoia*," p. 25.

6. "Chosen for its own sake" is a way that Aristotle characterizes *teleion* (see I.7.1097a30–b6 and X.7.1177b16–25). Though the phrase has a rather Kantian ring to it, Aristotle thinks the details and the particulars of moral life are too complex to admit the sort of rules that Kant advocates.

7. Christine M. Korsgaard ("Aristotle and Kant on the Source of Value," *Ethics* 46 [1986]: 490–95) examines the standard readings of this distinction—including maximal or "inclusive end" view (applied to I.7.1097a25–34). This latter is a quantitative interpretation. Korsgaard argues that Aristotle's distinction should rather be understood as a distinction between conditioned and unconditioned goods.

8. Usually Aristotle contrasts external goods with goods of the soul and with goods of the body (I.8.1098a12–14; *Politics* VII.1.1323a24–26). However, he insists that goods of the soul are most properly goods (*N.E.* I.8.1098a14–16), and in the subsequent discussion of what is needed for happiness he refers to at least one good of the body, good looks, as an external good (1099a31–b8). Here I shall follow the usage of this last important passage in taking external goods to be human goods that are not in the soul. See John M. Cooper, "Aristotle on the Goods of Fortune," *Philosophical Review* 44 (1985): 176–77.

9. John M. Cooper, "Aristotle on the Goods of Fortune," pp. 181–83.

10. This and other criticisms of Cooper are developed by Julia Annas in "Aristotle on Virtue and Happiness," *University of Dayton Review* 19 (1988-89): 12–14. Annas contrasts Cooper's view with the view that external goods are intrinsically valuable. She maintains that there is textual support for both views, and that Aristotle was of two minds on this issue. However, part of her case for Aristotle's recognition of the intrinsic value of external goods is vitiated by a confusion. She notes that Aristotle denies that virtue is sufficient for happiness because a virtuous person who was asleep or "broken on the wheel" would not be happy (p. 7), but she infers from this that Aristotle is committed to "the life of virtuous activity's not being on its own complete and self-sufficient" (p. 8). This is a non sequitur. The virtuous person who is asleep or "broken on the wheel" is not happy because happiness lies not in the *having* of virtue but in its *exercise* (see I.8.1098b31–1099a7—a passage similar to those Annas mentions). Virtue is a character state; external circumstances could impede its exercise. External goods are needed to insure that the exercise of virtue is neither obstructed nor impeded. Thus, that external

goods are needed for happiness does not show that the exercise of virtue is insufficient for happiness. Unfortunately, passages that point out the insufficiency of virtue for happiness are the only textual support Annas provides for her contention that Aristotle recognizes the intrinsic value of external goods. Since these texts do not support her position, her case rests on the implausibility of the alternative view.

11. Martha Nussbaum (*The Fragility of Goodness*, pp. 318-42) emphasizes the importance of chance for Aristotelian ethics. She claims that many of the external goods provide opportunities for virtuous actions—more or less the standard view—but she also claims (pp. 365–368) that friends are intrinsically valuable and that relationships inevitably involve risk.

12. Martha Nussbaum (*Fragility of Goodness*, pp. 329–32) argues against the attempt of Ross and Joachim to find a distinction between *eudaimonia* and *makariotēs* based on the latter's including external goods. She thinks both include the enjoyment of external goods, particularly friends.

13. Ironically, Cooper ("Aristotle on the Goods of Fortune," pp. 185–86) supports his interpretation by referring to Arius Didymus, the author of an epitome of Peripatetic ethics, and the Greek commentators Aspasius and Alexander of Aphrodisias, all of whom reject Stoicism. They define happiness as a kind of mixture of internal and external goods in opposition to the Stoic view that happiness only consists of internal goods, the virtues. Opponents in a controversy often share the same assumptions; we should wonder whether these commentators did not adopt Stoic assumptions, especially since the controversy was apparently initiated by Stoics. We should also wonder whether Cooper is right to think that these thinkers understand external goods instrumentally. (To pursue either of these questions here would take us too far afield.)

Annas ("Aristotle on Virtue and Happiness," pp. 9–10) remarks on the similarity of some of Aristotle's views to Kant's.

14. Korsgaard, "Two Distinctions in Goodness," *The Philosophical Review* 92 (1983): 169–95.

15. See *N. E.* I.9.1099b27–28. Commenting on this passage, J. A. Stewart (*Notes on the Nicomachean Ethics of Aristotle*, vol. 1 [New York: Arno Press, 1973], pp. 135–36) identifies bodily excellence as the necessary external good and mentions friendship among what is instrumental. (Stewart, p. 101, also speaks of our lower nature as the matter upon which reason, form, is impressed.) Likewise, Nussbaum (*Fragility of Goodness*, p. 327) claims that external goods could inhibit virtuous activity in the way that either a dam or sludge could block the flow of a river: they could completely block or merely impede virtuous activity. My proposal is that many of what we tend to call

external goods resemble the water of the river. Such goods are the material aspect of virtuous actions.

Chapter 5

1. The *Timaeus* uses the term *nous* not *epistēmē* (knowledge), but the passage from the *Republic* makes clear the near equivalence of these terms in this context.

2. "Time, Truth, and Knowledge in Ancient Greek Philosophy," *American Philosophical Quarterly* 4 (1967): 1–14.

3. Xenophanes may seem to be an exception, for he claims that even though God does not move, he thinks, sees and hears (B 24, 25, and 26). But these passages only show that he uses "motion" for local motion—not that he distinguishes actuality and motion.

4. Usually, though, Plato distinguishes *nous* from the movable and sensible (e.g., *Rep.* 509d).

5. Sometimes Aristotle reserves the term "motion" for accidental changes and uses the term "change" (*metabolē*) more broadly to include accidental motions and also change in the category of substance; e.g., *Phys.* V.1.225a35–b5; 5.229a30–32; b13–14. In other passages the term "motion" refers to substantial changes; e.g., III.1.210a9–16. In this chapter I will use these terms interchangeably.

6. 1048b22–23. Ross renders this claim: ". . . but that movement in which the end is present is an action." He takes *ekeinē* in line 22 to refer to motion. This translation supports my claim that actualities are a group of motions.

7. *Dilemmas* (Cambridge: Cambridge University Press, 1954), p. 102.

8. "Aristotle's Distinction between *Energeia* and *Kinesis*," in *New Essays on Plato and Aristotle*, edited by Renford Bambrough (London: Routledge & Kegan Paul, 1965), pp. 125–26.

9. Ibid., p. 127.

10. Ibid., pp. 128–33. Ackrill's interpretation has generated an extensive response among which are: M. M. Mulhern, "Types of Process According to Aristotle," *Monist* 52 (1968): 237–51; P. S. Mamo, "*Energeia* and *Kinesis* in *Metaphysics*Θ. 6," *Apeiron* 4 (1970): 24–34; and Ronald Polansky, "Aristotle's Demarcation of the Senses of *Energeia* in *Metaphysics* IX.6," *Ancient Philosophy* 3 (1983): 160–70.

11. As John Herman Randall, Jr. puts it: "There can be no science of all the many things an individual acorn can do, only of those that are 'natural' to the acorn, that belong to the nature of that kind, of the powers any acorn possesses 'by nature.' The rest are contingent, accidental, incidental to being an acorn." *Aristotle* (New York: Columbia University Press, 1968), pp. 176–77.

12. The idea that nature is a cause of motion is not new. It is accepted by the participants in the well-known medieval debate over whether nature is an efficient cause or a formal cause. As will soon be apparent, I side with Thomas Aquinas in accepting the latter view.

13. A possible exception is thinking. See *De Anima* III.5.

14. For an excellent discussion of the sense in which motions are actualities, see L. A. Kosman's "Aristotle's Definition of Motion," *Phronesis* 14 (1969): 40–62. My treatment complements Kosman's.

Chapter 6.

1. J. L. Ackrill, *Aristotle the Philosopher* (Oxford University Press, 1986).

2. Ibid., pp. 2–3.

3. Ibid., p. 11.

4. Ibid., pp. 31, 113.

5. Ibid., p. 10.

6. Ibid., p. 24.

7. Ibid., pp. 24–26.

8. Ibid., p. 27.

9. Ibid., pp. 27–28.

10. Ibid., p. 114.

11 Ibid., p. 115.

12. Ibid., p. 44.

13. Ibid., pp. 52–53.

Chapter 7

1. Though an important scholarly tradition credits Aristotle with laying the foundations for Euclid's mathematical axiomatic method (e.g., Kurt

von Fritz, "Die *APXAI* in der griechischen Mathematik," *Archiv für Begriffs-geschichte* 1 [1955]: 102–3; Oskar Becker, "Die *Archai* in der griechischen Math-ematik," *Archiv für Begriffsgeschichte* 4 [1959]: 210n.), it is recognized that Aris-totle's terminology is inconsistent with Euclid's, that mathematical proof long antedates Aristotle (A. Szabo, *The Beginnings of Greek Mathematics* [Dordrecht, Holland: D. Reidel, 1978], pp. 228–32; Thomas L. Heath, *The Thirteen Books of Euclid's Elements*, vol. 1 [New York: Dover, 1956], pp. 116–17), and that Aris-totle and Euclid conceive of geometry quite differently (Ian Mueller, "Aristo-tle on Geometrical Objects," in *Articles on Aristotle*, vol. 3: *Metaphysics*, edited by Jonathan Barnes, Malcolm Schofield, and Richard Sorabji [New York: St. Martin's Press, 1979], 104–5). See also note 3.

A fairly widespread stream of thought takes the biological writings as fundamental for his other work. After praising the accuracy of Aristotle's bio-logical works, D'Arcy W. Thompson ("Aristotle the Naturalist," in *Science and the Classics* [London: Oxford University Press, 1940] p. 70) suggests that Aris-totle "was a better biologist than physicist: . . . he lacked somewhat the math-ematical turn of mind which was intrinsic to the older schools of philoso-phy." See also: Marjorie Grene, *A Portrait of Aristotle* (Chicago: University of Chicago Press, 1963), pp. 32, 55–58; and the work of David Balme.

2. A useful compilation and discussion of Aristotle's mathematical texts is Thomas Heath's *Mathematics in Aristotle* (New York: Garland, 1980).

3. Ian Mueller, "Greek Mathematics and Greek Logic," in *Ancient Logic and its Modern Interpretations*, edited by John Corcoran (Dordrecht: D. Reidel, 1974), 35–70, esp. 37–42.

4. On the question of maximal length see: Friedrich Solmsen, *Aristo-tle's System of the Physical World: A Comparison with his Predecessors* (Ithaca, N.Y.: Cornell University Press, 1960), 160–73, esp. 173n.; and Jaakko Hintikka, *Time and Necessity* (Oxford: Clarendon Press, 1973), 118–21.

5. For a more detailed discussion of this distinction see my " 'Being *qua* Being' in *Metaphysics* Γ," *Elenchos* 8 (1987): 46–48, 57–60.

6. The notion that mathematical practice generates mathematical ontology lies behind Wittgenstein's well–known contention that "the mathe-matician creates *essence*" *(Remarks on the Foundations of Mathematics*, edited by G. H. von Wright, R. Rhees, and G. E. M. Anscombe [Cambridge, Mass.: M.I.T. Press, 1967], p. 13, § 32). A more conservative approach to the descrip-tion of mathematical methodology is Imre Lakatos's account of a mathemati-cal research program in *Proofs and Refutations: The Logic of Mathematical Dis-covery* (Cambridge: Cambridge University Press, 1976).

7. A number of scholars have maintained that mathematicals such as lines, points, planes, and solids are not attributes. Though it is not typically explained in this way, I suggest that this move is motivated, at least in part,

by the problems that I expound here. According to J. L. Ackrill (*Aristotle's "Categories" and "De Interpretatione"* [Oxford: Clarendon Press, 1979], 91–92) *Categories* 6 does not list or classify "quantitative properties"—as we might have expected from his discussion of qualities in chapter 9—but "the *owners* of quantitative properties," such as lines, surfaces, solids, and numbers. Ackrill presumes that quantitative predicates like "two cubits" or "three cubits" (cf. 4.1b28–29) are predicates of lines or the other entities discussed in *Categories* 6. Because none of these latter is a primary substance and because only primary substances admit of properties, the ontological status of lines and the others is unclear. Though Ackrill says only that Aristotle does not discuss their status in the *Categories*, what seems to follow from his remarks is the stronger claim that there is no coherent account of their status consistent with the *Categories*. Mueller ("Aristotle on Geometrical Objects," p. l04) proposes a status distinct from anything that we see in the *Categories*. He claims that lines, points, planes, and solids are indeterminate extension and, thus, the matter of geometric properties. Part of his support (pp. 102–3) for this move is Ackrill's remarks about *Categories* 6. (The antecedents of Mueller's interpretation are medieval discussions of prime matter; see the selection from Averroes in A. Hyman and J. J. Walsh [eds.], *Philosophy in the Middle Ages*, 2nd ed. [Indianapolis: Hackett, 1983], pp. 294, 318–19; cf. the Avicenna selection, pp. 248–49.) Whatever its merits, this approach is unable to account for numbers, "owners" of attributes such as odd and even.

Why does Ackrill think that the lines, points, planes, and numbers discussed in *Categories* 6 are the owners of properties? Apparently, the reason is that Aristotle uses abstract nouns for quantities here in *Categories* 6 but uses only the adjectival forms in referring to quantities in *Categories* 4. But Ackrill also recognizes an ambiguity of usage: "a line could be said *of* a certain length, but it could also itself be called a length" (p. 91). Why, then, does Ackrill insist that in *Categories* 6 the line (the referent of the noun) is the subject or bearer of properties? Ackrill notices that in that chapter Aristotle ascribes properties to lines (p. 92). Why, though, not say that although lines have attributes, they are themselves attributes of substances? Perhaps Ackrill realizes the difficulty in saying that attributes have attributes—my second problem. More likely, he is deterred by the difficulty of understanding how a line, plane, or point could be an attribute of a substance. Since they would not ordinarily be said to be "in a substance but not as a part" (1a24–25) nor would they be said of a substance, they seem inconsistent with the stipulation in *Categories* 2a34–35 that everything else be either in or said of a primary substance. But this is just a version of my first problem: how can quantities be attributes of substances as they should be?

There is no explicit evidence in *Categories* 6 for Ackrill's notion that lines, points, numbers and so forth are not quantitative properties of substances but the "owners" of quantitative properties. (Does he think that substances are *also* the owners of these properties?) Aristotle does not say lines, numbers, and so forth are not properties of substances. But unless the challenge of understanding how they could be attributes is met, we would be forced to accept Ackrill's solution: Aristotle's account of mathematicals is incoherent. In short, my aim in this portion of the chapter is to puzzle over problems that Ackrill and others take to be insoluble.

8. Jonathan Barnes, "Aristotle's Arithmetic" *Revue de Philosophie Ancienne* 3 (1985), 127–32. Barnes suggests "groups" or "sets" or "amounts" as renderings or meanings of *plēthē* (p. 128), and refers to them as "relatively ordinary objects" (p. 128). But the group studied by modern mathematics constitutes a special sort of entity, and in order for *plēthē* to have attributes they would need to be a group in this modern, special sense.

Mario Mignucci ("Aristotle's Arithmetic," in *Mathematics and Metaphysics in Aristotle*, edited by A. Graeser [Bern: Haupt, 1987], esp. p. 179) also maintains that numbers are groups of individuals. He dismisses a passage (XIII.3.1078a23–28) that implies that each arithmetical property belongs (*huparchein*) to some individual: "We must give a very loose sense to this verb and suppose that Aristotle is rather careless here. Arithmetical properties, being properties of groups of indivisibles, have something to do with, or are somehow related to, individual things in so far as they are indivisible" (p. 179). Is there any evidence for this view? The ascription of set theory to Aristotle (see esp. pp. 201–9) is surely problematic.

9. At *Politics* III.1.1274b41, Aristotle remarks that a city consists of some plurality (*plēthē*) of citizens. But this is a preliminary to investigating whether the state acts (1274b34–38), an affirmative answer to which shows that the citizens are more than just a plurality.

10. Someone might suppose that attributes of attributes are present in the underlying substances, as are the attributes of which they are attributes. It is easy to see the paradoxes that would result: a person who is short-sighted would, consequently, be short; someone with blue eyes would be blue; and someone whose knowledge was extensive would himself be extensive.

11. There are places where Aristotle speaks of attributes and composites of substance and attribute as universals (VII.4.1030b12–13); but he apparently takes the attribute to belong to some individual substance (VII.5.1030b20–21; 4.1029b14–15; cf. XII.5.1071a19–35).

12. M.-D. Philippe, "αφαίρεσιξ πρόσθεσιξ, χωρίζειν dans la Philosophie d'Aristote," *Revue Thomiste* 56 (1948): 461–79; Mueller, "Aristotle on Geometrical Objects," pp. 98–100; John J. Cleary, "On the Terminology of Abstraction in Aristotle," *Phronesis* 30 (1985): 13–45. Barnes ("Aristotelian

Arithmetic," pp. 110–12) denies that XIII.3 relies on abstraction, but in order to maintain this thesis he relies on an unaristotelian understanding of abstraction.

13. Gottfried Martin, *Die Klassische Ontologie der Zahl* (Cologne: Kolner Universität Verlag, 1956).

14. Jacob Klein, *Greek Mathematical Thought and the Origin of Algebra*, trans. Eva Brann Cambridge, Mass.: M.I.T. Press, 1968), pp. 100–13.

15. Ibid., pp. 48, 101–2.

16. Ibid., p. 107.

17. For a detailed discussion of these two chapters of the *Metaphysics*, see my *One and Many in Aristotle's Metaphysics: The Central Books* (Columbus, Ohio: Ohio State University Press, 1989).

18. Klein, *Greek Mathematical Thought*, pp. 107–9.

19. Horses in the barn is a sortal concept that allows us to count certain things and to ignore others. Its utility is not in question here. I am concerned to understand its ontological status. Neither Barnes nor Mignucci deals with this issue. It seems that both think they can avoid this sticky question because they connect the sortal with the *qua* locution and insist that the use of "*qua* does not presuppose or constitute an ontological level different from the level of perceptible things" (Mignucci, "Aristotle's Arithmetic," p. 176; cf. Barnes, "Aristotelian Arithmetic," pp. 104–5, 128–29). Though there may be some sense in which this is true, it is certainly misleading and cannot bear the weight Barnes and Mignucci would give it. We could not get very far if we tried to study a person "*qua* planet," "*qua* hurricane," or "*qua* unmoved mover" for the simple reason that a person is none of these things. Clearly, the *qua* locution does make some ontological presuppositions; it presupposes the division of beings into genera. Indeed, when Aristotle claims that we count instances of a single genus (X.1.1053a24–30; X.2.1054a4–9; XIV.1.1087b33–1088a14), he refers to an ontologically significant class, not to an arbitrary conceptual construct. I see no evidence to suppose that Aristotle takes instances of a genus to constitute a set.

Though neither Barnes nor Mignucci refers to Klein, I think their interpretations derive from Klein's view of the importance of counting in the definition of number.

20. See Julia Annas, *Aristotle's "Metaphysics": Books M and N* (Oxford: Clarendon Press, 1976), pp. 34–36.

21. Aristotle's claim at 207b8–9 that two and three are "derivative" terms might seem to be damaging to my position, but what he refers to there

is the two or three divisions of a line. His point is that though these divisions are called three, as is the number abstracted from them, three is applied to the divisions derivatively. I shall have more to say about this distinction later.

22. Klein (*Greek Mathematical Thought*, pp. 46–60, esp. p. 46) thinks that the Greek concept of *arithmos* inherently refers to something that is counted.

23. This point is also made by Barnes ("Aristotelian Arithmetic," p. 122).

24. In a very interesting paper, Stephen Gaukroger ("The One and the Many," *Classical Quarterly* 32 [1982]: 320) advances a similar account of what he calls "noetic numbers." But he distinguishes these from sensible numbers and takes the latter to be prior in knowledge and being (pp. 320–21). This distinction is based on Aristotle's claim at *Physics* IV.11.219b6–9 that what we count differs from what we count with (p. 312). Later, I shall show a different way to interpret this distinction. Though I do not think Aristotle's epistemology can sanction noetic entities with a nature distinct from that of sensibles (cf. *De Anima* III.7.431a1–2), Gaukroger's account of noetic number is close to what I propose here as the account of number.

In another paper ("Aristotle on Intelligible Matter," *Phronesis* 25 [1980]: 192–95), Gaukroger argues that lines are the intelligible matter of numbers. Would points on the line be a better candidate for intelligible matter? Or perhaps we should say that any geometric object could serve as intelligible matter? However we answer these questions, Gaukroger's approach is consistent with my account.

25. Passages where Aristotle applies numbers to attributes—such as his claims that time is a number of motion (*Physics* IV.11.220a24–26)—lend support for my contention that numbers exist in things. But they also seem to require that numbers be attributes; this difficulty, the second problem, will be resolved in the next paragraph.

26. My solution to the second problem bears some similarity to what Jonathan Lear has called a "predicate filter" ("Aristotle's Philosophy of Mathematics," *Philosophical Review* 91 [1982]: 168). According to Lear, to consider some thing *qua* triangle is to filter out all but those predicates that belong to the thing insofar as it is a triangle. What is nice about this notion is that it allows the predicates to belong to the substance rather than to the triangle. Yet a problem with his formulation is that the predicates, as they are ordinarily understood, do not belong directly to substances. Strictly speaking, the thing is not isosceles (as Lear claims, p. 172); the thing is an isosceles triangle (cf. *An. Po.* I.4.73a37–b3). To be predicated of substances, predicates typically need more than just a "filter"; they need to be combined with what we could call "intermediate per se attributes," such as number or triangle. Thus, predi-

cation is more complex than Lear's picture would allow. For additional criticisms of Lear's paper, see my " 'Being *qua* Being' in Metaphysics Γ," pp. 50–52.

27. A difficulty in the text of the second proof (1051a27–29) is that Aristotle speaks as though it were true universally of all inscribed triangles but—on the usual interpretation—provides us with the construction of only a single triangle, an isosceles right triangle. The problem is solved by altering the usual punctuation. The comma should be placed before rather than after *orthē* in line a28. Then the constructed line is the line from the center of the circle to the vertex of the inscribed triangle. This construction divides (cf. a22–23) the original triangle into two isosceles triangles. Thus, it is clear at a glance that the inscribed triangle is right because one of its angles is the sum of the other two and because the total is two right angles.

$(\alpha + \beta) + \alpha + \beta = 2$ right angles

$\alpha + \beta = \frac{1}{2} \cdot 2$ right angles $= 1$ right angle

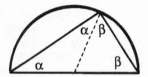

The problem is whether the rest of a28–29 can be understood in a way that is consistent with this interpretation. After interpreting the argument as I have here, Henry Mendell ("Two Geometrical Examples from Aristotle's *Metaphysics*," *Classical Quarterly* 34 [1984]: 366–67) examines several textual emendations that bring the text in accord with it (pp. 367–69). The simplest, his preference, is to delete *orthē* in a28. Any of the alternatives he mentions will do, but I prefer an interpretation that he does not mention. I suggest that a26–27 be punctuated as per Bonitz and Jaeger, and that the *dia ti* of the manuscripts be retained at a27 (instead of *dioti*) but taken with *orthē* in a28. Thus, at a26–27 Aristotle asks, "why, in general, is the angle in a semicircle a right angle?" He answers, "why—if three lines are equal (the base is two and the side set up from the middle)—[the angle] is right [would be] clear to one seeing if he knew the former [i.e., that the angles of a triangle are two right angles]." (We can understand *an ēn* in a28 from its parallel with a26.) Neither the former theorem by itself nor the construction is the middle, the answer to the "why" question. Aristotle's point is just that the construction makes clear what the middle is. The advantage of this interpretation is that it retains the text of the manuscripts and the natural punctuation of Jaeger and Bonitz. It or any of those Mendell mentions is preferable to supposing that *orthē* means right triangle in a27 but straight line in a28. The usual, incorrect punctuation is supported by Pseudo-Alexander's commentary. W. D. Ross (*Aristotle's*

"*Metaphysics*," vol. 2 [Oxford: Clarendon Press, 1958], pp. 270–71) and Heath (*Mathematics in Aristotle*, pp. 73–74) are overly influenced by Euclid's proof.

28. Cf. Lear, "Aristotle's Philosophy of Mathematics," pp. 179–82. Lear does not consider the dichotomy between such potentially existing objects and the mathematical characters actualized in physical things. Though the potential existence of mathematicals in physical objects supports Lear's central claim that mathematicals exist in sensibles; in an important way, it also undermines that claim. For if the mathematicals exist in sensibles only potentially, then the properties that they have could also only be expressed in the sensibles potentially, not actually as Lear requires. Even if some mathematicals are actualized in sensibles, other properties of the sensibles could mask the full expression of their properties, as the grain of the wood prevents the surface from being completely smooth.

Since Lear recognizes a potential existence for mathematical objects, he need not deny that numbers can be properties of objects, as he does on pp. 183–84.

29. Aristotle makes a parallel point at III.2.997b35–998a4. Lear ("Aristotle's Philosophy of Mathematics," p. 176), denies that this latter passage expresses Aristotle's view on the ground that, since it appears in the midst of *aporiai*, it can be read as a Platonist's response to a previously stated difficulty. Lear's aim is to show that sensible things perfectly instantiate mathematical properties. It is hard to see how infinite divisibility could exist in particular sensibles in any way that would be empirically useful for us, but it is just such utility that Lear proposes as the criterion of truth (p. 188).

30. There is at least one passage in the *Metaphysics* where Aristotle speaks of abstracting number from a line: at VII.11.1036a31–1036b23, he speaks of the Pythagorean abstraction of two from the line and their positing it as the essence of the line. Since the line does not occur without its form, this abstraction would be a separation "by thought" much like the abstraction of sphere from bronze (if all spheres were bronze) or man from flesh and bones (1036b2–7). Of course, Aristotle rejects the Pythagorean position, but it is significant that their mistake is not to abstract what is not present—apparently two *is* in the line—but to *abstract* excessively (1036b22–23).

31. Cf. *An. Po.* I.1.71a15–16: mathematics assumes existence of the unit—hence the process of abstraction of units falls outside the science of arithmetic.

32. John J. Cleary, ("On the Terminology of Abstraction," pp. 13–45) argues convincingly against what he terms an "epistemological theory of abstraction." He shows that abstraction does not give us knowledge of mathematicals but makes them available to mathematicians. My discussion is com-

patible with this result, but I try to explain more precisely what is involved in abstraction. In my account mathematicals are justly referred to as what is by abstraction.

33. *Philebus* 56d–e; Aristotle distinguishes measures in quantity from measures in other genera—*Metaphysics* X.1.1052b20–1053a14.

34. For alternative accounts, see the set-theoretic treatments of Aristotelian arithmetic by Barnes ("Aristotelian Arithmetic," pp. 130–32) and Mignucci ("Aristotle's Arithmetic," pp. 201–10).

35. Mueller ("Aristotle on Geometrical Objects," p. 105) offers an interesting alternative to the account that I offer here, one that also leans heavily on an active notion of abstraction. He claims that geometric objects result from [our] imposition of geometric properties on intelligible matter. There are two difficulties: (1) such objects are not directly connected with physical objects (as Lear also notices) and (2) this analysis does not apply to the objects of arithmetic.

36. Though the discussion of mathematicals in book III is dialectical, Aristotle relies on his own principles here, as elsewhere in III. It is on the ground that every kind of mathematical can be found in a single sensible substance (as Hermes is in the stone—1002a21–22) that he disputes the Pythagoreans. Were mathematicals substances, they would be actualities; how could every kind of mathematical actuality be present in the same place? Aristotle's own view that mathematicals are present potentially eliminates the problem.

37. Ross (*Aristotle's "Metaphysics,"* vol. 2, p. 418) maintains that mathematicals are in sensibles potentially and receive actual existence through the geometer's act of separation. Mignucci ("Aristotle's Arithmetic," p. 183), rejects this view on the ground that it represents a constructivism that is inconsistent with Aristotle's realism.

The treatment of ellipses and so forth as conic sections illustrates the idea that mathematicals exist in bodies potentially.

Edward A. Maziarz and Thomas Greenwood (*Greek Mathematical Philosophy* [New York: Federick Ungar, 1968], pp. 168–72) argue that "Aristotle combines abstraction and construction in order to give mathematical objects their being." It is the constructive aspect that enables Aristotle to distinguish mathematical objects from what we perceive (p. 172). To support this conclusion, they cite texts that show the necessity of demonstrating the existence of mathematicals and texts that are supposed to show the "hypothetical and relative character of mathematical principles." I do not think that Aristotle's mathematical principles are hypothetical and relative, except in the innocuous sense that they are the principles upon which demonstrations are based. Further, Maziarz and Greenwood understand "construction" as the technique of using ruler and compass. Thus, they deny flatly that mathematical objects exist in nature (p. 172). So even though their conclusion bears some resemblance to the position that I have taken here, it differs in crucial respects.

38. *Foundations of Arithmetic*, trans. J. L. Austin (Evanston, Ill.: Northwestern University Press, 1980), pp. 44-46.

39. Gaukroger ("The One and the Many," pp. 321–22) argues that Aristotle has a way around another of Frege's arguments, the argument that numbers could not be properties of things because numbers depend on the way we regard things. According to Gaukroger, this does not hold because Aristotle thinks numbers that belong to things belong by nature: each substance is one. True, one belongs by nature, but what about numbers? If my account is right, they too belong to substances by nature, but potentially.

40. At *An. Po.* I.27.87a31–34, Aristotle claims that arithmetic is more accurate than harmonics because it is not "in respect of a substrate." This does not mean that numbers do not exist as attributes of a substrate, but that the arithmetician need not consider the substrate. In contrast, the science of harmonics is concerned not merely with ratios but with the tones produced by instruments. Though the mathematician need not, in practice, consider the substrate of numbers, the existence of this substrate is metaphysically significant.

41. Mueller ("Geometrical Objects," p. 96–97) draws attention to Aristotle's distinction of mathematical ontology from mathematical epistemology.

Brumbaugh ("Aristotle as a Mathematician," in *Platonic Studies of Greek Philosophy: Form, Arts, Gadgets, and Hemlock* by Robert S. Brumbaugh [Albany, N. Y.: SUNY Press, 1989]) also argues that Aristotle mixes realism and constructivism: he sees Aristotle's application of mathematics as realistic (pp. 154–157) and his account of the nature of mathematical entities as constructivistic (pp. 157–60). The two perspectives are compatible, Brumbaugh contends, because Aristotle regards mathematical relations not as causes but as what needs to be explained (p. 161). This is essentially consistent with my account.

42. Ian Hacking, "Proofs and Eternal Truths," in *Philosophy through Its Past* (Middlesex, England: Penguin, 1984), p. 211. Hacking claims this contemporary view of proof has its source in Leibniz and is not to be found in Descartes. Aristotelian proof is even more distant from the contemporary notion than the Cartesian notion of proof.

Chapter 8

1. Baruch Spinoza (*The Ethics and Selected Letters*, trans. Samuel Shirley [Indianapolis: Hackett, 1982], p. 32) expresses the standard view when he lays down the axiom that "From a given determinate cause there necessarily follows an effect."

2. D. M. Armstrong (*What is a Law of Nature?* [Cambridge: Cambridge University Press, 1985], pp. 147–50) calls "iron laws" those that "tell us that given certain conditions, some further state of affairs is necessitated"; "oaken laws," in contrast, "need not issue in exceptionless uniformities." According to Armstrong, Newton's first law is "oaken" because it holds only if nothing interferes. It seems as though the condition that nothing interferes is part of the law, in which case the law is "iron," but Armstrong rejects this on the ground (I think) that infinitely many things would have to be excluded whereas any actual statement of the law must be finite (p. 149). He does not explain why a blanket exclusion of any interference could not be part of the law—this latter is what Newton surely intended. (Newton's first law is a dubious illustration of an oaken law because it states, on one formulation, that a body in motion *tends* to remain in motion unless another body acts upon it. This is a claim not about what it does but about what it would do if there were no interference from other things. A tendency is not inconsistent with the body's occasionally behaving differently.) In any case, Armstrong is making a very interesting distinction. We will see that, pressed in a certain way, it resembles Aristotle's account. But this is not the direction that Armstrong takes it. Though he thinks that an oaken law might have an infinite number of conditions, the set of conditions would still be "perfectly determinate." So far as I can see Armstrong does not really contemplate the case where *no* laws determine the outcome of events; it is rather that the conditions involved in some laws are too complicated to state fully.

3. Donald Davidson, "Causal Relations," *The Journal of Philosophy* 64 (1967): 694, 697–98. More specifications serve to pick out a particular individual cause; this in turn has a particular individual effect. The assumption is that a cause that is necessary for an effect is not a particular event but a particular type of event, and the effect for which a cause is sufficient is also an event of a particular type. That is, causal laws are relations of types of events. Davidson assumes that such laws govern events. The more a cause is specified, the less likely it is to be necessary but the more likely to be sufficient.

4. Richard Sorabji (*Necessity, Cause, and Blame: Perspectives on Aristotle's Theory* [Ithaca, N. Y.: Cornell University Press, 1980], pp. 27–29) takes the example from a lecture by G. E. M. Anscombe. Once decay occurs, the emitted electron or the nucleus is (or is not) a necessitating cause of the detector's

response. That is, whenever the nucleus causes the detector's response, it also necessitates the detector's response. The latter can be seen as unnecessitated only if the decay has not yet occurred. However, from this latter perspective, the detector's response is a matter of chance—it is ultimately uncaused, just as the decay is itself uncaused. The claim that the detector's response is both caused and not necessitated turns on adopting both perspectives concurrently: it is not necessitated from the perspective of the whole complex of events, but caused from the perspective of its immediate precursor. Clearly, this is a confusion. The mistake resembles a confusion of scope.

The example is much harder to conceive of than Sorabji supposes. We can gauge our difficulty in conceiving of it (and of quantum mechanics and random nuclear decay in general) by our tendency to suppose that there must be some hidden variables that account for the phenomenon.

Sorabji thinks that human behavior could also conceivably manifest non-necessitating causes; he ascribes determinism to faith (pp. 30–31). I suggest that David Hume's arguments that we have as much reason for ascribing causality to human behavior as to anything else provide a cogent response, *A Treatise of Human Nature* (London: Penguin, 1984), pp. 447–65.

5. Richard Sorabji, *Necessity, Cause, and Blame*, p. 5. Christopher Kirwan (*Aristotle's "Metaphysics": Books Γ, Δ, and E* [Oxford: Clarendon Press, 1971]) uses the term "coincidence" to translate both; rightly, I think.

6. To say that the storm "does not exist *qua* itself" is equivalent to saying that it is not per se (see *An. Po.* I.4.73b28–29).

7. Ross (*Aristotle's "Metaphysics,"* vol. 1, p. 360) understands the parallel argument at 1026b26–30 in this way, but he (inconsistently) takes 1027a8–11 as a "summary of what [Aristotle] has been arguing for since 1026b27" (p. 361). Kirwan, (*Aristotle's "Metaphysics,"* p. 193) also interprets both arguments as in the text.

8. Ross, *Aristotle's "Metaphysics,"* vol. 1, p. 361.

9. The passage speaks of the *ti estin* of the thing. Though this is literally the "what it is," here it refers to the essence (cf. 91a1 with *Cat.* 1a2 and *Metaphysics* VII.5.1031a12). G. R. G. Mure captures its sense by rendering it (at *Posterior Analytics* 90b36) as "essential nature" (*The Works of Aristotle*, edited by W. D. Ross, vol. 1 [Oxford: Clarendon Press, 1928]).

10. After two and a half pages of detailed discussion, Kirwan (*Aristotle's "Metaphysics,"* p. 198) declares that "the chapter has not yet received a satisfactory interpretation." Sorabji devotes an entire chapter of *Necessity, Cause and Blame* to VI.3. Arthur Madigan ("*Metaphysics* E 3: A Modest Proposal," *Phronesis* 29 [1984]: 123–36 reconstructs VI.3 as a series of responses made to objections raised against VI.2; as if the chapter were one side of a dialogue.

11. Pseudo-Alexander, p. 456.16–19. ("Pseudo-Alexander" refers to the author of the commentary on *Metaphysics* VI–XIV that has come down to us under Alexander of Aphrodisias's name; the commentary on books I–V is assumed to be authentic.) Sorabji does not mention this line, but he denies that the cause of the meeting is being thirsty and, by implication, eating spicy food (*Necessity, Cause, and Blame,* p. 9). More later on his interpretation of this passage.

12. Ross, *Aristotle's "Metaphysics,"* vol. 1, p. 363. Kirwan (*Aristotle's "Metaphysics,"* p. 196) thinks that the entire causal sequence is in the future and indeterminate for that reason; he supposes the initial cause in the sequence is timeless. I do not see any basis for thinking that the sequence is in the future, but even with this Kirwan is unable to make good sense of timeless causes, as he realizes. In any case, Kirwan seems to accept Ross's idea that once the initial cause comes to be, the rest must follow.

13. See the earlier discussion of Ross, *Aristotle's "Metaphysics,"* vol. 1, p. 361.

14. See, for example, Cynthia A. Freeland, "Accidental Causes and Real Explanations," in *Aristotle's "Physics:" A Collection of Essays,* edited by Lindsay Judson (Oxford: Clarendon Press, 1991), p. 69. Lindsay Judson ("Chance and 'Always or For the Most Part' in Aristotle," also in *Aristotle's "Physics,"* edited by Lindsay Judson, pp. 94–95) argues that accidental events are defined by their being "rare relative to natural and deliberative processes taking place in its subject." Freeland does not find it troubling to declare that an effect could have an indefinite number of real accidental causes (pp. 69–72). Judson recognizes that the cause must be external (pp. 93–94), but he does not see its significance because he focuses on a different issue.

15. Sorabji, *Necessity, Cause, and Blame,* pp. 7–8.

16. Ibid., pp. 10–11.

17. Ibid., p. 13.

18. Ross, Freeland, and Judson, take an accidental cause to be a real (or necessary) cause; Sorabji (pp. 5–9) speaks in close proximity of accidents having only accidental causes and of their having no cause. There is no reason to think that Aristotle's "accidental cause" fits under either of these two heads.

19. This point has often been noted. Speaking of Aristotelian science, A. N. Whitehead (*Adventures of Ideas* [New York: Macmillan, 1933], p. 169) declares it to be "beautifully simple. But it entirely leaves out of account the interconnections of real things." Whitehead exaggerates a bit; the interconnections appear in Aristotelian science as attributes, but some are accidental

attributes and thus unknowable. Whitehead also thinks that the reason for Aristotle's omission lies in the particular type of law that he employs. Neither Aristotle nor other Greek thinkers properly have laws that account for order in nature. Nevertheless, I think that Whitehead is right in a general way: it is Aristotle's conception of nature in terms of substances and attributes that leaves open the possibility of accidents.

20. See John M. Cooper, "Aristotle on Natural Teleology," in *Language and Logos: Studies in Ancient Greek Philosophy Presented to G. E. L. Owen*, edited by Malcolm Schofield and Martha Craven Nussbaum (Cambridge: Cambridge University Press, 1983), pp. 197–222, esp. 218–19 and n. 13. Cooper thinks that one type of Aristotelian teleological explanation consists of one species' acting for the sake of another. He denies that there are any ontological problems but notes Aristotle's neglect of this type of explanation.

21. Thomas Aquinas, *Commentary on the "Metaphysics" of Aristotle*, trans. John P. Rowan, vol. 2 (Chicago: Henry Regnery, 1961), VI. Lecture.3: Commentary 1215–1216.

22. Spinoza states this conclusion in corollary 1 of proposition 14, part I of his *Ethics*. (See Spinoza, *The Ethics and Selected Letters*, p. 40.) That Spinoza is concerned with the problem of interaction is clear from the propositions that precede this one; especially, propositions 3, 6, and 10.

23. Martha Nussbaum, *The Fragility of Goodness*, pp. 318–42. John M. Cooper, "Aristotle on the Goods of Fortune," pp. 173–96. Julia Annas, "Aristotle on Virtue and Happiness," pp. 7–22.

24. See chapter 4, "Two Problems in Aristotelian Ethics."

25. Compare this account with the discussion of Armstrong in the second note of this chapter. The characteristically abstract formulations of modern scientific laws mask the difficulty.

Chapter 9

1. Lawrence Hinman speaks of play as Nietzsche's fundamental category, *Philosophy Today* 18 (1974): 106–24.

2. Harold Alderman also thinks that this section is the key to the structure of the book, but he sees the three transformations as recurring in each of the sections, *Nietzsche's Gift* (Athens, Ohio: Ohio University Press, 1977), pp. 18–19, 31–36.

3. Monroe C. Beardsley (*Aesthetics from Classical Greece to the Present: A Short History* [New York: Macmillan, 1966], p. 253) writes: "For feeling, in the romantic theory of art, is . . . a source of knowledge. . . . It was the claim to this form of knowledge that gave rise to a new theory of the imagination—or, perhaps better, that was marked by a new extension of the term 'imagination,' to cover not only a faculty of inventing and assembling materials, but a faculty of seizing directly upon the truth."

4. Douglas Cooper (*The Cubist Epoch* [New York: E. P. Dutton, 1976], p. 263) describes Cubism as:

> a combination of vision, of understanding, of veracity, of modernism, and of a will to represent contemporary reality. Cubism was also the outcome of a conviction that the established methods and conventions of art (painting in particular) were outdated and false, and of an intuition that, if they willed it, a new generation of artists could discover or invent new means of pictorial expression.

Cooper does not quite say that the cubists valued newness for its own sake, but his iteration of the word "new" makes this conclusion difficult to avoid.

5. Arthur Danto, "The Artistic Enfranchisement of Real Objects: The Artworld," *Journal of Philosophy* 61 (1964): 576–77.

Chapter 10

1. See *Metaphysics* VII.12, especially 1038a25–26, and my discussion of this chapter in *One and Many in Aristotle's Metaphysics: The Central Books*, pp. 110–18. The same doctrine is implicit at *Categories* 3.1b16–24.

2. See the discussion at *Topics* VI.6.144a36–b3. Aristotle speaks of the genus's being predicated of the differentia; I have in mind the same relation when I speak of the differentia as included in the genus.

The Greek term that is usually rendered as "category" means literally "predicate." There are some passages where Aristotle may be thinking of the categories as mere predicates, but his considered view, expressed clearly in the *Metaphysics* (e.g., III.3.999a17–23 and V.6.1016b31–34) is that the categories are the highest genera of beings.

3. See, for example, J. L. Ackrill, *Aristotle's "Categories" and "De Interpretatione"*, pp. 85–87. Since "said of" is a transitive relation, if the differentia is said of a substance, then the categorial genus that is said of the differentia—the category under which it falls—must also be said of the substance. If

the differentia were a quality, as Aristotle sometimes says (*Met.* V.14.1020a33–b1), then quality would be "said of" a substance. In this case, substance would be an instance of the category of quality, and the distinction between the categories would dissolve. The basis of Aristotle's division of beings into categories is that each category is "said of" only its instances. Consequently, Ackrill and most other recent commentators have denied that Aristotle really thinks that differentiae are "said of" substances. Ackrill (p. 86) mentions as one source of the error Aristotle's principle that the differentia suffices to define the substance. He does not realize that this is a solid ground for including the differentia in the category of substance. Ackrill claims that Aristotle's mistake could be remedied by taking the differentia to be "in" a substance, just as other instances of nonsubstantial categories. But Aristotle denies that something that is "in" a substrate can be part of that substrate (2.1a24–25), whereas the differentia is a part of the substance because the substance cannot be without its differentia. Rational could not be in man because it is part of the species man, as well as part of an individual man. There are, then, good reasons for Aristotle to say that differentiae are "said of" substances. Presumably, Aristotle avoids the transitivity problem by denying that they fall under the category of quality, where they seem to belong, and instead including them somehow in the categorial genus of substance (cf. 3.1b10–15).

4. There is a parallel broadening of the category when Aristotle describes the object of a single science as a single genus (*Met.* IV.2.1003b19). More properly, the object is one genus and what belongs to it per se (*An. Po.* I.22). But this broadening is benign because the per se attributes that the science demonstrates do not belong to the essence of the genus.

5. Gilbert Ryle, *The Concept of Mind* (New York: Harper & Row, 1949), pp. 27–28, 40–41. This is a distinction that could, I think, be drawn quite sharply. Instead, Ryle emphasizes the open-ended character of the way we recognize instances of the distinction: knowing how apparently involves being "ready to detect and correct lapses, to repeat and improve upon successes, to profit from the examples of others and so forth."

6. Ludwig Wittgenstein, *Philosophical Investigations* (New York: Macmillan, 1971), I, sections 66–67.

7. Norman Kemp Smith (trans.), *Immanuel Kant's Critique of Pure Reason* (New York: St. Martin's Press, 1965).

8. Cf. Hegel's discussion of Kant in the *Encyclopedia* (esp. sections 45–46) (*Enzyklopädie*, pp. 121–24; *Hegel's Logic*, tr. William Wallace [Oxford: Clarendon Press, 1975], pp. 73–74). Subsequent references to Hegel's works

will mention the page number of the German edition followed by the page number of the English edition.

9. English translations in this paragraph are from A. V. Miller, *Hegel's Science of Logic* (London, George Allen & Unwin: 1969). *Logik* I, *Logik* II, and *Logik* III refer to books I, II, and III of Hegel's *Wissenshaft der Logik.* Page references following these are from, respectively, volumes 21, 11, and 12 of Hegel's *Gesammelte Werke* (Hamburg: Meiner, 1978, 1981, and 1985).

10. For a concise account, see sect. 114 of the *Encyclopedia (Enzyklopädie,* pp. 235–36; *Hegel's Logic,* pp. 165–66).

11. This is Miller's translation with the substitution of "differentiae" for his "differences."

BIBLIOGRAPHY

Ackrill, J. L. "Aristotle on *Eudaimonia*." In *Essays on Aristotle's Ethics*, edited by A. O. Rorty, pp. 18–28.

————. *Aristotle's "Categories" and "De Interpretatione."* Oxford: Clarendon Press, 1979.

————. "Aristotle's Distinction between *Energeia* and *Kinesis*." In *New Essays on Plato and Aristotle*, edited by Renford Bambrough. London: Routledge & Kegan Paul, 1965, pp. 121–41.

————. *Aristotle the Philosopher.* Oxford: Oxford University Press, 1981.

Alderman, Harold. *Nietzsche's Gift.* Athens, Ohio: Ohio University Press, 1977.

Alexander of Aphrodisias. *In Aristotelis Metaphysica*, edited by Michael Hayduck. Berlin: George Reimer, 1891. Vol. 1 of *Commentaria in Aristotelem Graeca*.

Allen, R. E. *The Euthyphro and Plato's Earlier Theory of Forms.* London: Humanities Press, 1970.

————. "Plato's Earlier Theory of Forms." In *The Philosophy of Socrates: A Collection of Critical Essays*, edited by G. Vlastos, pp. 319–34.

Annas, Julia. "Aristotle on Virtue and Happiness." *University of Dayton Review* 19 (1988–89): 7–22.

————. *Aristotle's "Metaphysics": Books M and N.* Oxford: Clarendon Press, 1976.

Aristotle. *Nicomachean Ethics.* Translated by Martin Ostwald. Indianapolis: Bobbs-Merrill, 1962.

243

Armstrong, D. M. *What is a Law of Nature?* Cambridge: Cambridge University Press, 1985.

Barnes, J., M. Schofield, and R. Sorabji, eds. *Articles on Aristotle*, vol. 3: *Metaphysics*. New York: St. Martin's Press, 1979.

Barnes, J. "Aristotelian Arithmetic." *Revue de Philosophie Ancienne* 2 (1985): 97–133.

Beardsley, Monroe C. *Aesthetics from Classical Greece to the Present: A Short History*. New York: Macmillan, 1966.

Becker, Oskar. "Die *Archai* in der griechischen Mathematik." *Archiv für Begriffsgeschichte* 4 (1959): 210–26.

Brumbaugh, Robert S. "Aristotle as a Mathematician." In *Platonic Studies of Greek Philosophy: Form, Arts, Gadgets, and Hemlock* by Robert S. Brumbaugh. Albany, N. Y.: SUNY Press, 1989. Originally published in *Review of Metaphysics* 8 (1954): 511–21.

Cleary, J. J. "On the Terminology of Abstraction in Aristotle." *Phronesis* 30 (1985): 13–45.

Cooper, Douglas. *The Cubist Epoch*. New York: E. P. Dutton, 1976.

Cooper, John M. "Aristotle on Natural Teleology." In *Language and Logos: Studies in Ancient Greek Philosophy Presented to G. E. L. Owen*, edited by Malcolm Schofield and Martha Craven Nussbaum. Cambridge: Cambridge University Press, 1983, pp. 197–222.

———. "Aristotle on the Forms of Friendship." *Review of Metaphysics* 30 (1977): 619–48.

———. "Aristotle on the Goods of Fortune." *Philosophical Review* 44 (1985): 173–96.

———. "Friendship and the Good in Aristotle." *Philosophical Review* 86 (1977): 290–315.

———. *Reason and Human Good in Aristotle*. Cambridge, Mass.: Harvard University Press, 1975.

Corcoran, John, ed. *Ancient Logic and its Modern Interpretations*. Dordrecht: D. Reidel, 1974.

Danto, Arthur. "The Artistic Enfranchisement of Real Objects: The Artworld." *Journal of Philosophy* 61 (1964): 571–84.

Davidson, Donald. "Causal Relations." *The Journal of Philosophy* 64 (1967): 691–703.

Frede, Dorothea. "The Impossibility of Perfection: Socrates' Criticism of Simonides' Poem in the *Protagoras.*" *Review of Metaphysics* 39 (1986): 729–53.

Freeland, Cynthia A. "Accidental Causes and Real Explanations." In *Aristotle's "Physics:" A Collection of Essays,* edited by Lindsay Judson, pp. 49–72.

Frege, G. *Foundations of Arithmetic.* Translated by J. L. Austin. Evanston, Ill. Northwestern University Press, 1980.

von Fritz, Kurt. "Die *APXAI* in der griechischen Mathematik." *Archiv für Begriffsgeschichte* 1 (1955): 13–103.

Garver, Eugene. "Aristotle's Geneology of Morals." Philosophy and Phenomenological Research 44 (1984): 471–92.

Gaukroger, S. "Aristotle on Intelligible Matter." *Phronesis* 25 (1980): 187–97.

———. "The One and the Many." *Classical Quarterly* 32 (1982): 312–22.

Gauthier, R. A., and J. Y. Jolif. *L'Éthique à Nicomaque.* 2nd. ed. Louvain: Publications Universitaires, 1970.

Graeser, A., ed. *Mathematics and Metaphysics in Aristotle.* Bern: Haupt, 1987.

Grene, Marjorie. *A Portrait of Aristotle.* Chicago: University of Chicago Press, 1963.

Gulley, Norman. *The Philosophy of Socrates.* London: Macmillan, 1968.

Hacking, I. "Proofs and Eternal Truths." In *Philosophy through Its Past,* edited by Ted Honderich. Middlesex, England: Penguin, 1984, pp. 211–24.

Halper, Edward. " 'Being *qua* Being' in *Metaphysics* Γ." *Elenchos* 8 (1987): 43–62.

———. *One and Many in Aristotle's "Metaphysics": The Central Books.* Columbus, Ohio: Ohio State University Press, 1989.

Hardie, W. F. R. *Aristotle's Ethical Theory.* 2nd ed. Oxford: Clarendon Press, 1980.

———. "The Final Good in Aristotle's *Ethics.*" *Philosophy* 40 (1965): 277–95. Reprinted in *Aristotle: A Collection of Critical Essays,* edited by J. M. E. Moravcsik, pp. 296–322.

Heath, Thomas L. *Mathematics in Aristotle.* New York: Garland, 1980.

———. *The Thirteen Books of Euclid's "Elements,"* vol. 1. New York: Dover, 1956.

Hegel, G. W. F. *Enzyklopädie der philosophischen Wissenschaften im Grundrisse (1830). Erster Teil. Die Wissenschaft der Logic. Mit den mündlischen Zusätzen.* Vol. 8 of *Werke.* Frankfurt: Suhrkamp, 1970.

——. *Hegel's Logic.* Translated by William Wallace. Oxford: Clarendon Press, 1975.

——. *Hegel's Science of Logic.* Translated by A. V. Miller. London, George Allen & Unwin: 1969.

——. *Wissenschaft der Logik.* Edited by Friedrich Hogemann and Walter Jaeschke. Vols. 11, 12, and 21 of *Gesammelte Werke.* Hamburg: Felix Meiner, 1978, 1981, and 1985.

Hinman, Lawrence M. "Nietsche's Philosophy of Play." *Philosophy Today* 18 (1974): 106–124.

Hintikka, Jaakko. *Time and Necessity.* Oxford: Clarendon Press, 1973.

——. "Time, Truth, and Knowledge in Ancient Greek Philosophy." *American Philosophical Quarterly* 4 (1967): 1–14.

Hoerber, Robert G. "Plato's *Lysis.*" *Phronesis* 4 (1959): 15–28.

Hume, David. *A Treatise of Human Nature.* London: Penguin, 1984.

Hyman, A. and Walsh, J. J., eds. *Philosophy in the Middle Ages.* 2nd ed. Indianapolis: Hackett, 1983.

Irwin, Terence H. "The Metaphysical and Psychological Basis of Aristotle's Ethics." In *Essays on Aristotle's Ethics,* edited by A. O. Rorty, pp. 35–53.

——. *Plato's Moral Theory: The Early and Middle Dialogues.* Oxford: Clarendon Press, 1974.

Judson, Lindsay, ed. *Aristotle's "Physics": A Collection of Essays.* Oxford: Clarendon Press, 1991.

——. "Chance and 'Always or For the Most Part' in Aristotle." *In Aristotle's "Physics",* edited by Lindsay Judson, pp. 73–99.

Kant, Immanuel. *Immanuel Kant's Critique of Pure Reason.* Translated by Norman Kemp Smith. New York: St. Martin's Press, 1965.

Kenny, A. *The Aristotelian Ethics.* Oxford: Clarendon Press, 1978.

Keyt, David. "Intellectualism in Aristotle." In *Essays in Ancient Greek Philosophy,* vol. 2, edited by J. P. Anton and A. Preus. Albany: SUNY Press, 1983, pp. 364–87.

Kirwan, Christopher. *Aristotle's "Metaphysics": Books* Γ, Δ, *and* E. Oxford: Clarendon Press, 1971.

Klein, Jacob. *Greek Mathematical Thought and the Origin of Algebra*. Translated by Eva Brann. Cambridge, Mass.: M.I.T. Press, 1968.

Korsgaard, Christine M. "Aristotle and Kant on the Source of Value." *Ethics* 46 (1986): 486–505.

————. "Aristotle on Function and Virtue." *History of Philosophy Quarterly* 3 (1986): 169–95.

————. "Two Distinctions in Goodness." *The Philosophical Review* 92 (1983): 169–95.

Kosman, L. A. "Aristotle's Definition of Motion." *Phronesis* 14 (1969): 40–62.

Lakatos, I. *Proofs and Refutations: The Logic of Mathematical Discovery*. Cambridge: Cambridge University Press, 1976.

Lear, Jonathan. "Aristotle's Philosophy of Mathematics." *Philosophical Review* 91 (1982): 161–92.

Loux, Michael. "Aristotle on Transcendentals." *Phronesis* 18 (1973): 225–39.

McDowell, John. "Virtue and Reason. " *Monist* 42 (1979): 331–50.

Madigan, Arthur. "*Metaphysics* E 3: A Modest Proposal." *Phronesis* 29 (1984): 123–36.

Mamo, P. S. "*Energeia* and *Kinesis* in Metaphysics Θ. 6." *Apeiron* 4 (1970) : 24–34.

Martin, G. *Die Klassische Ontologie der Zahl*. Cologne: Kolner Universität Verlag, 1956.

Maziarz, E. A., and T. Greenwood. *Greek Mathematical Philosophy*. New York: Federick Ungar, 1968.

Mendell, H. "Two Geometrical Examples from Aristotle's *Metaphysics*." *Classical Quarterly* 34 (1984): 359–72.

Mignucci, M. "Aristotle's Arithmetic." In *Mathematics and Metaphysics*, edited by A. Graeser, pp. 175–211.

Moravcsik, J. M. E., ed. *Aristotle: A Collection of Critical Essays*. Notre Dame, Ind.: University of Notre Dame Press, 1968.

Mueller, Ian. "Aristotle on Geometrical Objects." *Archiv für Geschichte der Philosophie* 52 (1970): 156–71. Reprinted in *Articles*, vol. 3, edited by Barnes, Schofield, and Sorabji, pp. 96–107.

————. "Greek Mathematics and Greek Logic." In *Ancient Logic*, edited by Corcoran, pp. 35–70.

Mulhern, M. M. "Types of Process According to Aristotle." *Monist* 52 (1968): 237–51.

Nietzsche, Friedrich. *The Birth of Tragedy and The Genealogy of Morals.* Translated by Francis Golffing. Garden City,N.Y.: Doubleday, 1956.

————. *Thus Spoke Zarathustra.* Translated by Walter Kaufmann. New York: Penguin, 1980.

Nozick, Robert. *Philosophical Explanations.* Cambridge, Mass.: Belknap Press, 1981.

Nussbaum, Martha. *The Fragility of Goodness.* Cambridge: Cambridge University Press, 1986.

O'Connor, David. "Two Ideals of Friendship." *History of Philosophy Quarterly* 7 (1990): 109–22.

Owen, G. E. L. "*Tithenai ta Phainomena.*" In *Aristote et les Problèmes de Méthode,* edited by S. Mansion. Louvain: Publications Universitaires de Louvain, 1961, pp. 83–103. Reprinted in *Aristotle: A Collection of Critical Essays,* edited by J. M. E. Moravcsik, pp. 167–90.

Penner, Terry. "The Unity of Virtue." *Philosophical Review* 82 (1973): 35–68.

Philippe, M.-D. "αφαίρεσιξ πρόσθεσιξ, χωρίζειν dans la Philosophie d'Aristote." *Revue Thomiste* 56 (1948): 461–79.

Polansky, Ronald. "Aristotle's Demarcation of the Senses of *Energeia* in *Metaphysics* IX.6." *Ancient Philosophy* 3 (1983): 160–70.

Randall, John Herman, Jr. *Aristotle.* New York: Columbia University Press, 1968.

Robinson, Richard. *Plato's Earlier Dialectic.* 2nd ed. Oxford: Clarendon Press, 1953.

Rorty, A. O., ed. *Essays on Aristotle's Ethics.* Berkeley: University of California Press, 1980.

Ross, W. D. *Aristotle's "Metaphysics."* 2 vols. Oxford: Clarendon Press, 1958.

————, ed. *The Works of Aristotle.* 12 vols. Oxford: Clarendon Press, 1928.

Ryle, Gilbert. *The Concept of Mind.* New York: Harper & Row, 1949.

————. *Dilemmas.* Cambridge: Cambridge University Press, 1954.

Saunders, T. J. *Plato: Early Socratic Dialogues.* Harmonsworth, England: Penguin, 1987.

Sedley, David. "Is the *Lysis* a Dialogue of Definition?" *Phronesis* 34 (1988): 107–8.

Solmsen, F. *Aristotle's System of the Physical World: A Comparison with his Predecessors.* Ithaca, N.Y.: Cornell University Press, 1960.

Sorabji, Richard. "Aristotle on the Role of Intellect in Virtue." In *Essays on Aristotle's Ethics,* edited by A. O. Rorty, pp. 201–19.

————. *Necessity, Cause, and Blame: Perspectives on Aristotle's Theory.* Ithaca, N.Y.: Cornell University Press, 1980.

Spinoza, Baruch. *The Ethics and Selected Letters.* Trans. Samuel Shirley. Indianapolis: Hackett, 1982.

Stewart, J. A. *Notes on the Nicomachean Ethics of Aristotle.* 2 vols. New York: Arno Press, 1973.

Stokes, Michael. *Plato's Socratic Conversations: Drama and Dialectic in Three Dialogues.* Baltimore: Johns Hopkins University Press, 1986.

Szabo, A. *The Beginnings of Greek Mathematics.* Dordrecht, Holland: D. Reidel, 1978.

Taylor, A. E. *Plato: The Man and his Work.* New York: Dial Press, 1936.

Thomas Aquinas. *Commentary on the "Metaphysics" of Aristotle.* Translated by John P. Rowan. 2 vols. Chicago: Henry Regnery, 1961.

Thompson, D'A. W. "Aristotle the Naturalist." In *Science and the Classics.* London: Oxford University Press, 1940.

Versenyi, Laszlo. "Plato's *Lysis.*" *Phronesis* 20 (1975): 185–98.

Vlastos, Gregory. "The Argument in *La.* 197E ff." Appendix to "The Unity of the Virtues in the *Protagoras.*" In *Platonic Studies,* pp. 266–69.

————. "The Individual as an Object of Love in Plato." In *Platonic Studies,* pp. 3–34.

————. "Introduction: The Paradox of Socrates." In *The Philosophy of Socrates,* edited by G. Vlastos, pp. 1–21.

————, ed. *The Philosophy of Socrates.* Garden City, N.Y.: Doubleday, 1971.

————. *Platonic Studies*. Princeton: Princeton University Press, 1973.

————. "Socrates' Disavowal of Knowledge." *The Philosophical Quarterly* 138 (1985): 1–31.

————. *Socrates, Ironist and Moral Philosopher*. Ithaca, N.Y.: Cornell University Press, 1991.

————. "The Unity of the Virtues in the *Protagoras*." *Review of Metaphysics* 25 (1972): 415–58. Reprinted in *Platonic Studies*, pp. 221–65.

White, Stephen A. "Is Aristotelian Happiness a Good Life or the Best Life?" *Oxford Studies in Ancient Philosophy* 8 (1990): 103–43.

Whitehead, A. N. *Adventures of Ideas*. New York: Macmillan, 1933.

Williams, Bernard. *Morality*. New York: Harper & Row, 1972.

Wittgenstein, Ludwig. *Philosophical Investigations*. New York: Macmillan, 1971.

————. *Remarks on the Foundations of Mathematics*. Edited by G. H. von Wright, R. Rhees, and G. E. M. Anscombe. Cambridge, Mass.: M.I.T. Press, 1967.

Young, Charles M. "Aristotle on Temperance." *Philosophical Review* 97 (1988): 521–42.

A

Absolute, 206

Abstraction
  as mathematical construction,
    144–45
  of mathematical entities, 7,
    136–37, 138, 146, 148–49, 153,
    229–30 233–34, 234–35
  nature of, 136, 144

Acceleration, 116. *See also* Motion,
  unchanging

Accident (accidental being). *See also*
  Accidental cause
  existence (possibility) of, 90–91,
    158, 160–62, 166, 169–73, 178,
    181
    denials of existence, 156, 161,
      167, 168, 176
  no knowledge (science of), 111,
    112–113, 115, 160, 170, 181–82
  not always or for the most
    part, 160–61, 165, 167, 238
  occasions for ethical acts, 88,
    177–78, 179
  posterior to nature (substance),
    159–60, 165–66, 167, 169

privations of nature or art,
  164–66, 180–81
reality of, 158, 167, 172 –74
as two events, 8, 171–72
types of, 158–59, 164 , 166–67

Accidental cause, 7–8, 155–84. *See
  also* Accident
  account of, 173–74, 181–82
  affects outcome of events, 164,
    171, 181
  atemporal, 162– 64
  denials of, 167–68, 173, 238
  incompatible with modern
    notion of cause, 155, 157–58,
    168
  indeterminate (infinite), 159,
    181–82
  lies in some other thing, 159–60,
    163–64, 170–71, 173, 177–78,
    179, 238
  reality of, 172–73, 238
  spicy food example, 162–64,
    170–71, 238
  types of pluralities involved in,
    173–74

Ackrill, J. L., 6–7, 98, 117–30, 219,
  220, 222, 223, 225, 226, 228–29,
  240–41